IMAGES
of America

CONSTITUTION ISLAND

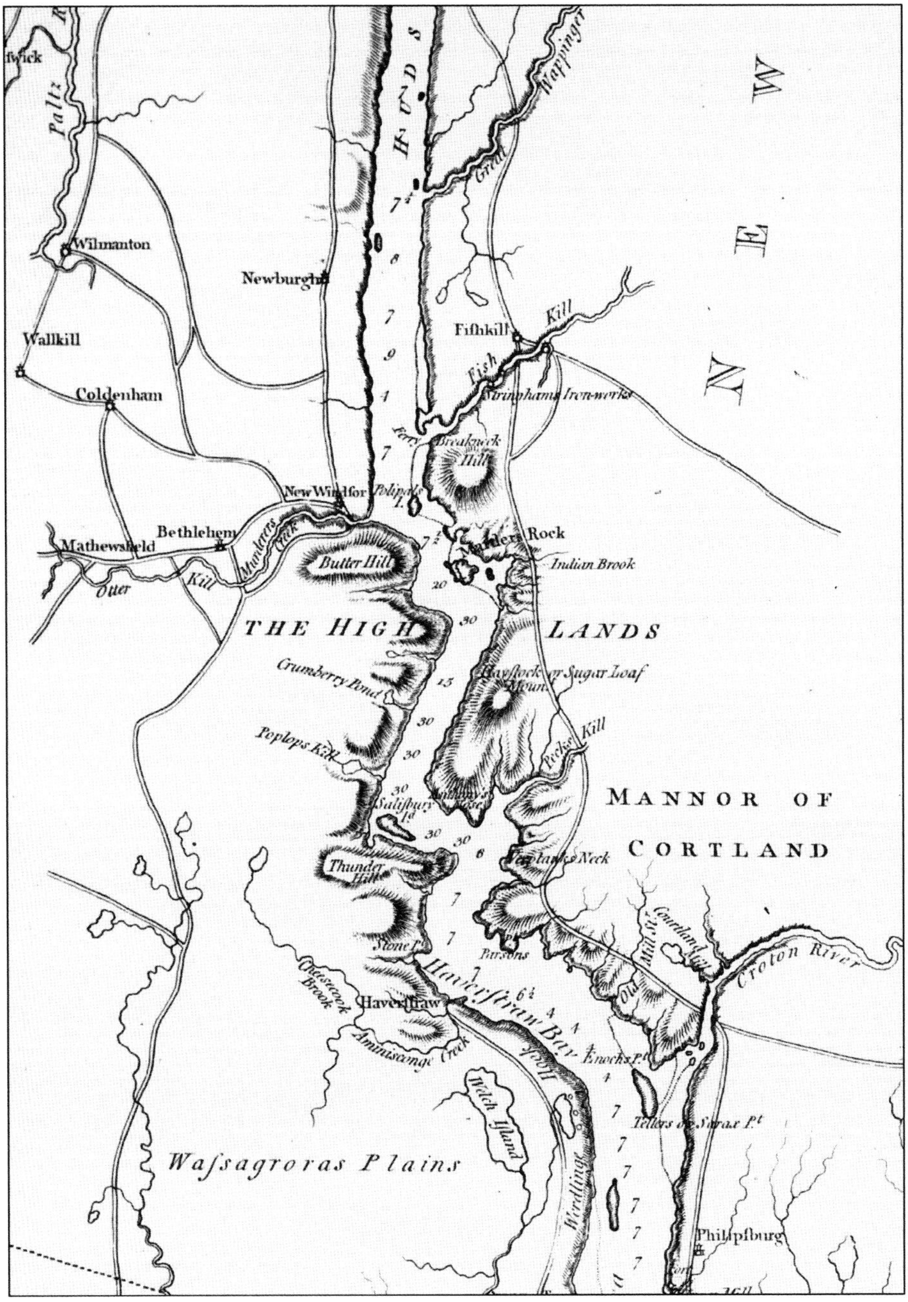

TOPOGRAPHICAL MAP. Cartographers Claude Sauthier and William Faden drew this topographical map of the Hudson about 1776. They charted the entire river from Sandy Hook to Fort Edward. This section of the map traces the Hudson River as it passes through the Highlands in a dramatic curve. It narrows to one-quarter mile across, and its depth, in places, is 200 feet. "Martlers Rock" on the east side of the river is now known as Constitution Island. (United States Military Academy Library.)

On the cover: Please see page 101. (Constitution Island Association.)

IMAGES *of America*

CONSTITUTION ISLAND

Ronnie Clark Coffey

ARCADIA PUBLISHING

ISBN 978-0-7385-5673-4

Published by Arcadia Publishing
Charleston SC, Chicago IL, Portsmouth NH, San Francisco CA

Printed in the United States of America

Library of Congress Catalog Card Number: 2007943798

For all general information contact Arcadia Publishing at:
Telephone 843-853-2070
Fax 843-853-0044
E-mail sales@arcadiapublishing.com
For customer service and orders:
Toll-Free 1-888-313-2665

Visit us on the Internet at www.arcadiapublishing.com

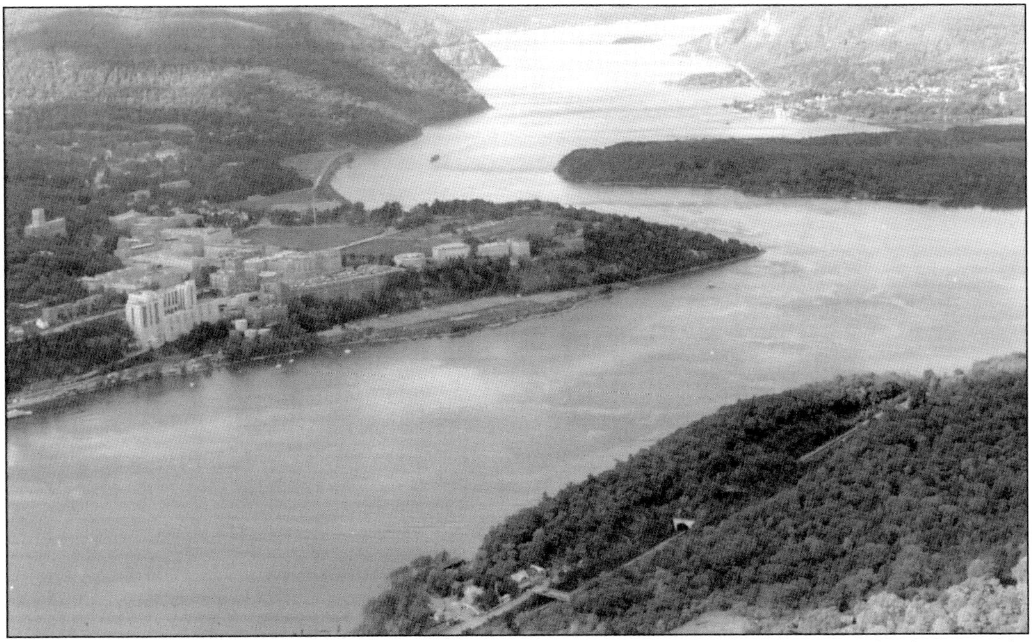

S-CURVE. The renowned S-shaped curve of the Hudson River is seen in this view looking north. The United States Military Academy is at left. One can easily see how West Point got its name. Jutting into the river on the east side is Constitution Island. In the 1600s, Dutch sailors divided the river into sections called "reaches." This one was known for dangerous currents and winds and was called Martelaer's Rach or Martyr's Reach. The island was originally called Martelaer's Island.

Contents

ACKNOWLEDGMENTS

This book is dedicated to my daughters, Veronica Clark Coffey and Juliet Elizabeth Coffey, with whom I have spent so many happy days on Constitution Island. I became a volunteer at the island in 1989. Volunteer organizations are constantly in need of workers, so through the years, they joined me on the island to help in the bookshop and later "graduated" to become costumed docents. During the years that I served as executive director, they assisted me in countless ways. Sometimes they rambled over the island like the Warner sisters, returning with sun-ripened berries for me to eat. My husband, Kevin, graciously did any task I "volunteered" him for as well. I thank them. Together our own family history became happily entwined in the history of this remarkable place.

I begin by thanking the Constitution Island Association whose board chairperson Elizabeth Pugh and executive director Richard DeKoster were supportive from the very start of my project. I am indebted to Faith Herbert, research chairperson and archivist of the Constitution Island Association's collection. I am not the first researcher who has been the beneficiary of her beautifully organized archives. Images not otherwise attributed were loaned to me by the Constitution Island Association (noted as CIA). I am indebted to the following individuals and organizations: Elaine McConnell, Casey Madrick and the staff of the Special Collections and Archives of the United States Military Academy (USMA) Library, under the direction of Suzanne Christoff; Suzanne Brahm, director of the Highland Falls Library and her professional staff; island caretaker Roddy MacLeod and Deb MacLeod; USMA harbormaster Richard Camarda; Lillian McGuinness, of the Putnam County Historical Society; Susan Smith of the Palisades Interstate Park Commission (PIPC); and the New York Historical Society. I was most fortunate to be able to draw from the extensive private collections of Peter Carroll, James Donnery, June and John Gunza, and William "Bird" Vacek, who generously loaned images. My thanks go to Dr. Jane Weiss for her annotated transcription of Susan Warner's journals. Anna Warner's biography, *Susan Warner*, was an important primary source. Both works are liberally quoted. Again I thank my husband, Kevin Coffey, for his many hours of scanning, planning, and layout. Veronica Coffey helped with typing, and Juliet Coffey with encouragement. Peter Clark, Cathy Kelly, Frank and Phyllis Murphy, Anne Sidamon-Eristoff, and the Parry family provided images or assistance.

Finally I gratefully acknowledge the continued efforts of the volunteer docents, gardeners, and board members of the CIA who, since 1916, have devoted their time and energy to preserving the history of the island, the Warner family, and the treasure which is the Warner House.

—Ronnie Clark Coffey

INTRODUCTION

At an S-shaped bend of the Hudson River, 50 miles north of New York City, lies a rugged island, separated from the eastern shore by a salt marsh. Today it is known as Constitution Island, hinting at one of the many roles it has played in history. It is a place with many stories to tell.

Evidence of Native American habitation, such as spear points and hammer stones, have been unearthed throughout the island, attesting to human activity going back about 6,000 years. These 280 acres served them for hunting and fishing. Pottery shards tell us that cooking and eating took place here; so the dense oak forest undoubtedly sheltered their sharing, storytelling, and laughter.

Dutch sailors traveling up the river in the 1600s broke the Hudson River into sections, or "reaches," for reference. This one was known for dangerous currents and winds and was called Martelaer's Rach or Martyr's Reach. The island came to be known as Martelaer's Rock or Martelaer's Island. When England took control of Dutch lands in New York State, the island became part of a land grant to the Philipse family who maintained ownership through the 18th and early 19th centuries.

In those days, the Hudson River was the major navigation highway of the colonies. All day long, square-rigged sloops darted around larger, slower ships, delivering goods and passengers. This lively commerce united the colonies with wheat and corn, news, and ideas. As thoughts of revolution turned from words into actions, the Continental Congress ordered fortifications to be built in the Hudson Highlands to protect this vital highway. Because of its strategic location at a narrow bend of the river, the patriots chose Martelaer's Rock as the site of the first fortification to guard the Hudson-Champlain route. It was called Fort Constitution, which gave the island a new name, Constitution Island. Batteries and a blockhouse were constructed. As expected, the British came up the Hudson in 1777. After a fierce daylong battle in the Hudson Highlands, British forces captured Forts Clinton and Montgomery two miles south of the island. Then they occupied Constitution Island as well.

After three weeks, the British left the island, and the Americans reclaimed it. A revised strategy designed by engineer Thaddeus Kosciuszko put the larger forts at West Point with smaller redoubts at Constitution Island, forming a formidable defensive system. Barracks were built for soldiers. A massive chain was installed across the river to increase its defenses. The great chain was in use until the end of the war in 1783. A young soldier named Joseph Plumb Martin, who helped construct the forts on the island, later described his experiences in a memoir titled *Private Yankee Doodle*.

At the conclusion of the war, the island remained in the Philipse family for two more generations and was used by tenant farmers. In 1836, it was sold to a wealthy lawyer from New York City named Henry Warner. Warner had learned about the island during visits to his brother, Thomas Warner, a chaplain and professor at the United States Military Academy at West Point. Henry and Thomas dreamed of erecting an elegant tourist hotel and commissioned noted architect Alexander Jackson Davis to draw up the plans. Meanwhile, Henry added rooms to the farmhouse already on the island to serve as a summerhouse for his family who resided in an elegant townhouse at St. Mark's Place in New York City.

This family consisted of Henry, a widower, his sister Fanny, and his two daughters, Susan and Anna, five years younger. The girls had been raised with all the comforts of upper-middle-class society—servants, dressmakers, private tutors, dancing school, church attendance, horses, carriages, and a busy social life of visiting and receiving friends. A vacation home was just another luxury. Then the economic panic of 1837 began its gradual devastation of Henry's financial status, ending in his need to sell his New York City home and other investments and move his family permanently to Constitution Island in 1838. At first, the family maintained a fairly comfortable lifestyle that enabled them to spend the winters in New York City. But soon it was necessary to sell off possessions and reduce spending as they sank from privilege into poverty. Necessity became the mother of creativity. Anna invented a game to sell. Susan did something rare for a woman of that time; she wrote a book to earn money. Susan's first novel, *The Wide, Wide World*, was an enormous success, leading her to write more books. Anna too began to write. Occasionally they collaborated but most often wrote their own works. Their literary output totaled about 100 books. Anna also wrote hymn lyrics, the most famous being "Jesus Loves Me." Writing paid the bills but never made them rich. Ineffective copyright laws and unwise money management conspired against them.

Religion had always played an important part in the sisters' lives. After Henry's death in 1875, Susan began teaching Bible classes across the river to West Point cadets. In the winter, classes were held on the post, but in summer, the cadets rowed to Constitution Island to have class. Susan died in 1885, and Anna continued the Bible classes for the next 30 years. Through these classes, both women had a deep and lasting affect on their students. They remained in touch with many graduates, sending them comforting letters and gifts of books as they served their country in faraway posts.

Because of this strong connection to the military academy, it was the ardent wish of the two sisters that their island would become a permanent part of West Point—a place where cadets could relax and find peace. In her old age, Anna lived in reduced circumstances, shunning offers from entrepreneurs who wanted to buy the island. In 1908, philanthropist Margaret Sage found out about Anna through one of her former students and arranged with her to buy the island for $150,000 and, with Anna, bequeath it to the federal government. This enabled Anna to spend her last seven years free of financial worries for the first time since her childhood. Upon her death in 1915, she also gave the military academy a painting of George Washington painted by Gilbert Stuart that the Warners had owned. Both Susan and Anna are buried at the military cemetery at West Point.

Shortly after Anna's death, a group of her friends formed an association dedicated to preserving the history of the island and the Warner House. It is known today as the Constitution Island Association and, through active volunteerism, continues to interpret the history and maintain the beauty of this special place. School tours of the Warner House and the ruins of the fortifications are given during the spring. Public tours are given during the summer. Volunteers retell the remarkable stories of Constitution Island so they will not be forgotten.

One

Martelaer's Rock

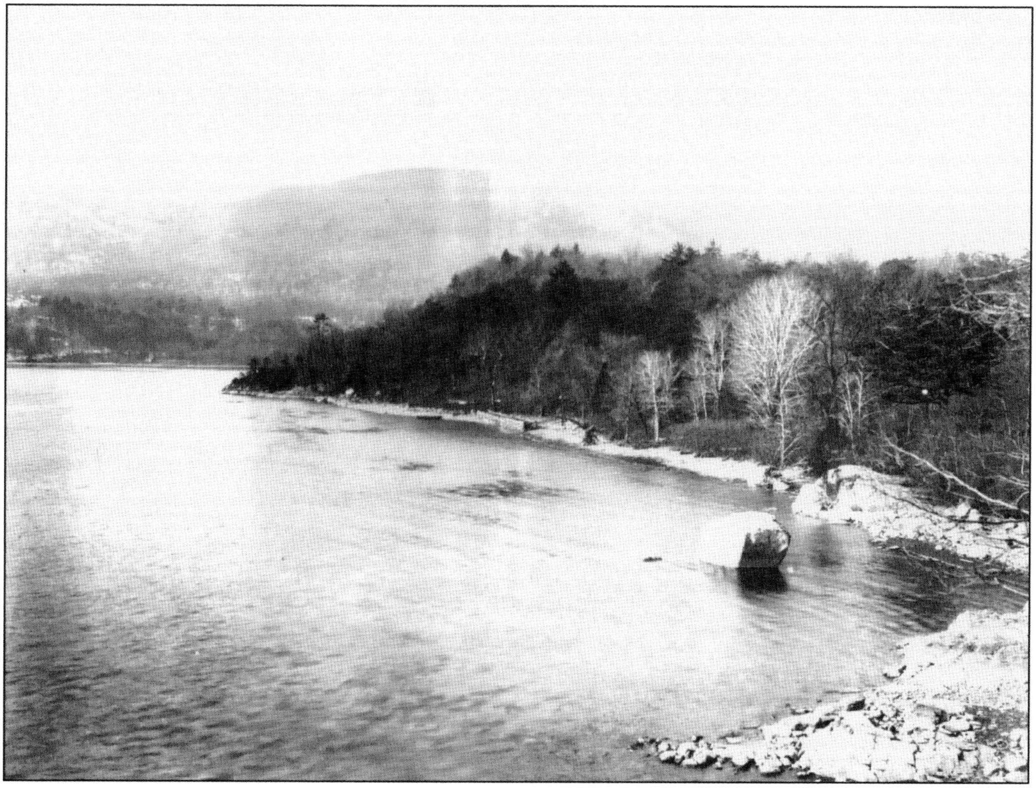

Native Americans. With its thick forest sloping down into deep water, Constitution Island made a perfect hunting and fishing ground for Native Americans. Archaeological evidence reveals a presence that dates back about 6,000 years from the archaic through the woodland periods. Projectile points, grinding stones, net sinkers, and pottery shards indicate that hunting, fishing, and gathering took place on the island. The river was used for trade and transportation.

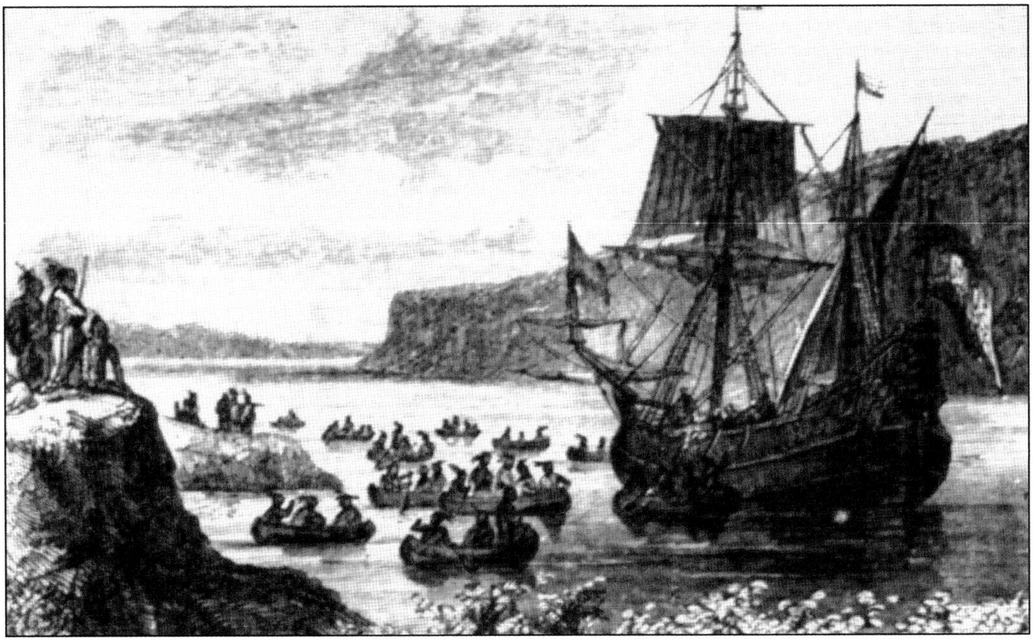

HALF MOON. On his famous exploration voyage, Henry Hudson anchored the *Half Moon*, in an impressive spot along the river. Ship's officer Robert Juet described it: "The high land hath many points and a narrow channel." One of those points was Constitution Island. Native American presence soon gave way to Dutch settlers, but by the late 17th century, the English took control. The island became part of a land grant to the Philipse family.

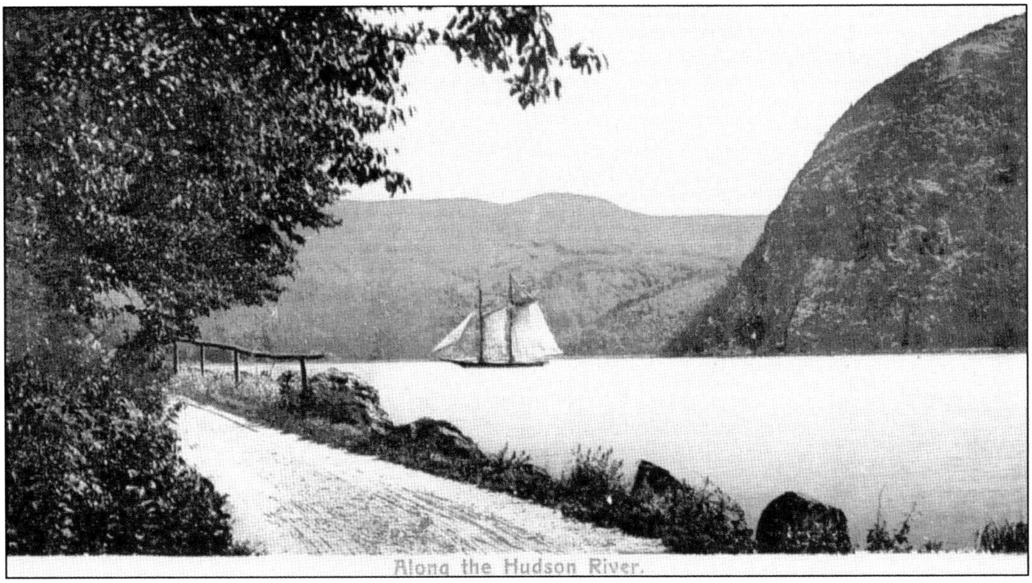

NAVIGATION HIGHWAY. In the 1700s, the North River, later called the Hudson River, was the major navigation highway of the colonies, linking New England with the middle and southern colonies. Sailing ships like this one and smaller sloops delivered goods and passengers, uniting the colonies with wheat and corn, news, and information. Ideas about independence from England began to spread. (Gunza collection.)

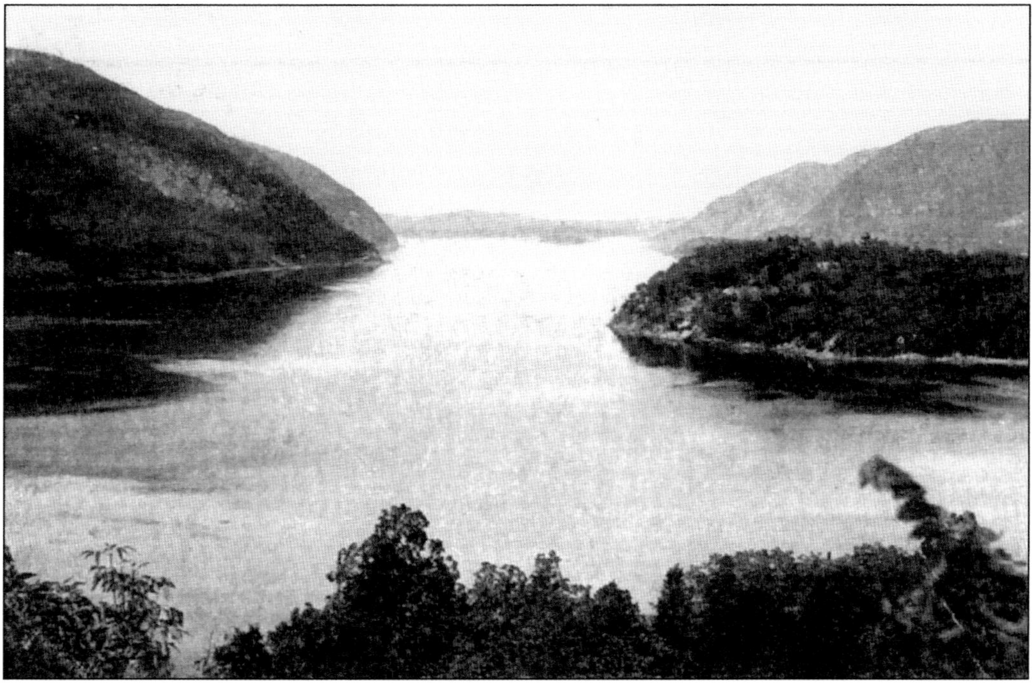

FORT CONSTITUTION. In 1775, as thoughts of revolution turned from words into actions, the Second Continental Congress drafted orders that forts be built in the Hudson Highlands to protect the colonists "and that security to their persons and property which is derived from the British Constitution." Martelaer's Rock was chosen for the first fortification, which was called Fort Constitution. The island was soon commonly called Constitution Island. (Donnery collection.)

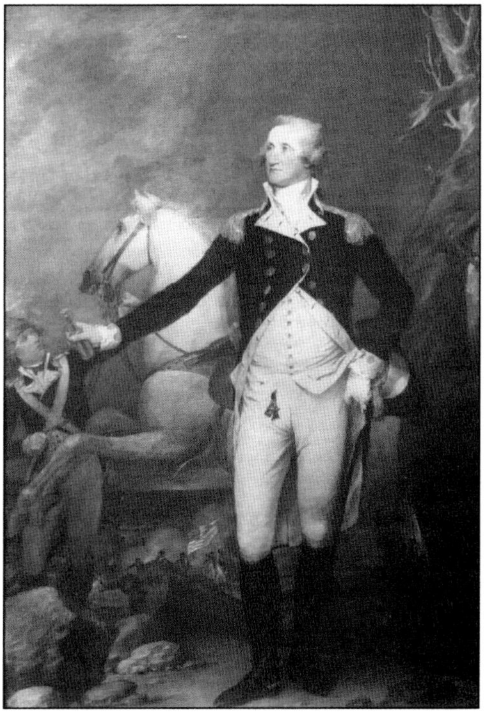

GEORGE WASHINGTON. It was Gen. George Washington who recommended to the Second Continental Congress that forts be built in the Hudson Highlands. The Congress responded, "Resolved, that a post be taken in the Highlands on each side of Hudson's River and batteries erected in such a manner as most effectually prevent any vessels passing that may be sent to harass inhabitants." (USMA Library.)

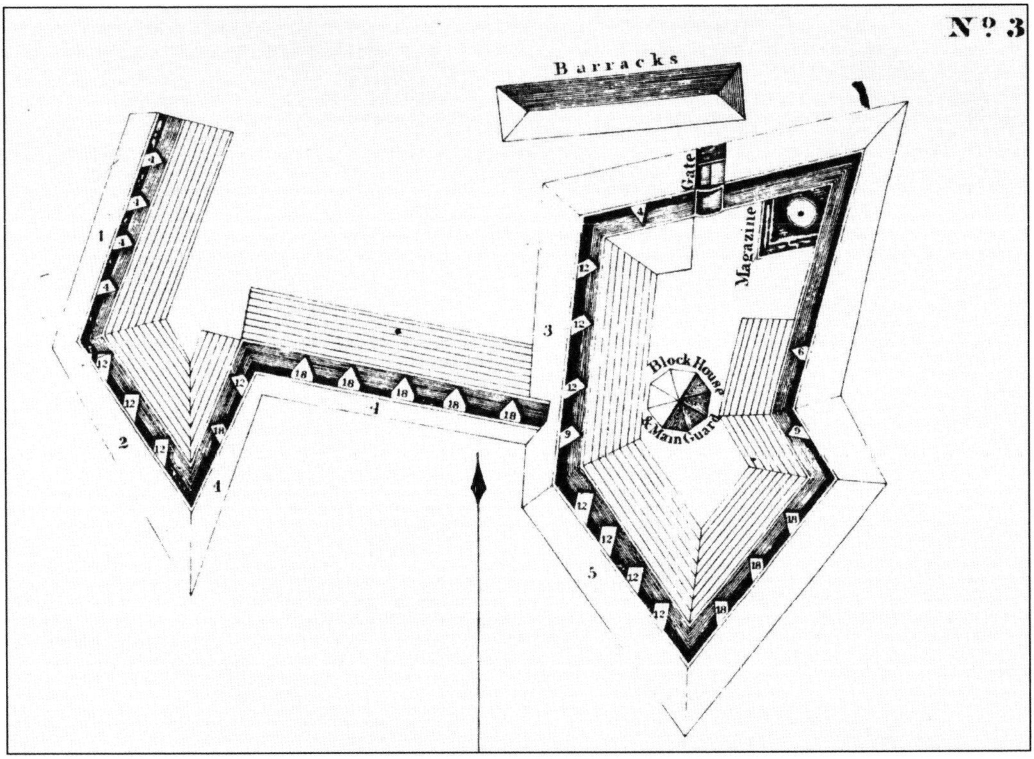

FORT PLAN. Engineer Bernard Romans was appointed to construct the fortifications at Constitution Island. He designed a massive fort with a blockhouse and powder magazine surrounded by angled batteries. Begun in the winter of 1775, parts of it were completed but were destroyed by the British in 1777. As seen in this illustration from Merle Sheffield's *The Fort That Never Was*.

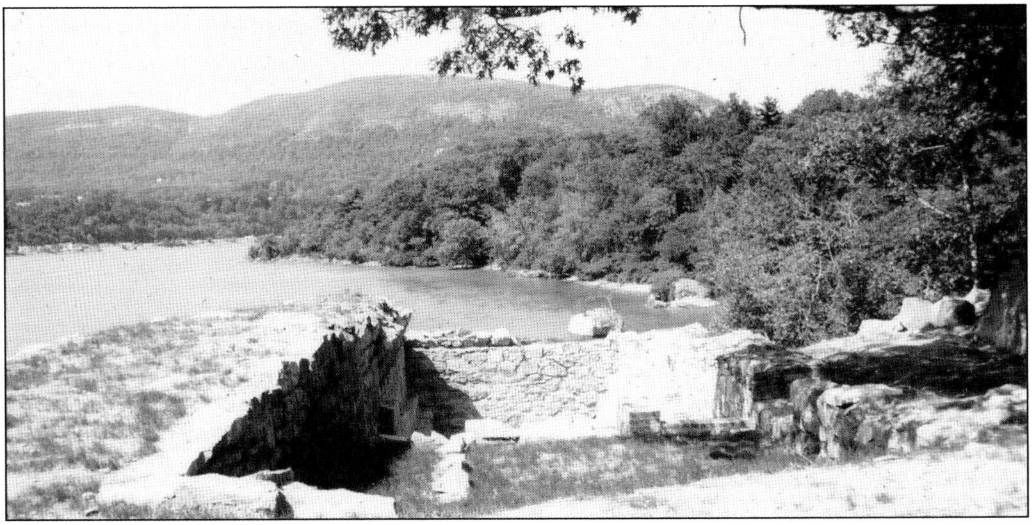

ROMANS BATTERY. This battery, now called Romans Battery, was 200 feet long, supporting 14 cannons. Additionally it contained a powder magazine. For common soldiers like Joseph Plumb Martin, the construction work was difficult. "Our duty was wheeling dirt upon a stone building intended for a magazine. . . the weather became so hot, it was difficult to breathe. I was never so glad to get clear of any duty as I was of that."

REENACTOR. A Revolutionary War reenactor demonstrates the operation of an 18th-century cannon. Officers monitored the training of young soldiers in procedures for firing the cannons. One of the artillery officers stationed at Constitution Island was Capt. David Bushnell, inventor of the first submarine. (Photograph by Gina Gascon.)

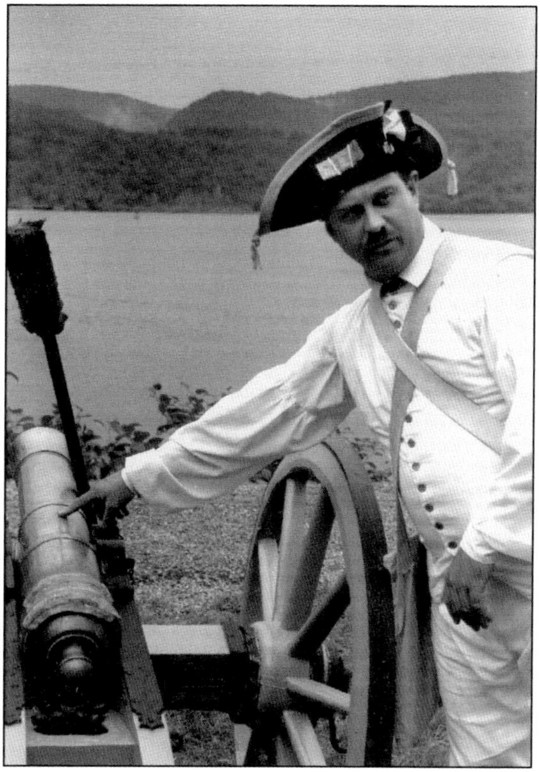

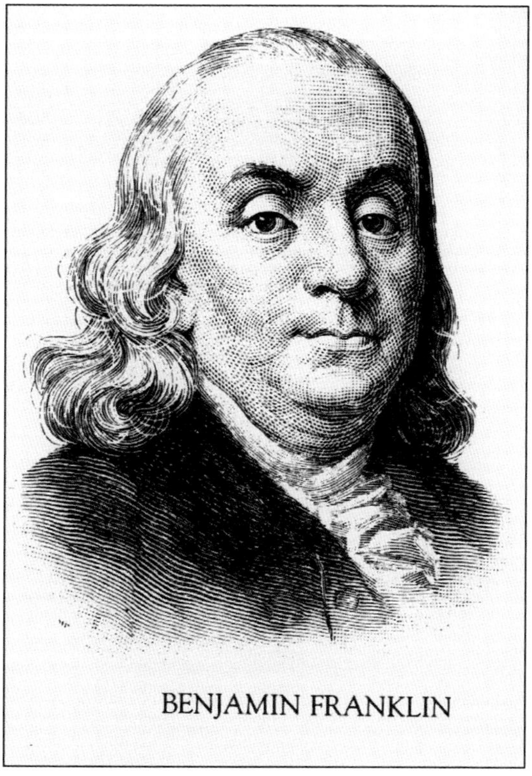

BENJAMIN FRANKLIN. In April 1776, a committee from the Second Continental Congress stopped at Fort Constitution en route to a meeting in Canada to persuade the Canadians to unite with the colonies. The group, composed of Benjamin Franklin, Samuel Chase, and Charles Carroll, recorded that there were three companies of minutemen, totaling 124 men and an artillery inventory of 22 cannons.

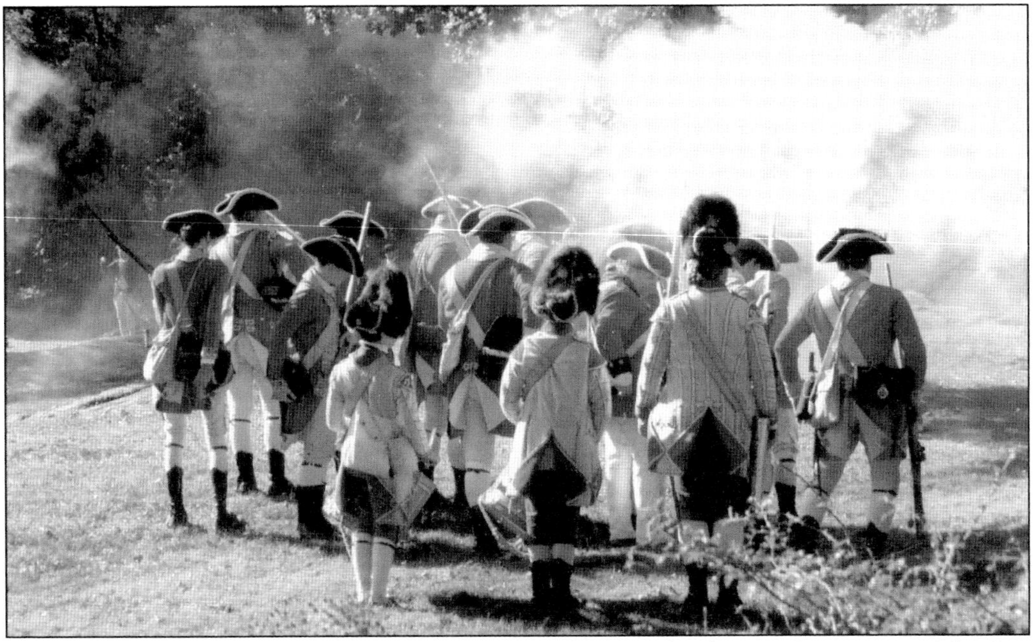

REDCOATS. Firearms ready, reenactors portray British troops landing at Constitution Island in 1777. Actually at the time, the British encountered no resistance. After their October victory at nearby Fort Montgomery, the British sent a surrender request to the American forces at the island. A shot was fired at the truce flag. When the British arrived the following morning to attack, they found the island abandoned. They remained 20 days and left, dismantling the fortifications but leaving masonry intact.

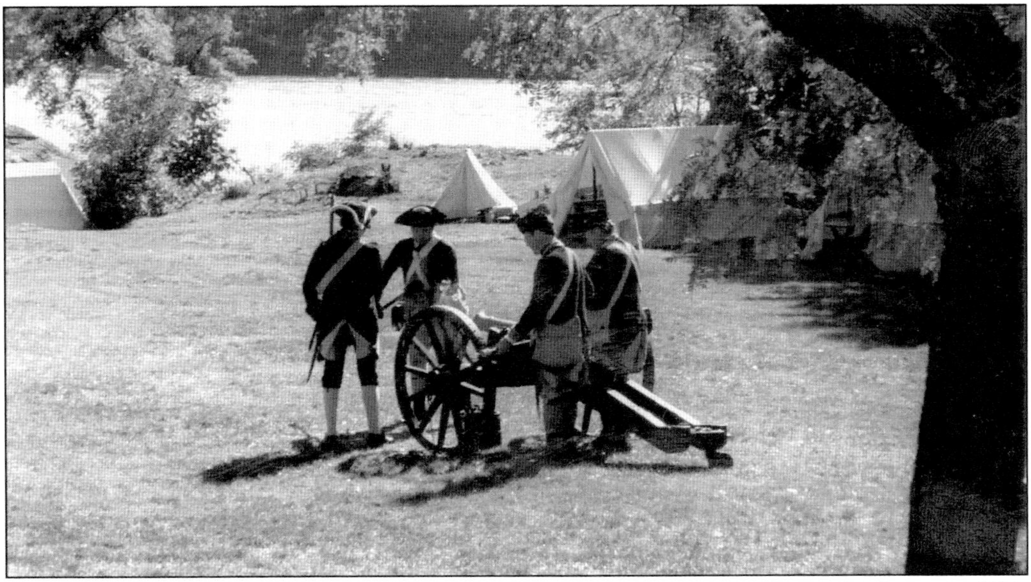

AMERICANS RETURN. Reenactors position a cannon opposite West Point. In January 1778, the Americans returned after the British occupation, revising the plan of one large fortress at Constitution Island in favor of several smaller redoubts and batteries. West Point, commanding higher ground, became the focus of an improved defensive system designed by engineer Thaddeus Kosciuszko.

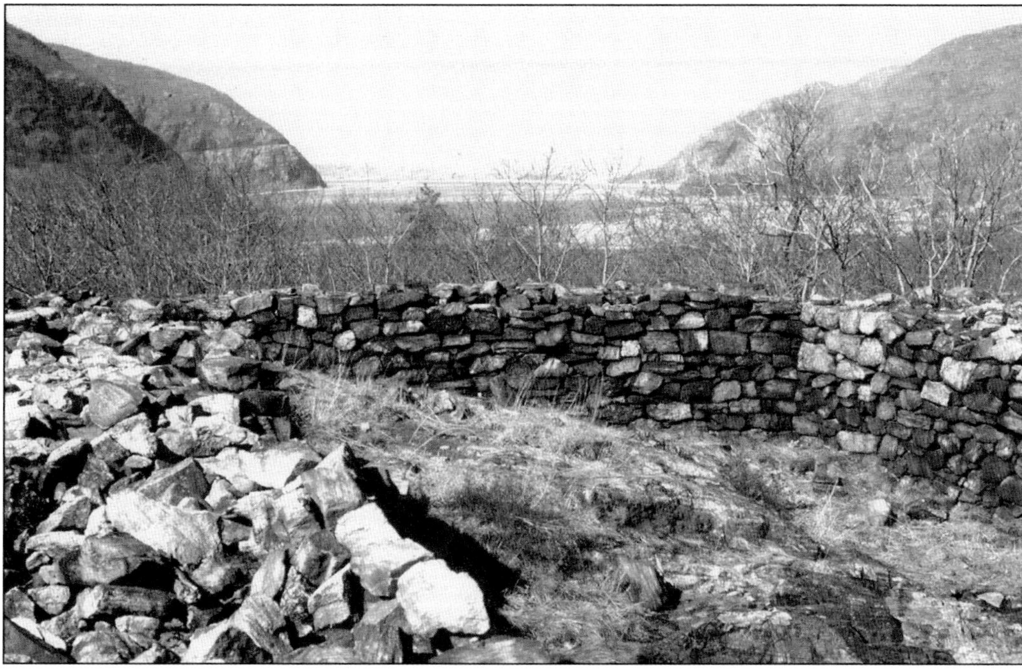

Redoubt No. 6. A redoubt is a small fortification created to protect a single feature such as a hill or a pass. On Constitution Island, Redoubt No. 6 protected against a marsh-side attack on the great chain; 120 men lived in huts outside its walls. Cannons were positioned inside. Built in 1779, its dry masonry remains intact more than 220 years later.

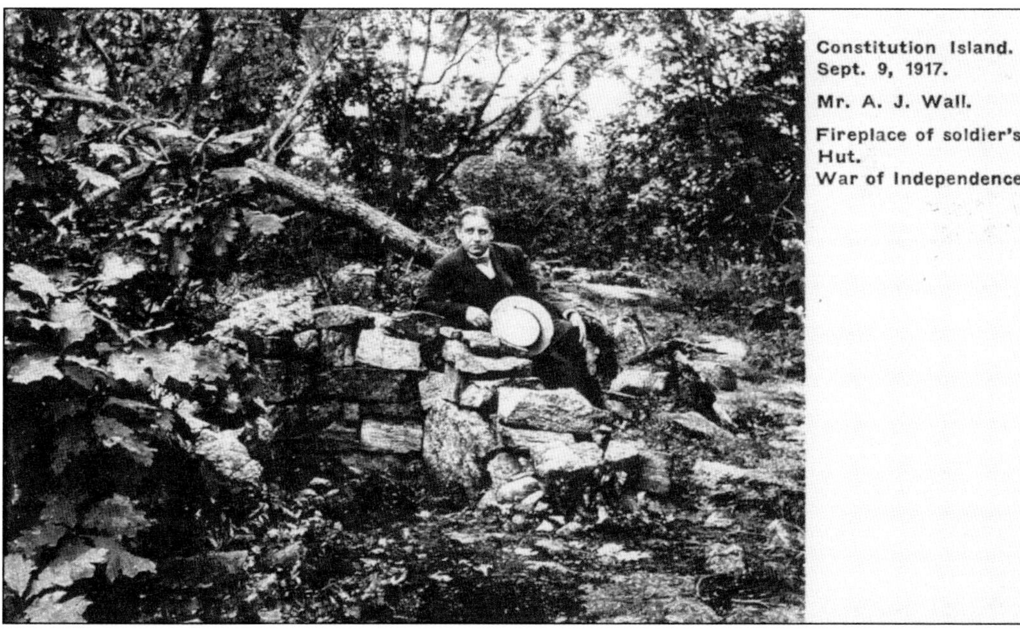

Archaeological Dig. An archaeological dig in 1917 unearthed the fireplace of a Revolutionary War soldier's hut on the island. Evidence showed that there was a camp, consisting of about 25 huts, about 200 yards from a clearing on the island called Washington's Parade Ground. (Gunza collection.)

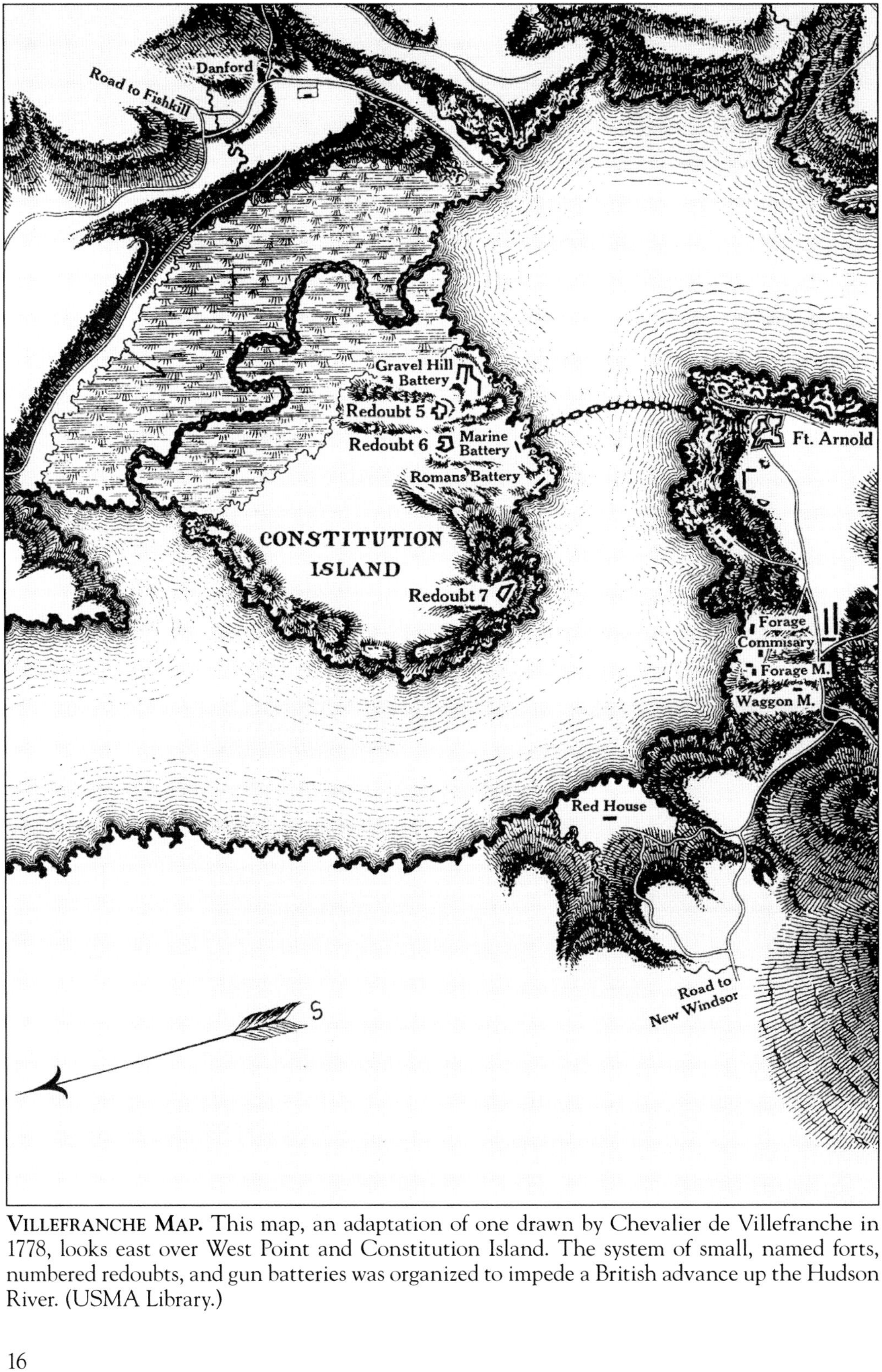

VILLEFRANCHE MAP. This map, an adaptation of one drawn by Chevalier de Villefranche in 1778, looks east over West Point and Constitution Island. The system of small, named forts, numbered redoubts, and gun batteries was organized to impede a British advance up the Hudson River. (USMA Library.)

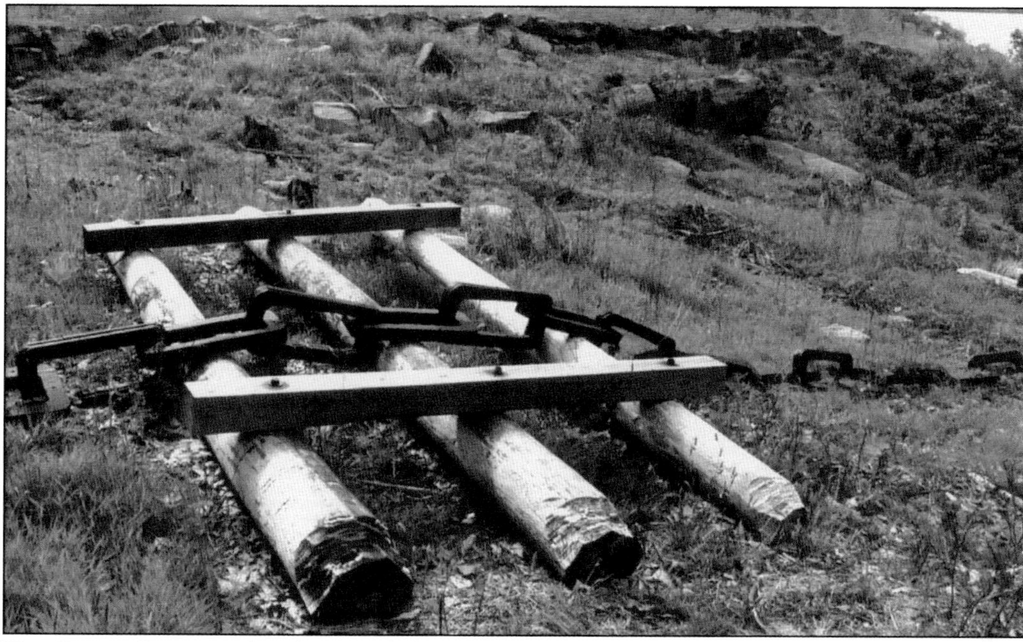

THE GREAT CHAIN. After the British destroyed the first Hudson River chain at Fort Montgomery, a stronger one called the great chain was positioned between West Point and Constitution Island. A re-creation of the chain is on exhibit at the island. Each link was about two feet long and two inches thick. A swivel joint allowed the chain to move with the tides. It was supported on log rafts to keep it afloat on the surface of the river. Seen below, on display at West Point in 1920, is a portion of the chain mounted on upturned cannons. During the Revolutionary War, it was removed in the winter and repositioned in April. Soldiers charged with this duty called it "Washington's Watch Chain." Its strength was never tested. After 1778, the war moved south ending in 1783. (Below, PIPC Archives.)

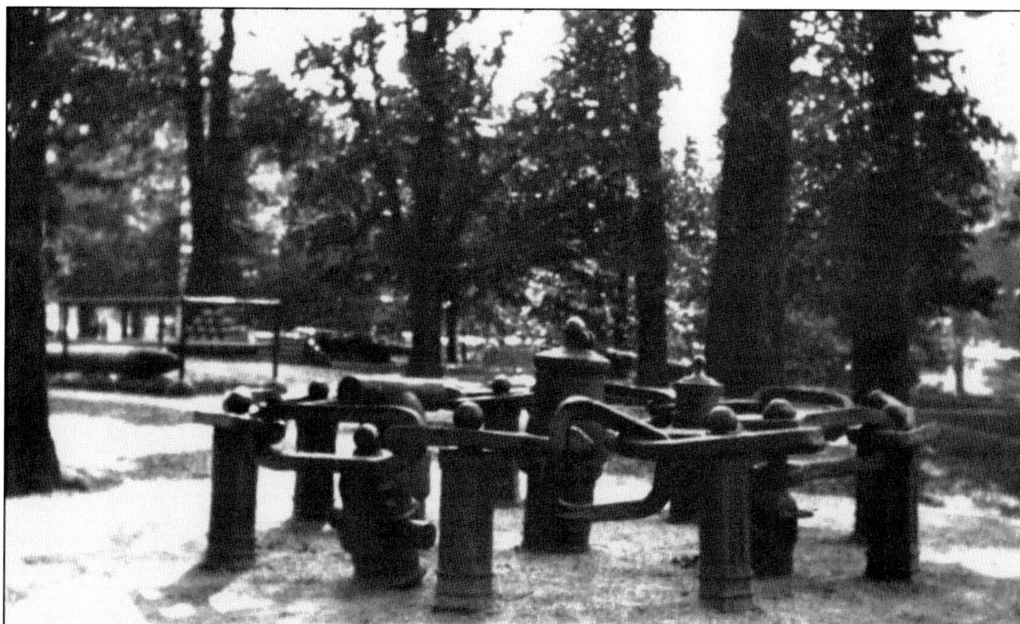

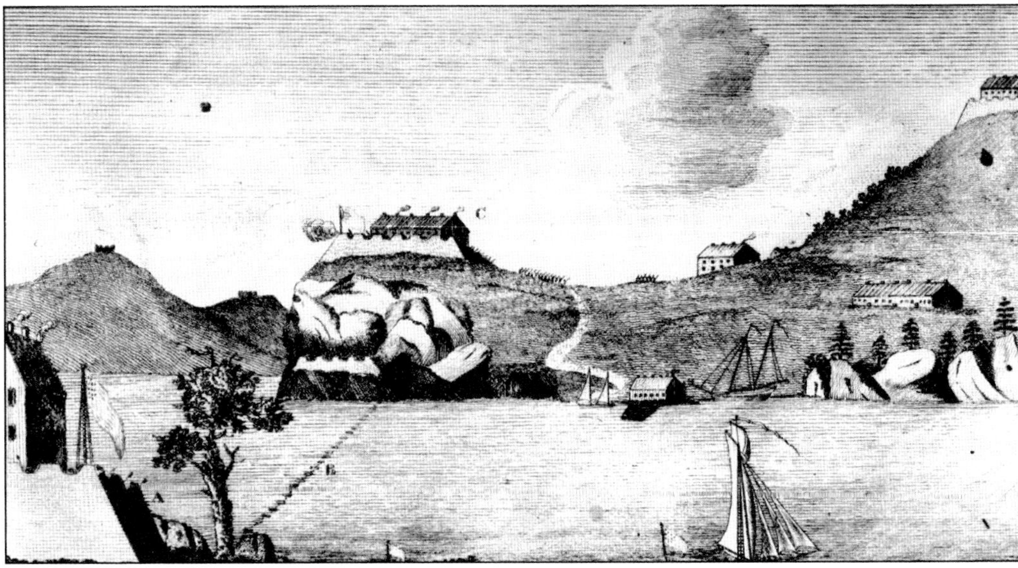

WEST POINT. This 18th-century drawing is sketched from Fort Constitution, looking toward West Point. Directly across on the center hill is Fort Arnold, renamed Fort Clinton in 1780 after Benedict Arnold's treason. The great chain is clearly marked in the river below. At the center of the picture, the building at the water line is the North Dock. On the hill at right is Fort Putnam. (USMA Library.)

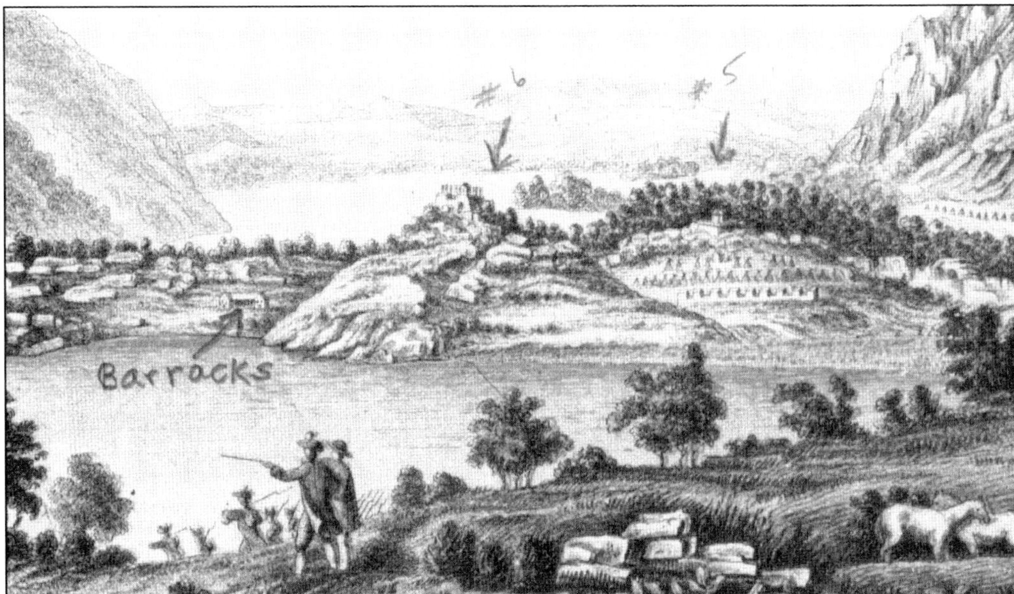

CONSTITUTION ISLAND. Looking in the opposite direction toward Constitution Island, this artistic rendition of a drawing by military engineer Pierre L'Enfant shows the system of small forts envisioned by Thaddeus Kosciuszko. Redoubts Nos. 5 and 6 occupy the hills. The barracks site is the location of the Warner house. This illustration is from Merle Sheffield's *The Fort That Never Was*.

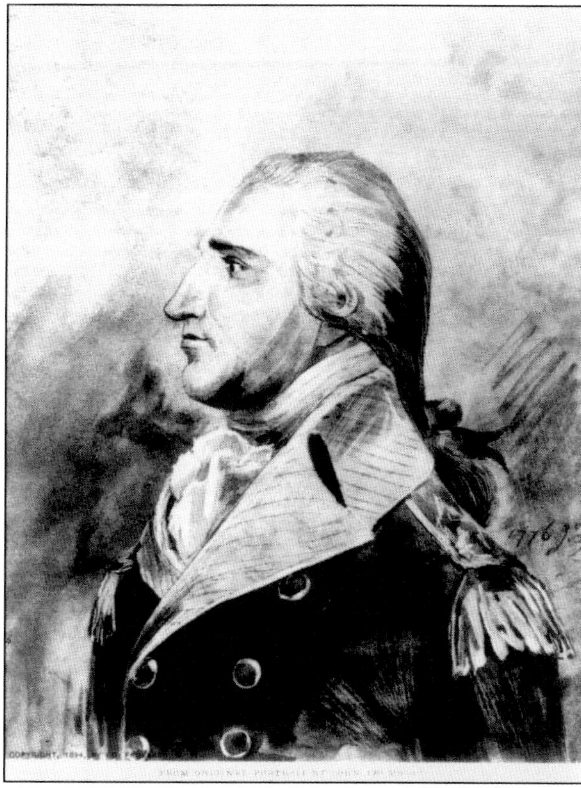

ARNOLD AND ANDRE. In 1780, the American hero, Benedict Arnold, became commander of West Point. After distinguished service to the colonies, he changed sides and schemed to turn West Point and Constitution Island over to the British for the sum of £20,300 and a commission as a brigadier general. His treason was discovered when his contact, Maj. John Andre was captured in possession of the plans with a pass signed by Arnold. Upon learning of Andre's capture, pictured below, Arnold fled to England. The documents discovered in Andre's boot listed the troop strength of each fort at West Point and Constitution Island. Andre, who was traveling in disguise when he was caught, was hanged as a spy in Tappan, New York. (Below, Library of Congress.)

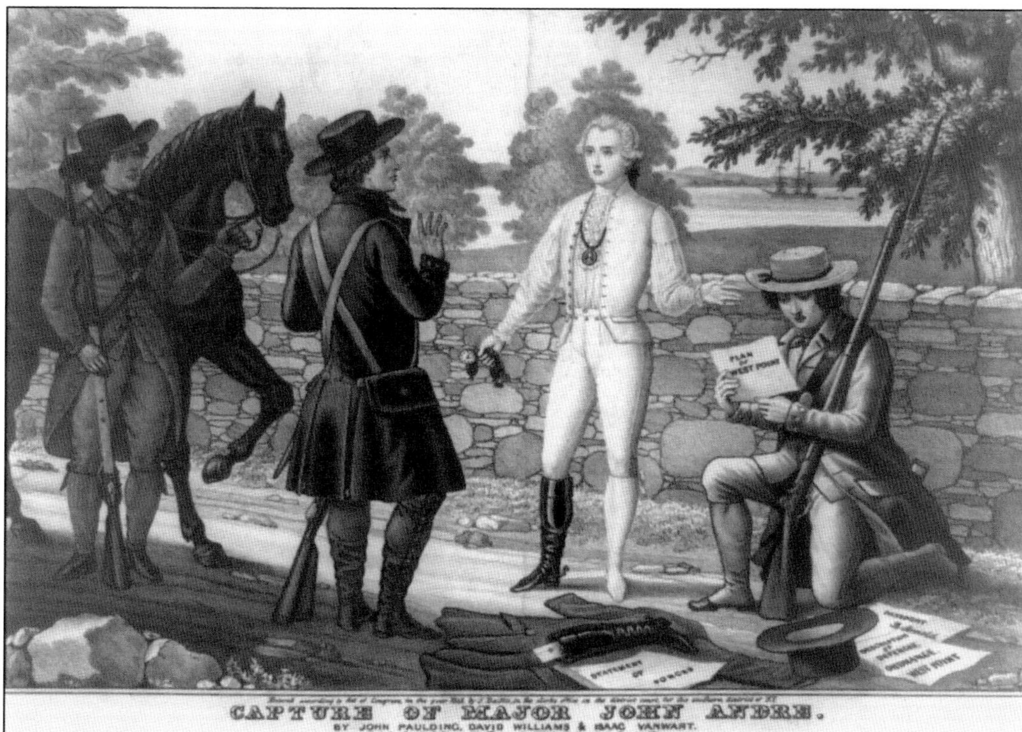

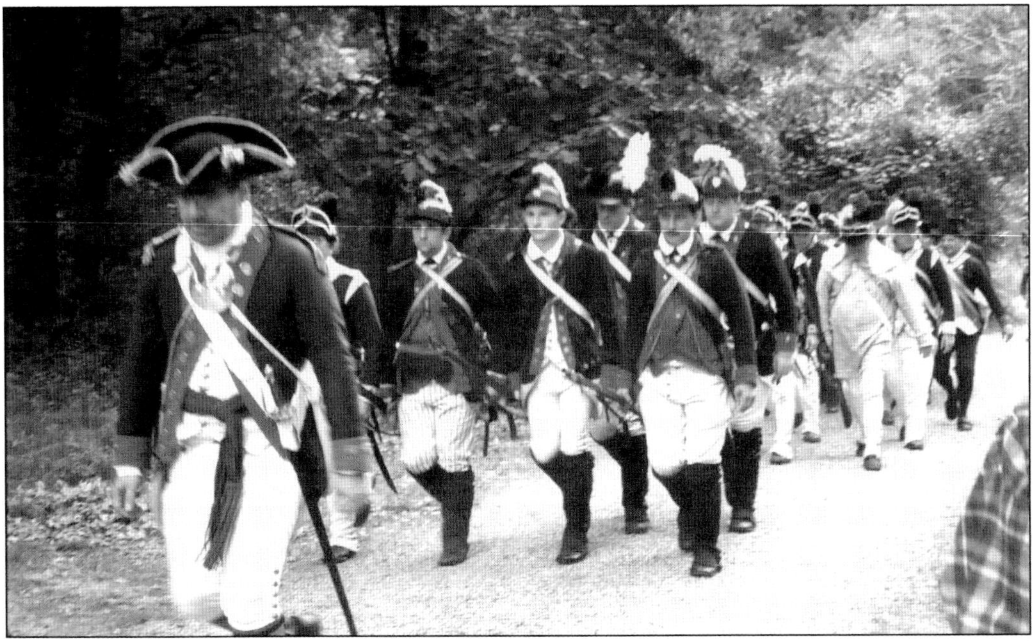

War's End. Reenactors portraying Continental Army soldiers march along a wooded island path. Two interesting units lived on Constitution Island at the end of the war. In 1782, an invalid corps was formed of men recovering from illness or wounds who were not ready for active duty. They spent six months of the year at West Point and six months on the island. The last unit to occupy the island was Washington's Life Guard, 64 soldiers who escorted the general as the British withdrew from New York in 1783. They were disbanded in December 1783. The soldier's barracks remained until 1788 when they were torn down and the materials sold. Mr. Bunn, a Philipse tenant before and after the war, requested that one-fifth of one barracks be left as his home. This part of the Warner house, below, is believed to be that portion of the barracks.

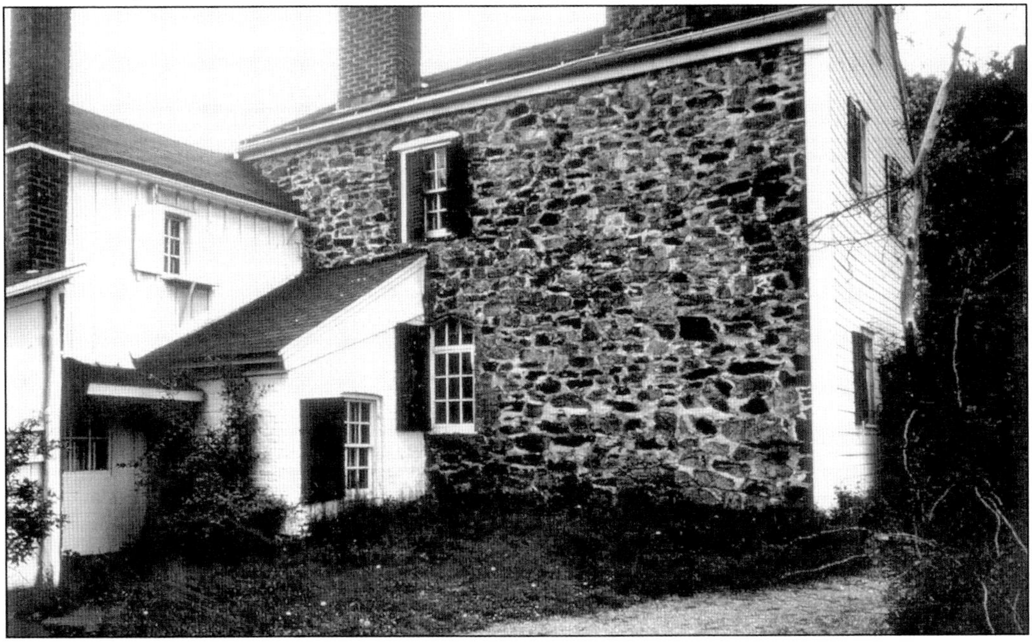

Two

THE WARNER FAMILY

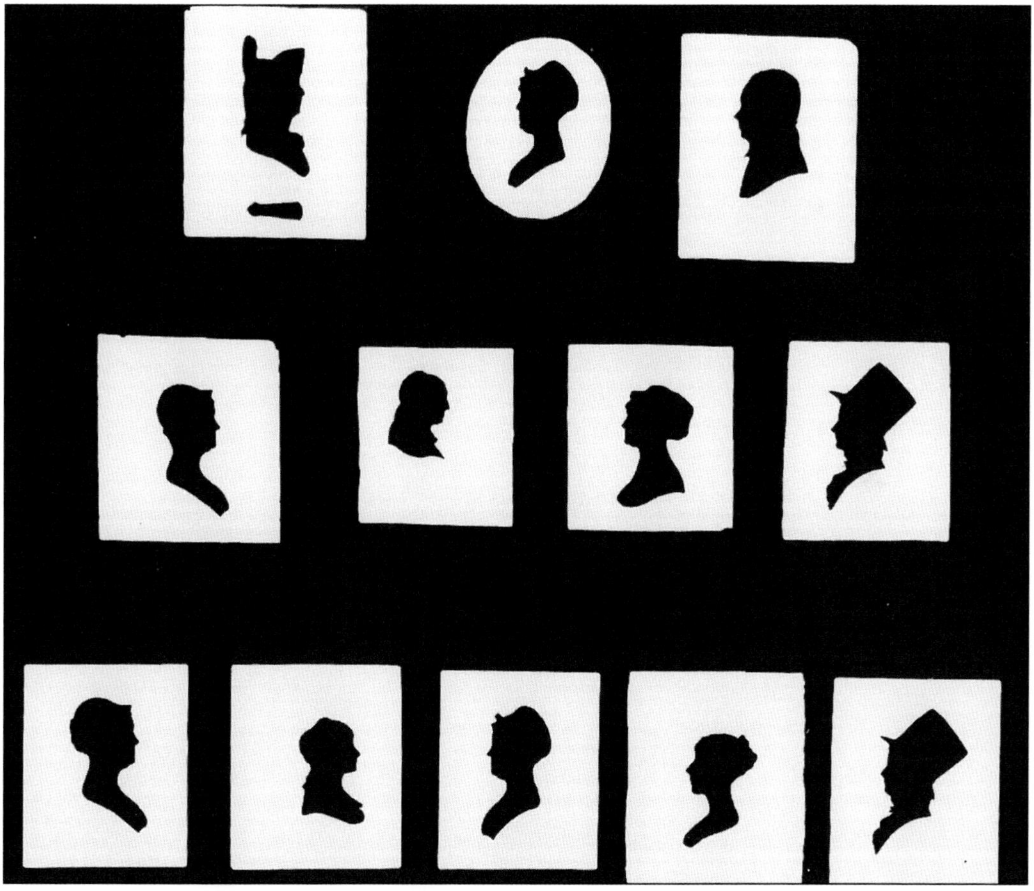

SILHOUETTES. Constitution Island became the home of the Warner family 55 years after the Revolutionary War. Their ancestors are represented by this framed collection of silhouettes that hangs in their island home, now a museum. Descended from 17th-century settlers in New England, their family members included hard-working pioneer farmers and businessmen as well as soldiers who had fought in the Revolutionary War.

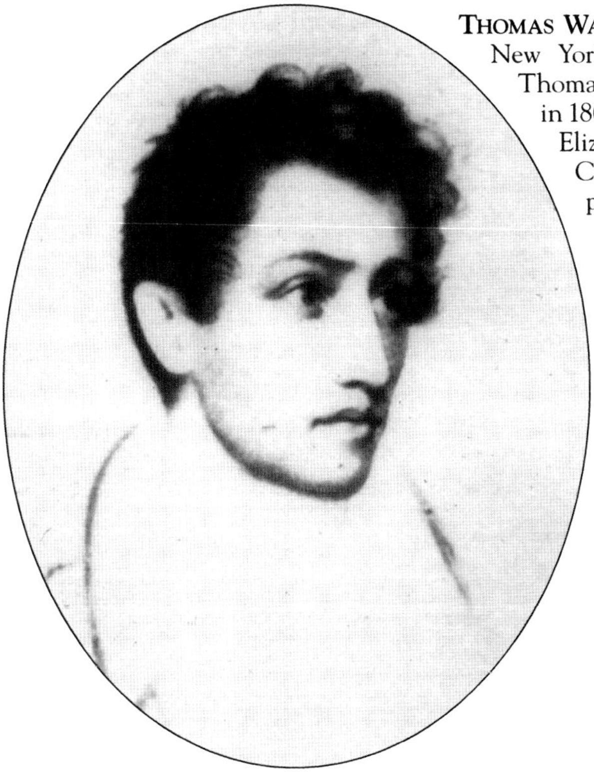

THOMAS WARNER, 1784–1848. Raised in Canaan, New York, with his brother and two sisters, Thomas Warner graduated from Union College in 1808 with a degree in theology. He married Elizabeth McDougal while living in St. Croix. Thomas served as chaplain and professor of geography, history, and ethics at the United States Military Academy (USMA) from 1828 to 1838. Family members visited him often during his tenure at the academy.

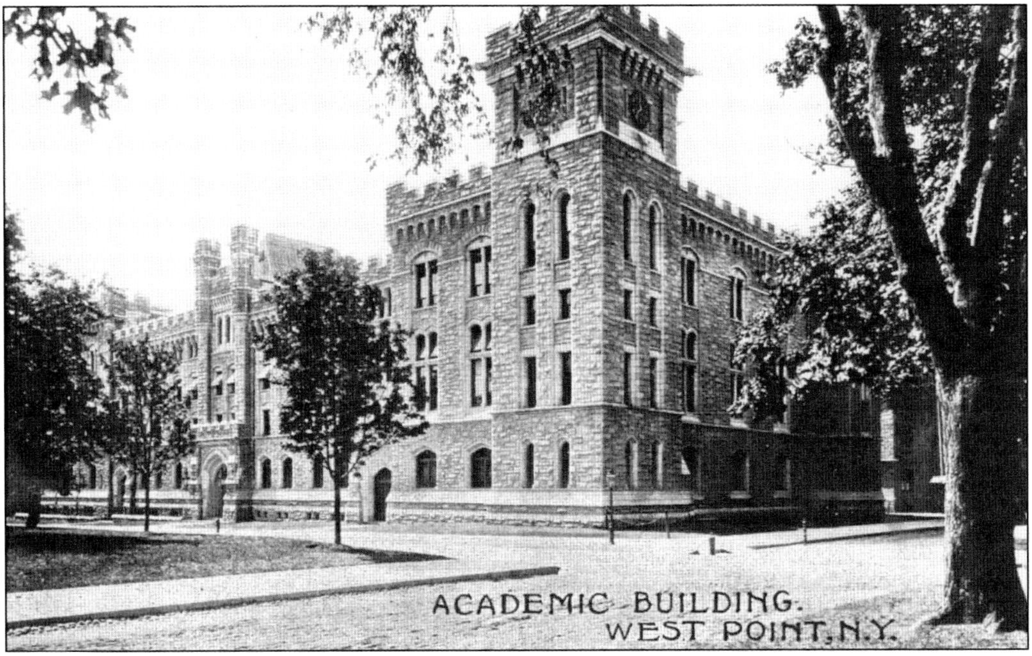

OLD WEST POINT. When Thomas began teaching at West Point, the academy had only been in existence for 26 years. The superintendent was Sylvanus Thayer, a friend of Thomas. During the 1800s, the original three- and four-story wooden buildings were gradually replaced by gray granite structures like the academic building shown here. (USMA Library.)

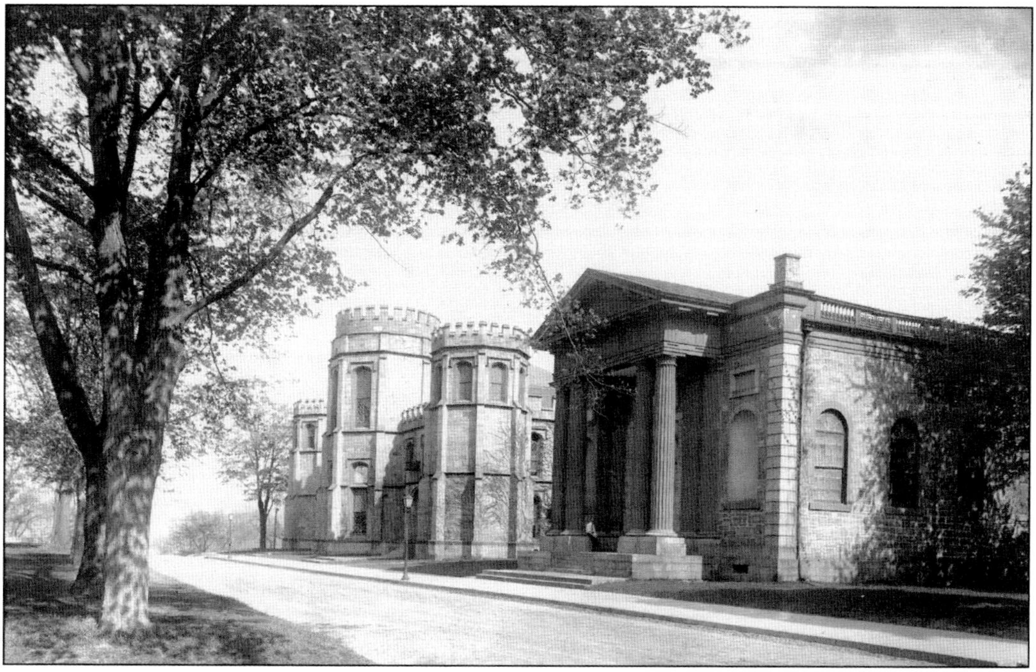

LIBRARY AND CHAPEL. As chaplain, Thomas gave the first service in the Cadet Chapel, right, when it was completed in 1836. His family attended the historic occasion. Now referred to as the Old Cadet Chapel, the building stands inside the West Point Cemetery. At left is the old library. (USMA Library.)

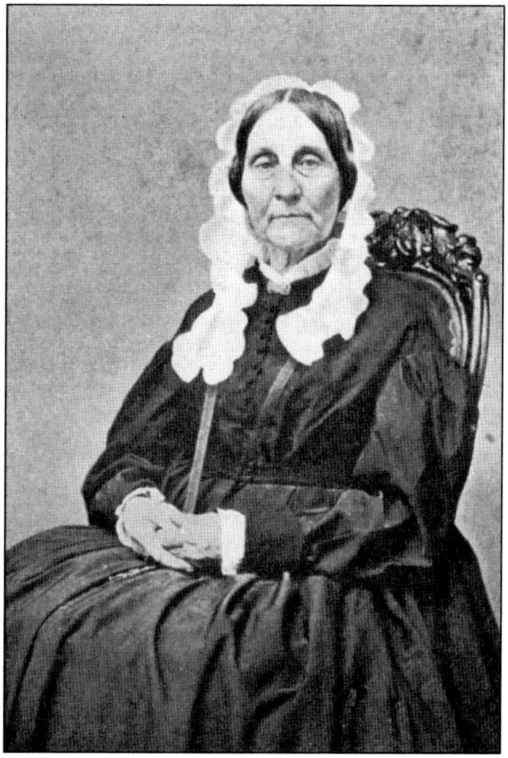

FRANCES L. WARNER, 1802–1885. Sister of Thomas and Henry Warner, Frances came to live with Henry after the death of his wife. She cared for his two daughters, Susan and Anna. She was only 23 years old at the time, and she remained with them until her death at age 83. She was beloved by her brothers and nieces who called her Aunt Fanny. Anna described her as handsome, quick, high-spirited, energetic, and devoted.

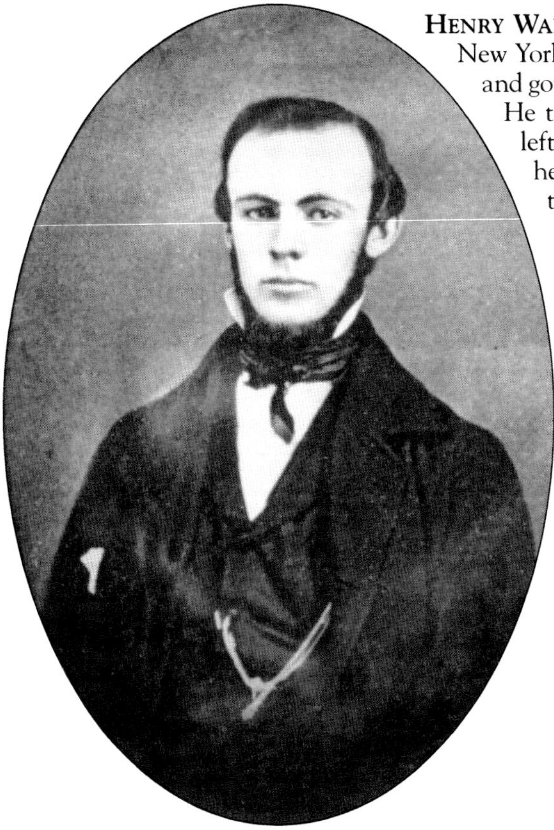

HENRY WARNER, 1787–1875. Raised in rural Canaan, New York, Henry Warner preferred study to farming and got his law degree from Union College in 1801. He taught for a time at the college. In 1811, he left to join a New York City law firm. In 1814, he established his own successful practice that often required him to go to Albany. Handsome and well mannered, Henry married the lovely Anna Bartlett in 1817.

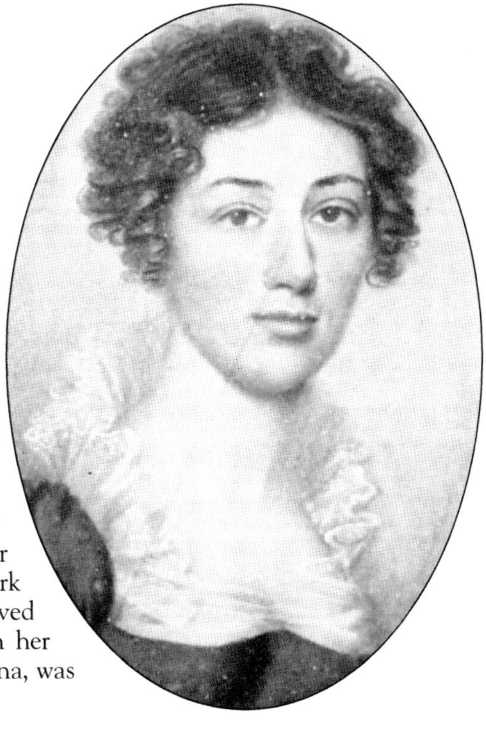

ANNA MARSH BARTLETT, 1792–1826. Born in Rhode Island to a wealthy family, Anna Marsh Bartlett was raised in Jamaica, New York, by her mother and stepfather, Cornelius Bogert. After her marriage to Henry in 1817, they moved to New York City. They had five children, but only two survived to adulthood. Anna Marsh died at age 34 when her daughter, Susan, was almost 7 and her infant, Anna, was 17 months old.

SUSAN BOGERT WARNER, 1819–1885. Eldest child of Henry and Anna, Susan was raised by her father and aunt in New York City but traveled often to Canaan, Jamaica, and West Point to visit relatives. As was customary among upper-middle-class families, she was educated by private tutors in French, Latin, Italian, singing, and piano. As a child, Susan loved to read, write, and tell stories.

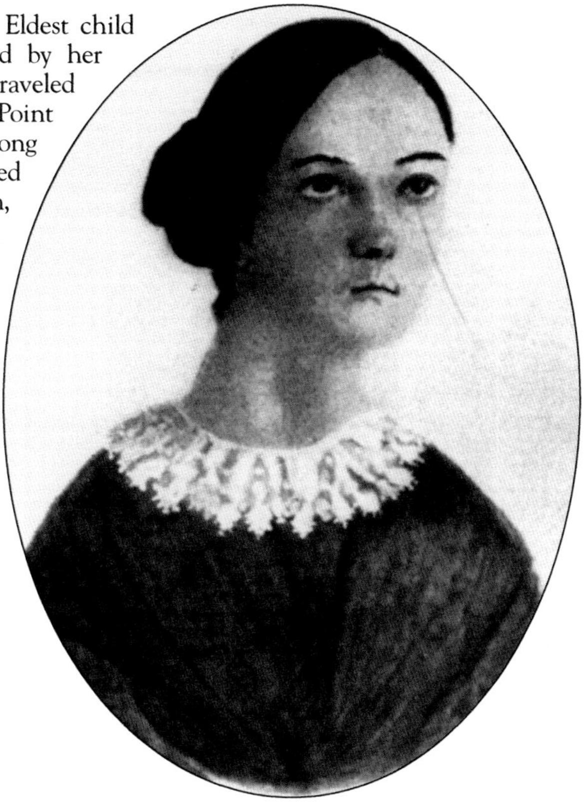

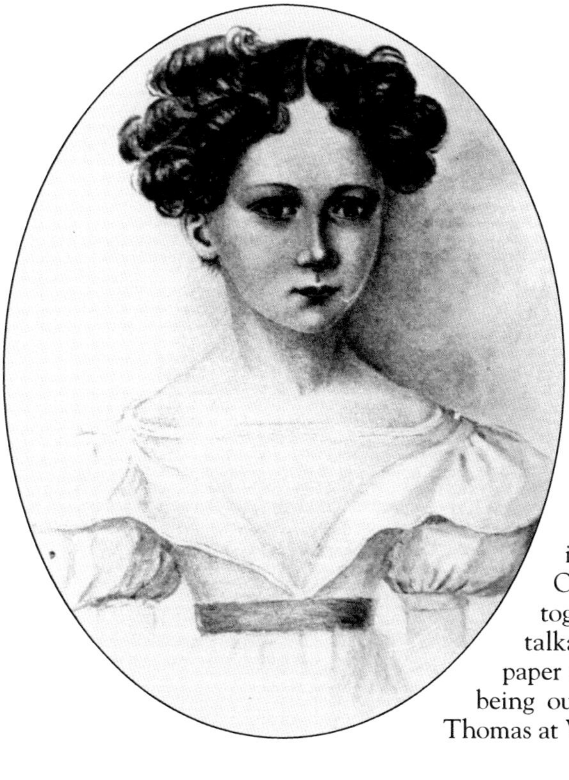

ANNA BARTLETT WARNER, 1824–1915. Like her sister, Anna was born in New York City and tutored at home. Henry oversaw his daughters' education and instructed them in history and geography. On Sundays, the family attended church together and visited friends. Vivacious and talkative, Anna enjoyed playing cards and paper dolls with Susan, but she especially loved being outdoors. She delighted in visits to Uncle Thomas at West Point.

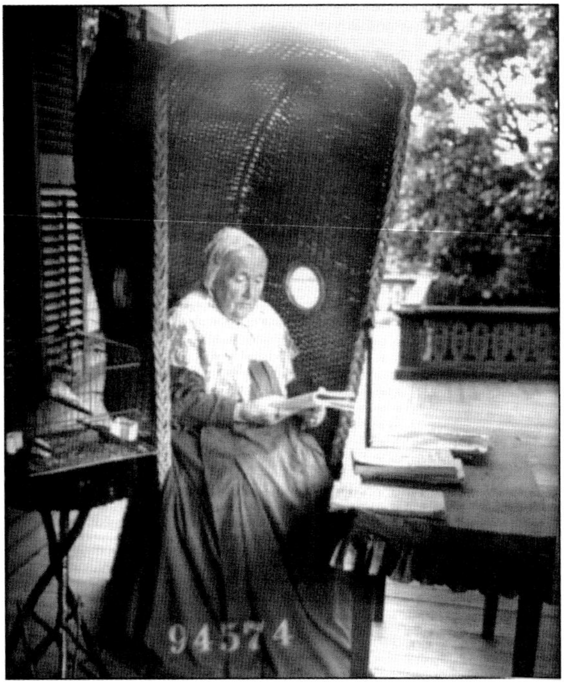

JULIA WARD HOWE. As children living in New York City, Susan Warner and Julia Ward Howe were well acquainted and visited each other socially. Howe, who became a social activist and abolitionist, wrote the *Battle Hymn of the Republic* in 1862. In another interesting literary connection, the Warner sisters were cousins, on their mother's side, of Sarah Power Whitman, the Rhode Island poet romantically involved with Edgar Allan Poe. (Library of Congress.)

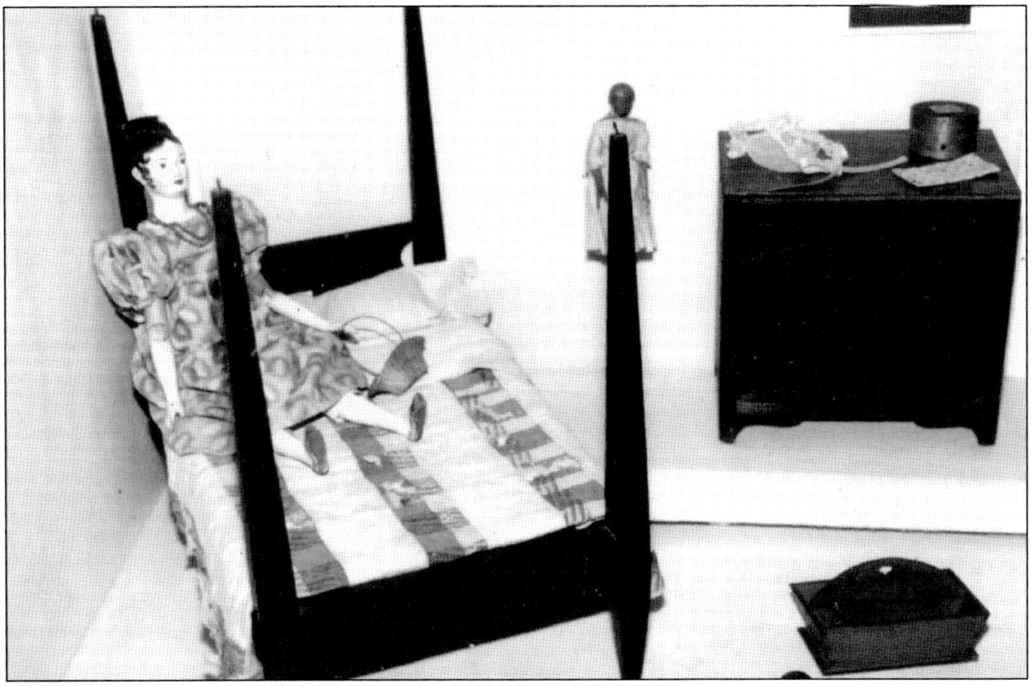

TOY EXHIBIT. An exhibit now in the Warner House indicates the close and caring relationship of the family. Susan's journal entry on September 1, 1830, states, "Yesterday was Anna's birthday . . . after breakfast Grandma presented her with the doll. When I brought down the bedstead, the child was nearly overcome." Years later, Anna recalled the happy moment. "A little high post bedstead made by my father's own hands. Curtains, bolster, sheets and quilt were all my sister's gift. And each was perfectly well made."

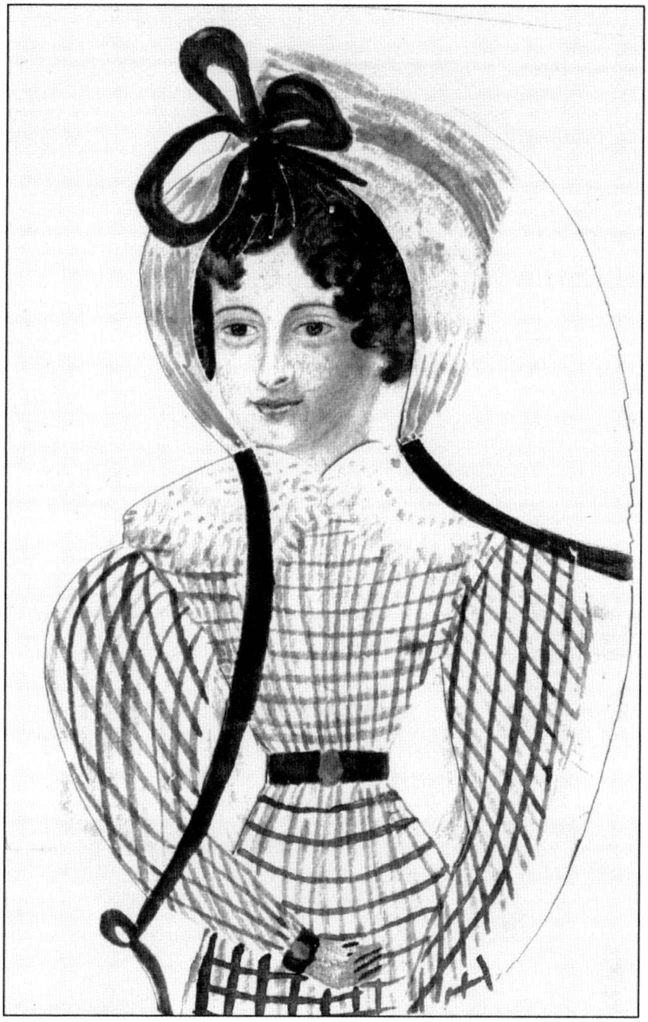

PAPER FASHIONS. Children of the 19th century created their own entertainment. Susan was fond of designing and playing with paper dolls or "cardbabies." In a journal entry at age 12 she writes, "Soon after we got home I began to draw. After dinner I cut one or two little things out of card and then told stories with Anna." Interestingly the face of the doll at right bears a striking resemblance to her mother (page 25). Styles depicted here date back to the 1830s. The two sisters also used their artistic talents to draw, paint, embroider, and sew. Real fashion was equally interesting to them. Prior to 1837, a dressmaker came to their home each season to sew new clothes, always cause for excitement.

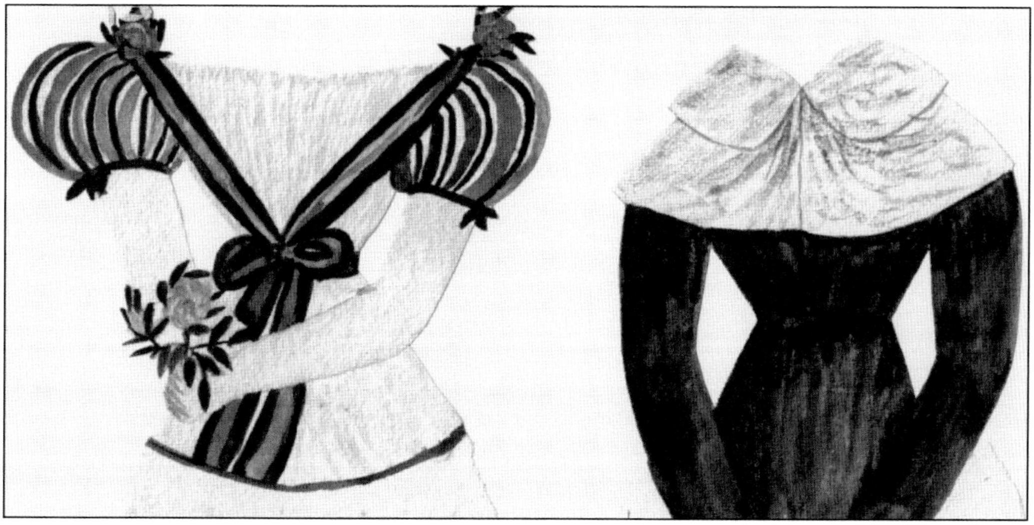

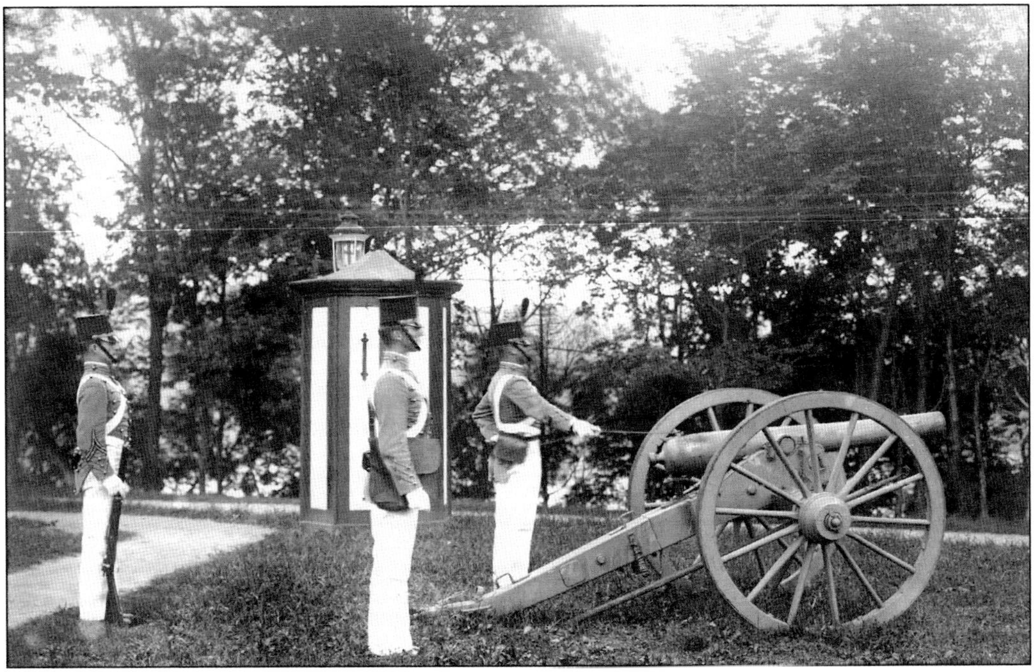

EVENING GUN. During summer visits to Thomas Warner at West Point, the family took late afternoon walks near the cadet encampments. Every night there was a cannon firing known as the "evening gun," pictured here. Susan, at age 15, recorded her reaction in her diary; "One thing disturbs me a little. I am afraid of the gun-fire . . . but I suppose I should not mind it after a little time." (USMA Library.)

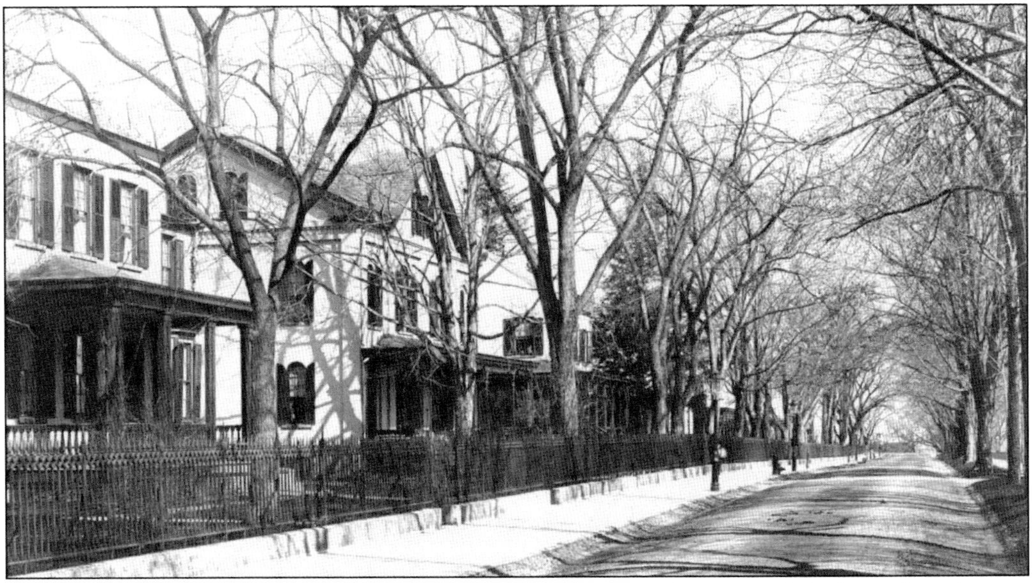

PROFESSORS' ROW. The superintendent and the academy professors resided along this pleasant street west of the parade ground. While visiting their uncle Thomas, the sisters were often invited to tea by the officers' wives who lived in these homes. After one such tea in June 1836, the Warners attended the graduation parade and then watched fireworks from the porch of the West Point Hotel. (USMA Library.)

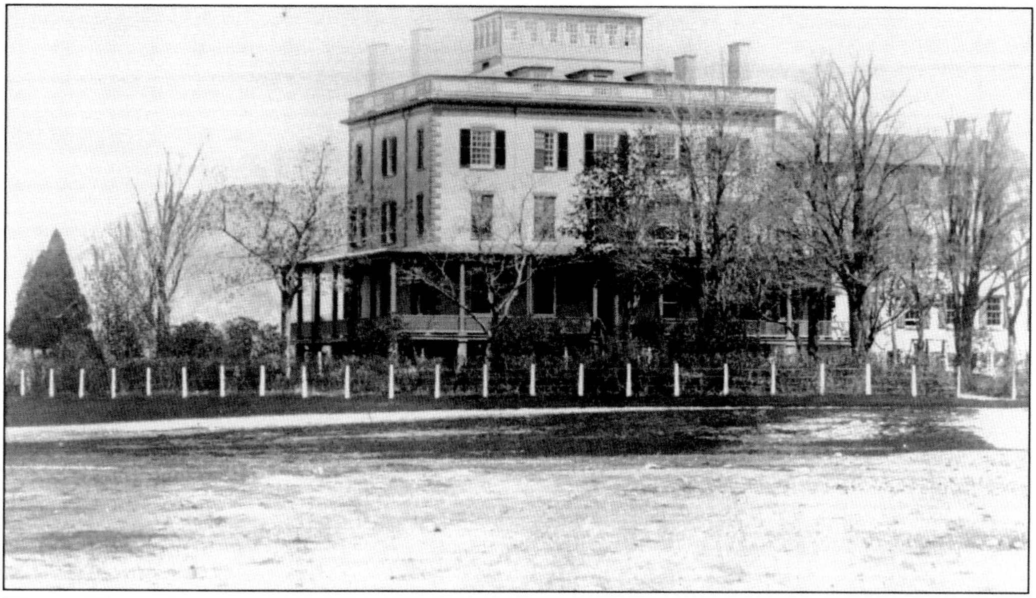

HOTEL VIEW. Commanding a magnificent view of the Hudson Highlands from Trophy Point, the West Point Hotel, above, served visitors from 1829 to 1911. Tourists, distinguished visitors, and relatives and friends of cadets were accommodated here for 82 years. Among the notables who stayed here during the 19th century were Ulysses S. Grant, Robert E. Lee, James McNeill Whistler, and Edgar Allan Poe. A wide porch wrapped around the building affording a view on the north side similar to the view below. At right is Constitution Island. It was Thomas who first conceived of buying Constitution Island. He thought it would be a smart investment for Henry Warner, whose wealth had increased through real estate speculation. After much lobbying from Thomas, Henry bought the island in 1836 for $48,000 from a descendant of the Philipse family. (Above, USMA Library.)

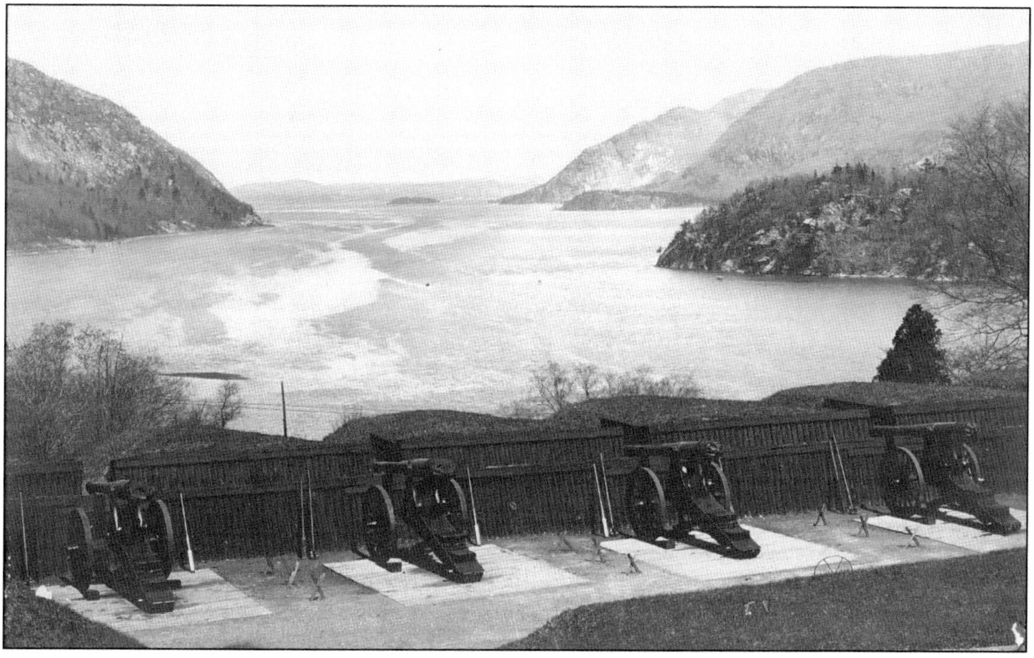

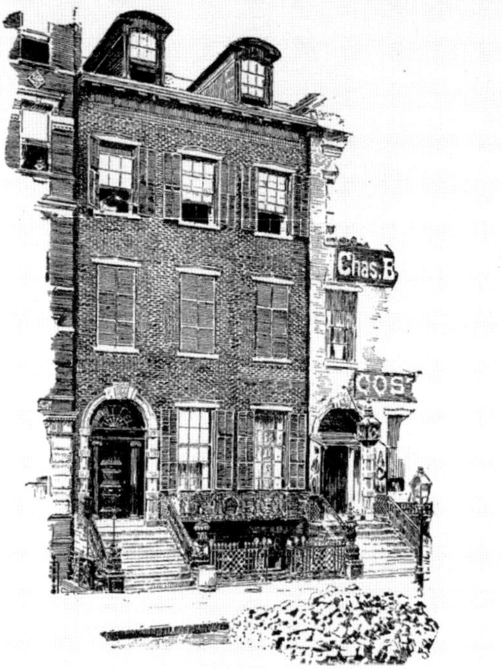

NO. 6 ST. MARK'S PLACE, NEW YORK.

Where James Fenimore Cooper wrote "Homeward Bound" and "Home as Found."

ST. MARK'S PLACE. One year before he purchased Constitution Island, Henry Warner had moved his family into an elegant townhouse in New York City. No image of their fashionable residence at 10 St. Mark's Place exists, but it stood two doors down from this presumably identical house belonging to James Fenimore Cooper at 6 St. Mark's Place. (The New York Historical Society.)

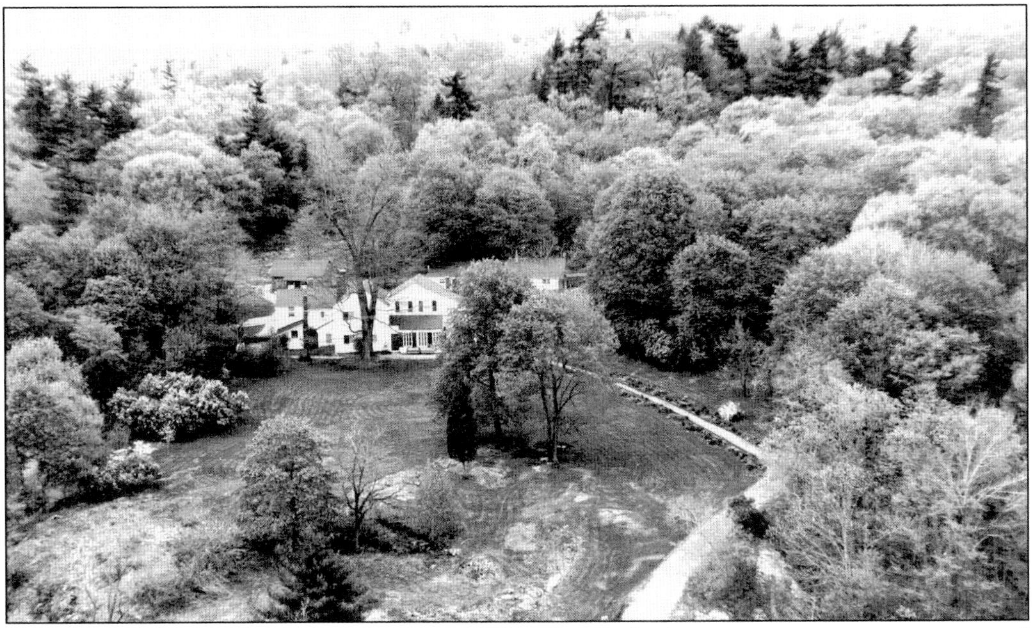

ISLAND PROPERTY. Thomas and Henry were excited with the new investment property and dreamed of building an elaborate hotel on the north side of the island. Meanwhile on the south side, Henry put a large addition on the existing farmhouse to create the summer residence for his family. But the nationwide depression known as the panic of 1837 changed everything, and soon the rugged island opposite West Point became the Warners' permanent home.

Three

The Warner House

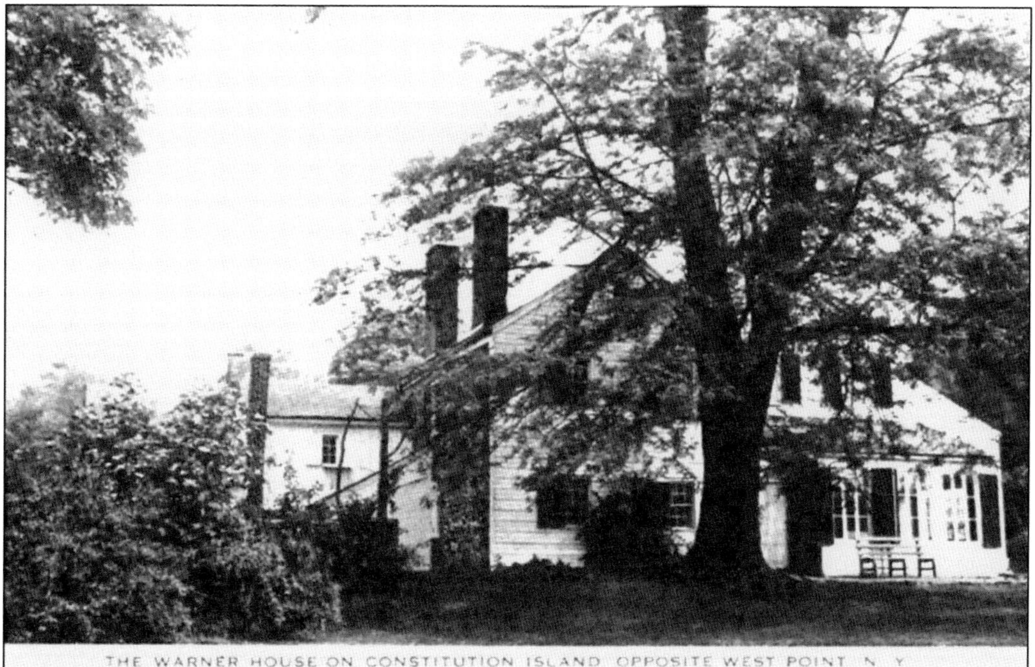

Warner House. After purchasing the island in 1836, Henry Warner enlarged the two-story, 18th-century farmhouse, left of tree, with a spacious addition that included a parlor, dining room, library, office, three bedrooms, and an enclosed front porch. Henry named their completed house Wood Crag. His plan was to spend eight months of every year on the island and four months in the comfortable luxury of the New York City townhouse. (Gunza collection.)

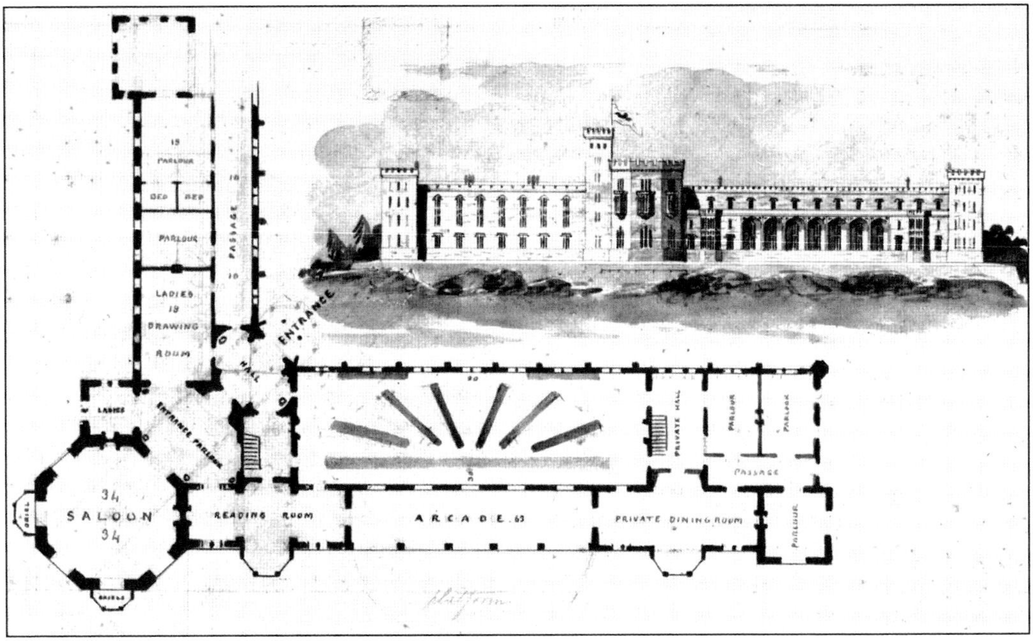

HOTEL PLAN. Constitution Island was purchased as an investment property. Thomas and Henry Warner commissioned a design for an elegant hotel with smaller resort cottages to attract wealthy tourists from New York City. Architect Alexander Jackson Davis prepared these plans, which included an octagonal saloon, reading room, ladies drawing room, private dining room, parlors, and an arcade. The project was abandoned for financial reasons.

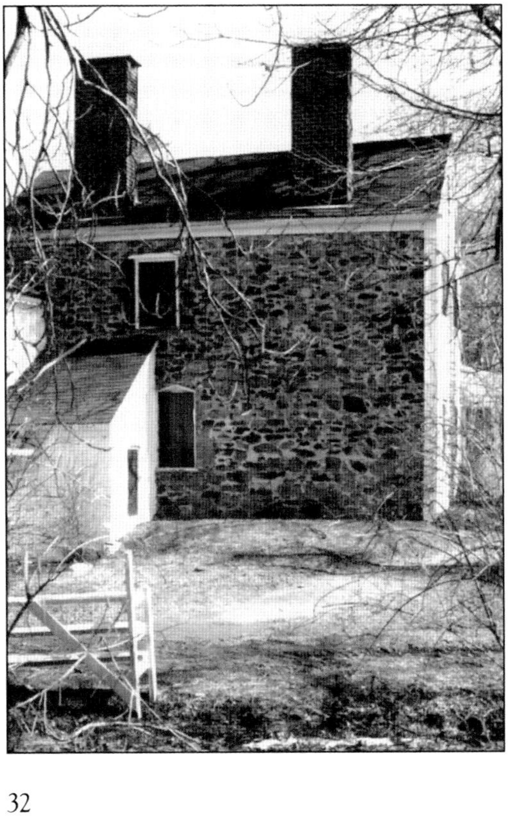

OLD BARRACKS. The oldest parts of the Warner house are the wall seen here and the rooms immediately behind it. They are believed to be part of the Revolutionary War period soldiers' barracks dating from 1778. Henry's financial crisis resulting from the panic of 1837 required him to sell the elegant New York City townhouse to pay debts and move his family to the island in 1838.

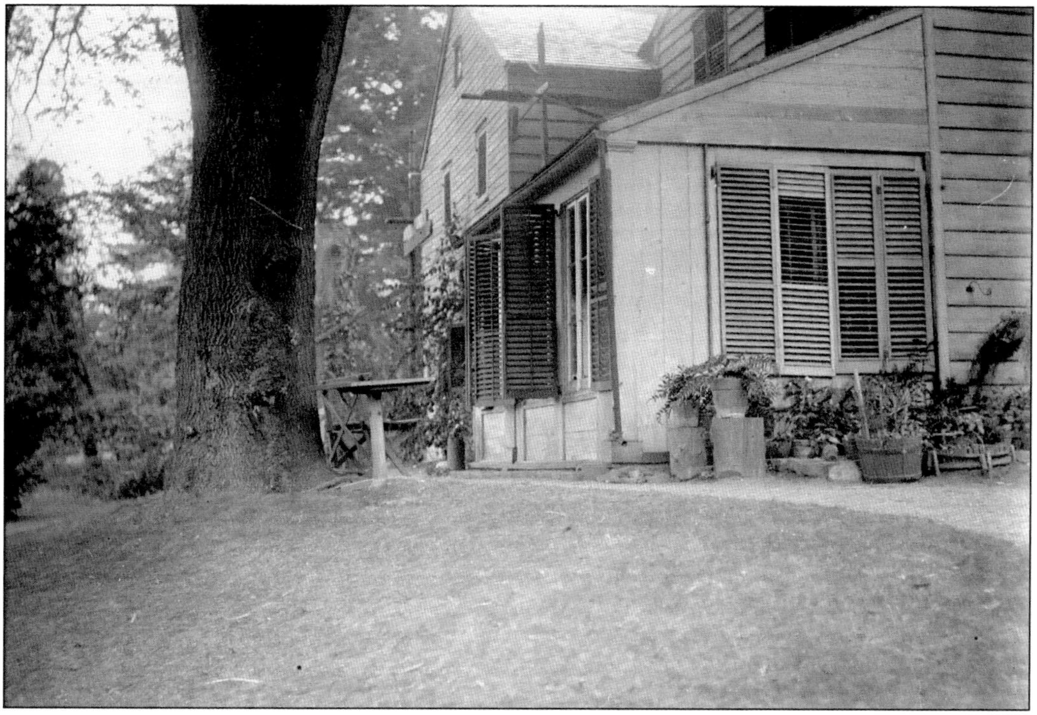

PIAZZA. Susan and Anna Warner called their glass-enclosed porch "our little glazed piazza." It was used for sitting, sewing, and reading. Potted plants were displayed in summer and the room served as a greenhouse in the winter. From this delightful porch, they looked out on the Hudson River, busy with boat traffic. (Below, Historic American Buildings Survey, Library of Congress.)

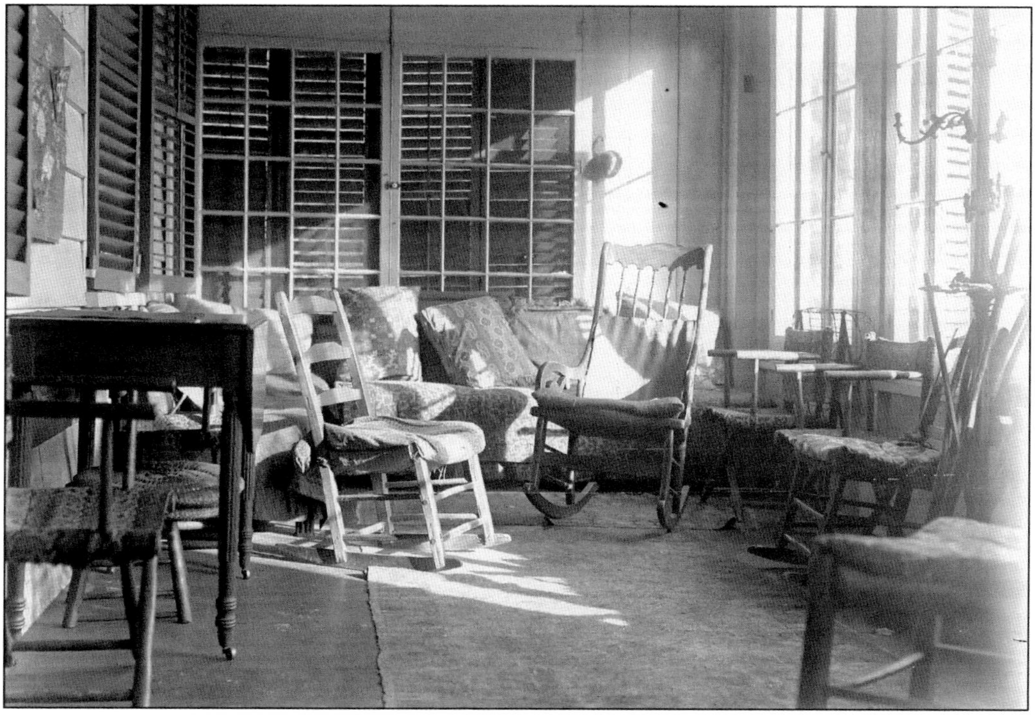

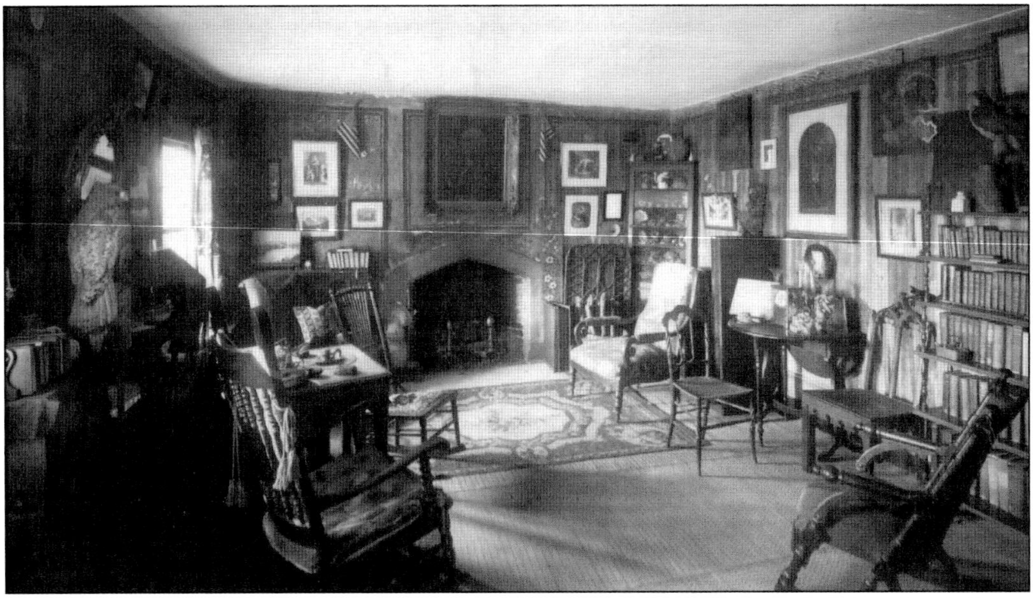

Revolutionary Sitting Room. The photographs of this room were taken by William Stockbridge, West Point's official photographer, in 1908. In true Victorian fashion, surfaces of walls and furniture are cluttered with mementos and pictures. The centerpiece is the treasured portrait of George Washington by Gilbert Stuart, flanked by flags. The family's love of books is evident here and throughout the house. In later years, Anna Warner described the sisters' daily routine in her biography, *Susan Warner.* Anna habitually woke at 4:30 a.m., made the fire, and prepared tea. Susan soon joined her. "Here in the old Revolutionary room that was our study . . . two busy pens kept company in delightful work. No disturbing doors or questions, no creaking shoes or stairs, no unsympathetic knocks. The fire snapped, the coals dropped softly; the noiseless pens covered sheet after sheet with their black marks."

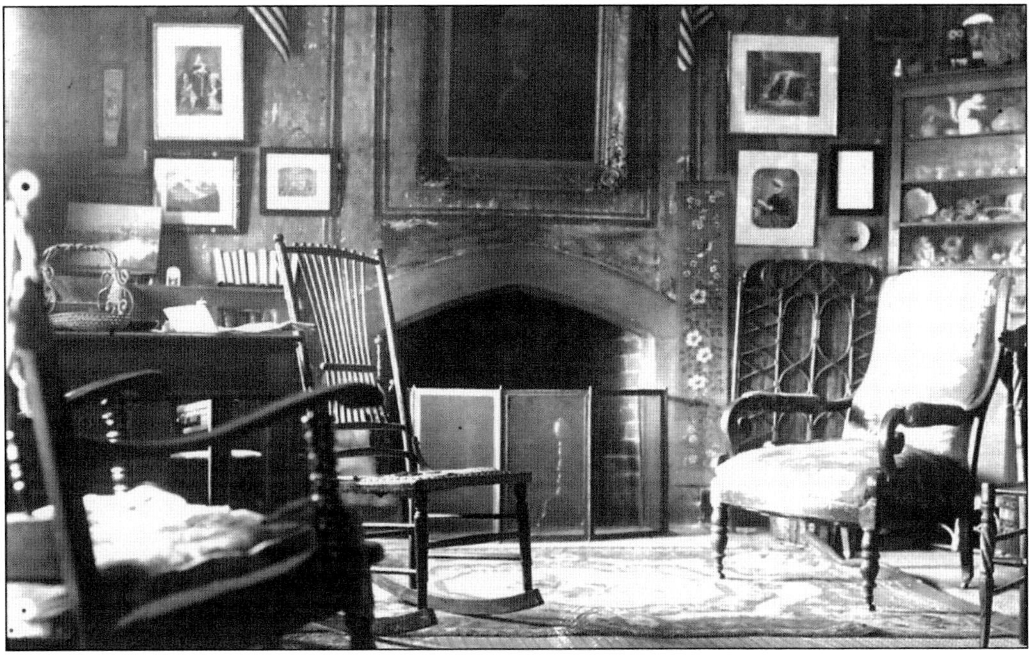

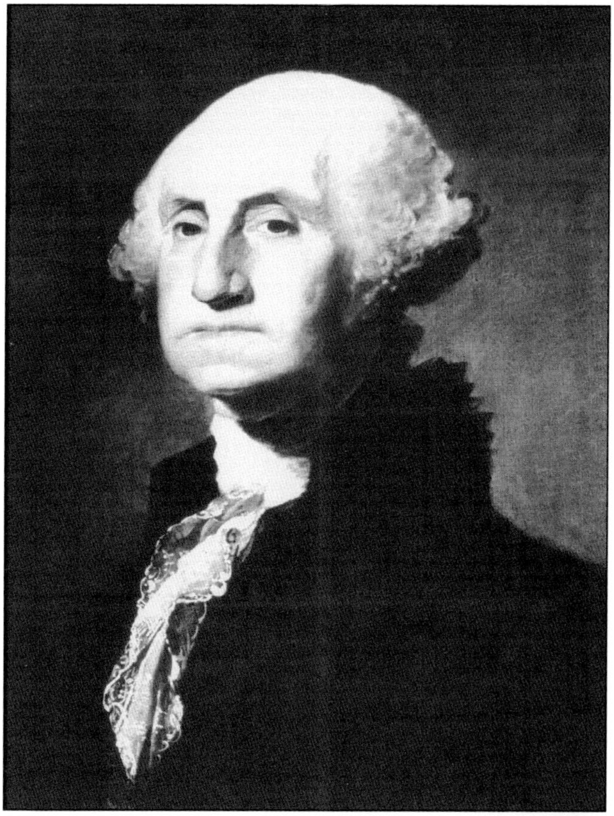

WASHINGTON PORTRAIT. A prized possession of the Warner family was their portrait of Washington by Gilbert Stuart. Henry Warner traded seven other paintings to acquire it in 1840. Years later when the family's valuables were auctioned off to pay debts, the painting was in the home of a friend as collateral for a loan. The loan was never repaid, but in 1851, the painting, in an act of kindness, was returned to the family.

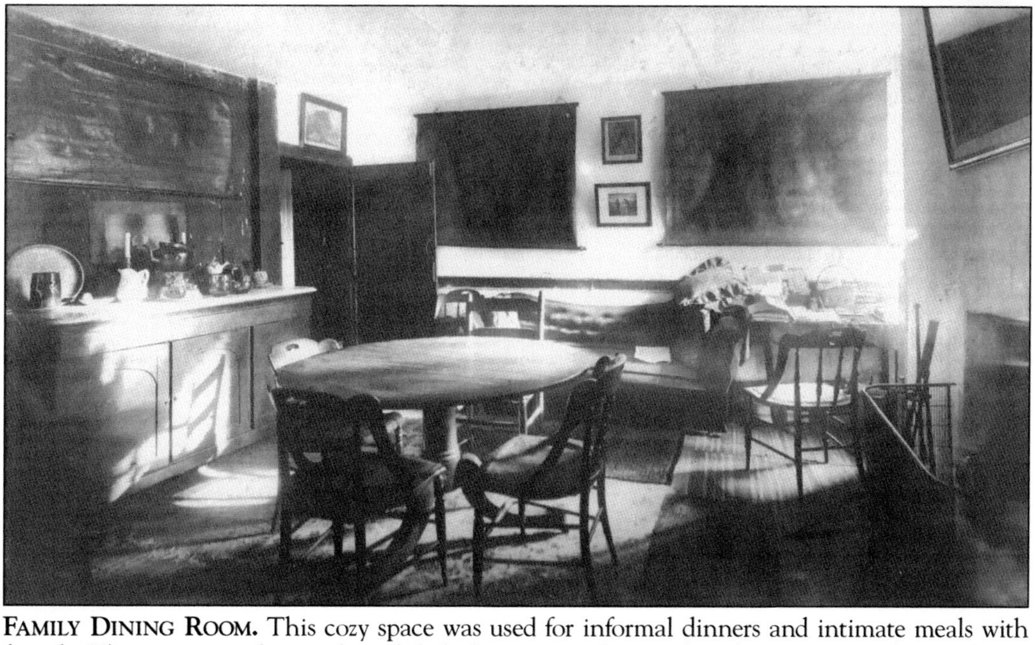

FAMILY DINING ROOM. This cozy space was used for informal dinners and intimate meals with friends. The presence of a couch and desk, however, indicates that this was more than a dining room. Anna wrote that it was here, while the women were washing dishes, that Aunt Fanny urged Susan to try writing a book. Susan began that night to write her first novel, *The Wide, Wide World.*

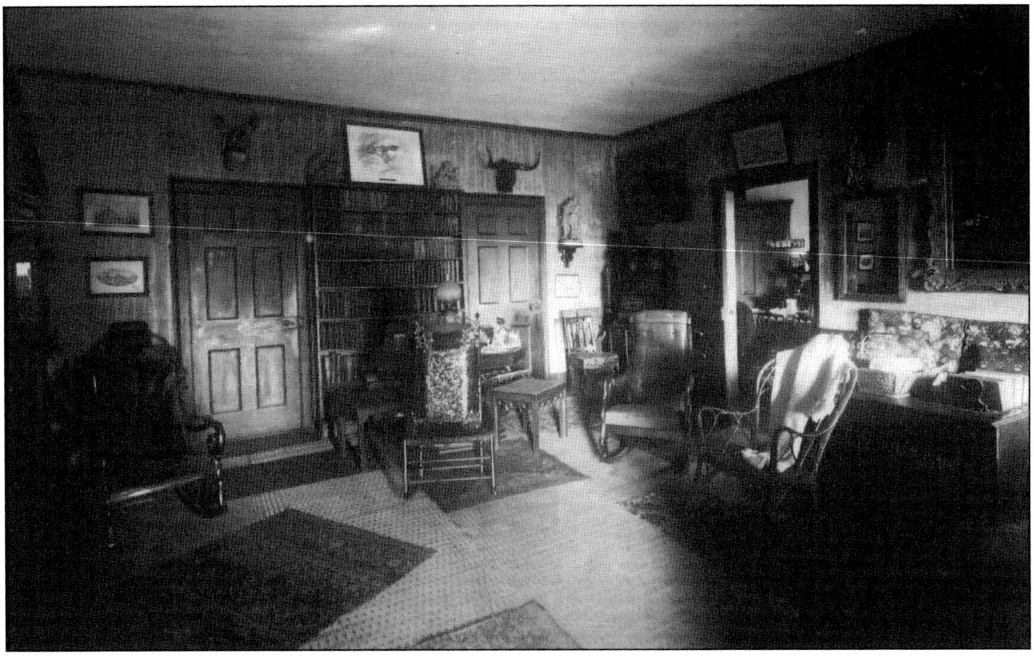

FORMAL PARLOR. This spacious parlor was part of the 1837 addition. The high ceiling and absence of a fireplace indicate that the house was to be a summer residence. This room was used to entertain guests and for reading and study. Taxidermy specimens over doorways to the library, left, and study, center, had to be handled with care, as arsenic was a commonly used preservative. The Warners were fond of rocking chairs; note that there are four. The photograph below shows the opposite side of the room with its elegant Gothic revival bookcase and matching table and chairs.

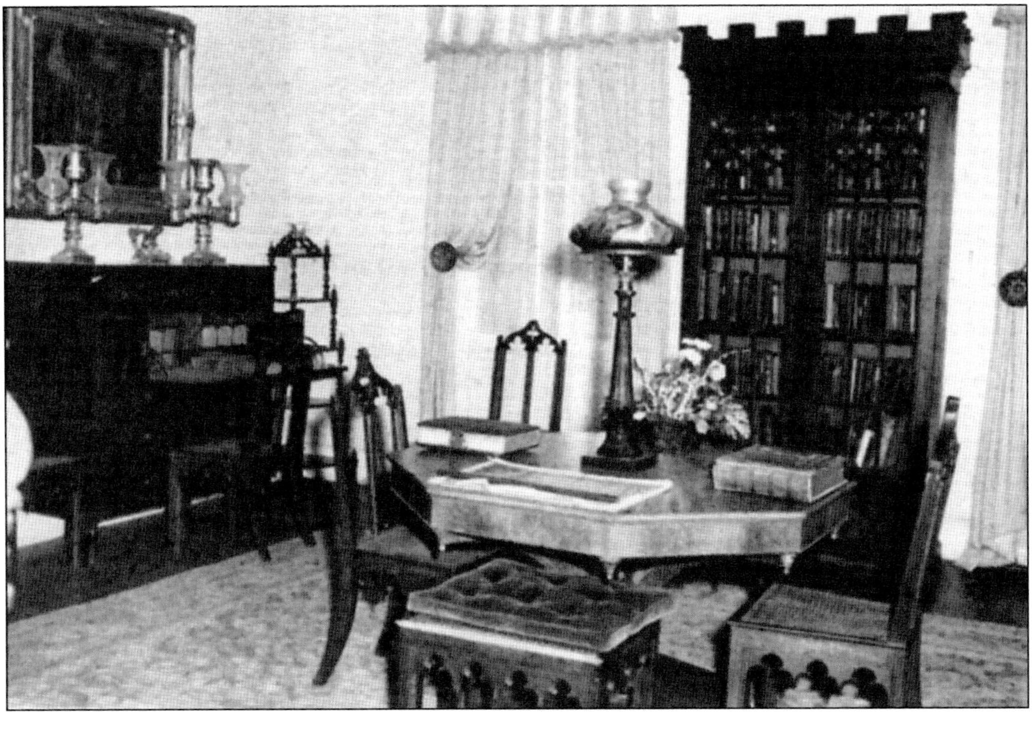

HENRY WARNER'S STUDY. The sturdy mahogany desk in this study reminds the visitor that Henry Warner was both a scholar and a lawyer. Case notes and court appearances were neatly recorded in leather bound ledgers. Legal work done for members of the Tiffany, Roosevelt, and other prominent New York families are mentioned in his records. He was also the author of a legal treatise, a thesaurus, and a play.

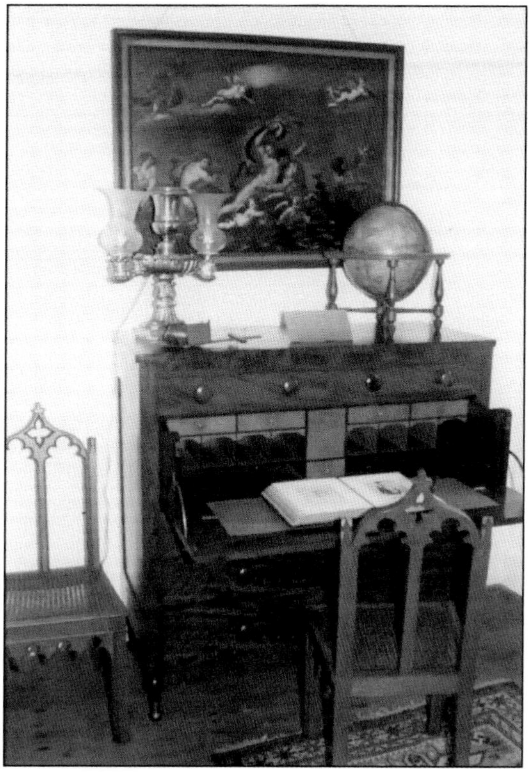

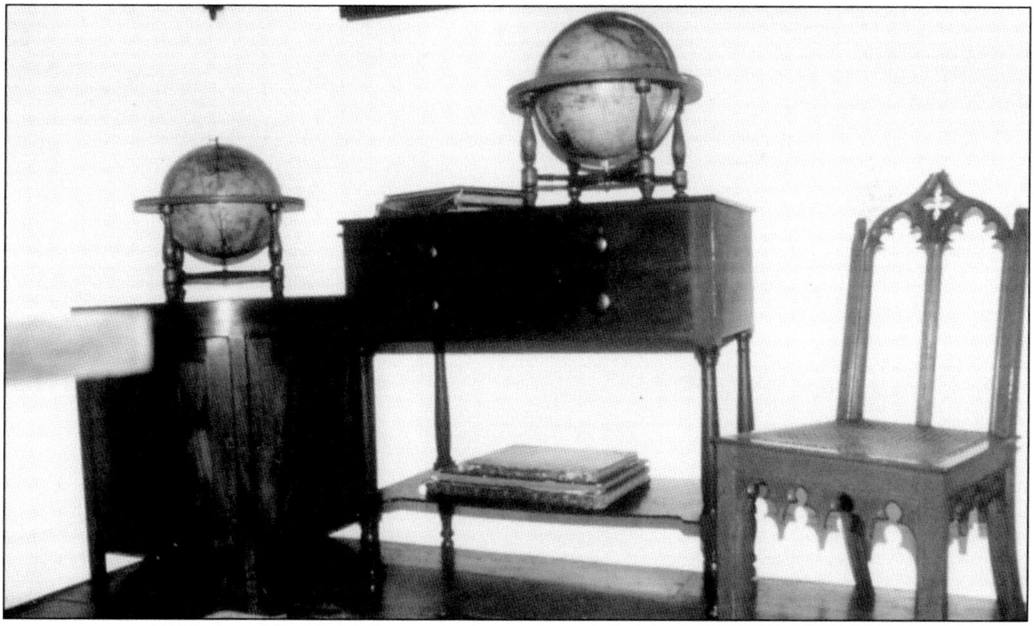

GLOBES. On display in the study are Henry's set of celestial and terrestrial globes. They were manufactured by James Wilson of Albany, one of the first American globe makers, and are dated 1826 and 1828 respectively. Henry used them to tutor his daughters in geography. In a journal entry at age 13, Susan remarked that her father had given her "five problems on the globes today. Not very difficult."

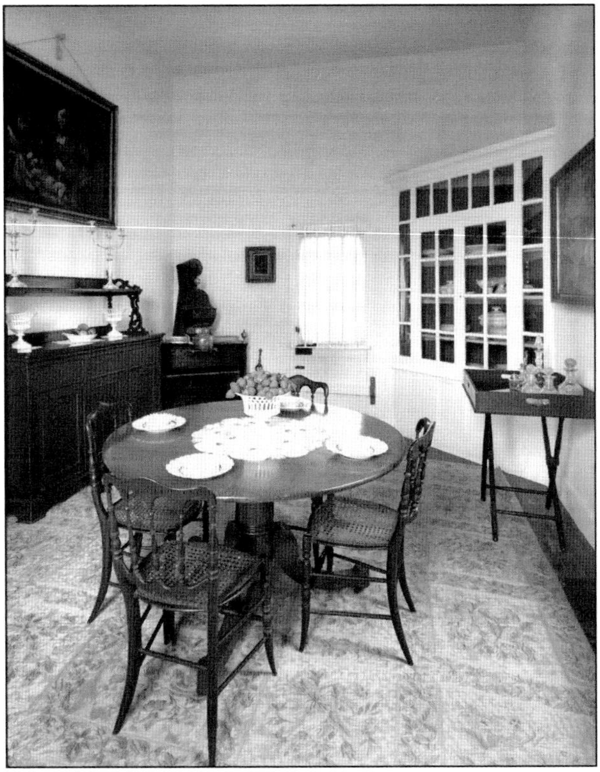

Formal Dining Room. Warner friend Olivia Phelps Stokes described this space as "a light pleasant room with a fine Franklin stove in one corner." It was here where guests dined with the Warners and where cadets adjourned for light refreshments after Bible class. The original table was rectangular and accommodated about 20 people. A corner cupboard holds Anna Bartlett Warner's graceful white china. (Historic American Buildings Survey, Library of Congress.)

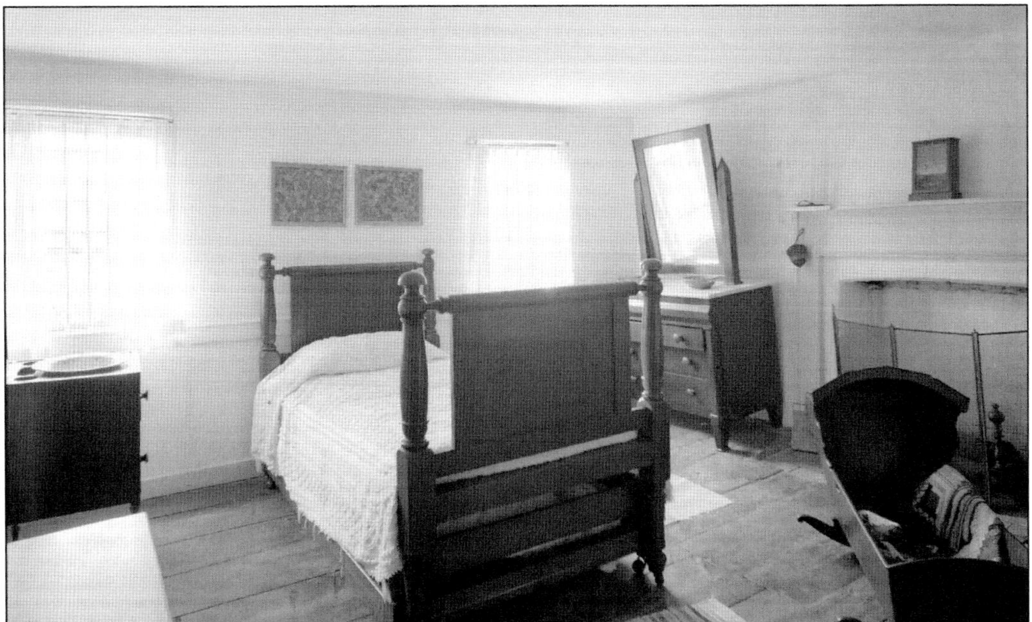

Guest Room. With its white walls and white dimity counterpane, this guest room was referred to as "the old white room." Two intricate needlepoint creations by Susan Warner are displayed over the bed. Wide plank floorboards indicate that this bedroom is in the 18th-century part of the house. (Historic American Buildings Survey, Library of Congress.)

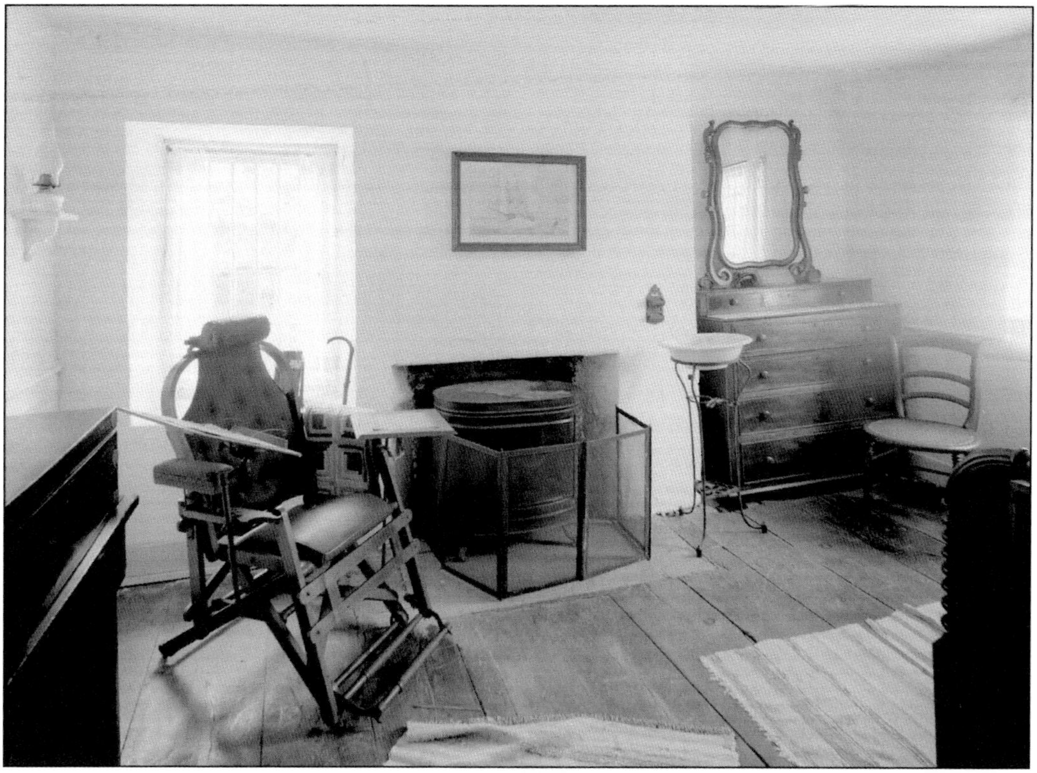

HENRY'S BEDROOM. This unusual invalid chair, with an apparatus for holding reading material, is in Henry Warner's bedroom. An elegant match holder is mounted on the wall beside the fireplace. At the foot of Henry's bed is the medicine chest seen below. In her journal, Susan mentions several 19th-century medical practices. Occasionally Aunt Fanny was bled by the local doctor. Susan took stibium (also known as antimony), a metallic substance used in matches and gunpowder, for a cold and found it very effective. Once Aunt Fanny treated Susan's earache by putting pieces of onion in her ear before bedtime. Susan reported that upon waking, she was better. (Above, Historic American Buildings Survey, Library of Congress.)

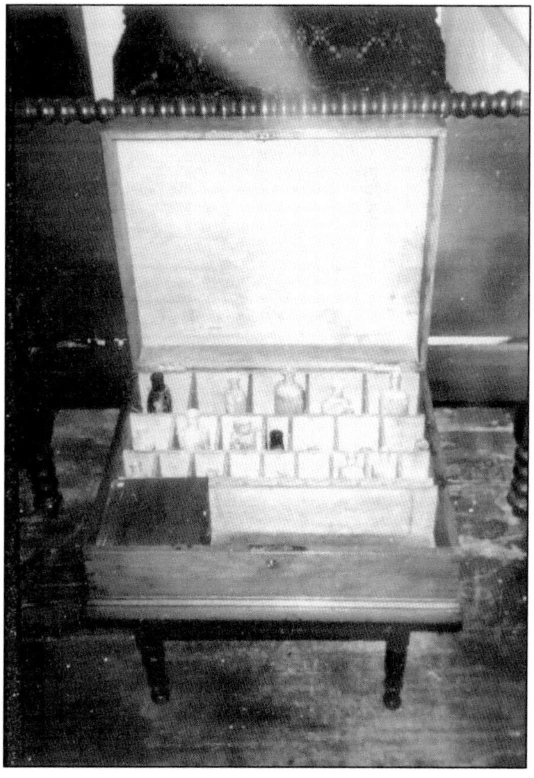

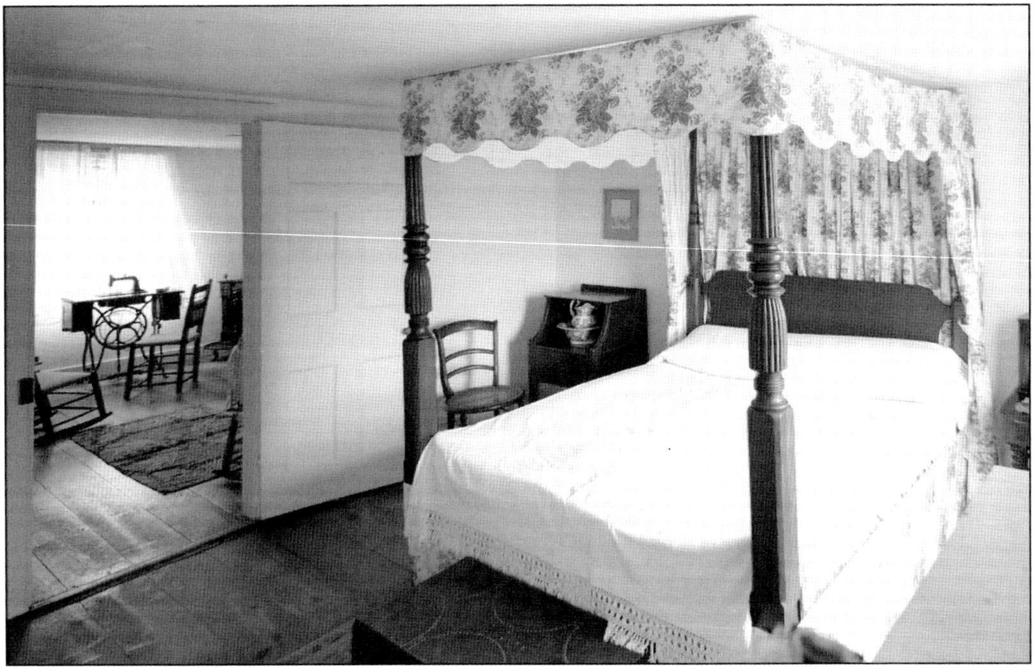

SUSAN'S BEDROOM. From the time she was 19, Susan Warner occupied this bedroom with its old-fashioned high-post bed with testor rings. At left is a commode with pitcher and bowl for washing. Through the doorway is Aunt Fanny's room with its Wilson sewing machine. (Historic American Buildings Survey, Library of Congress.)

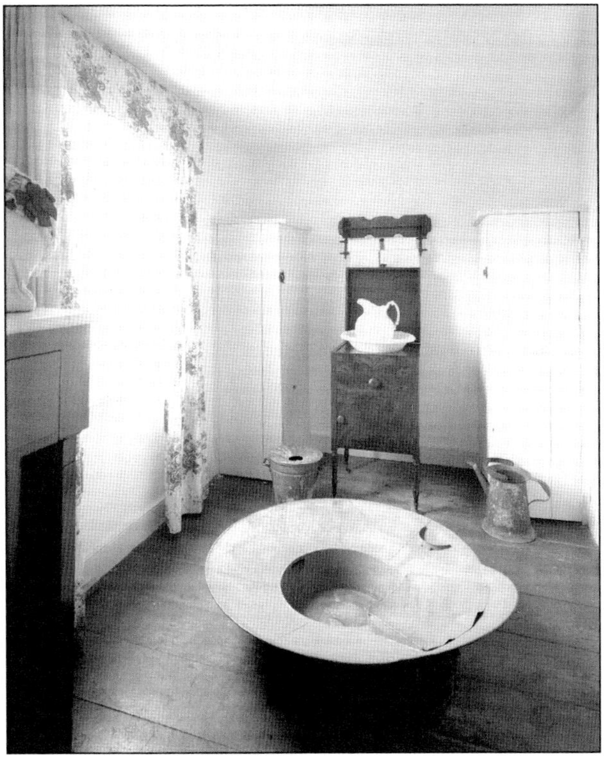

ALCOVE. The alcove off Susan's bedroom is arranged as a bathing room. In 19th-century homes, water was warmed downstairs and carried upstairs for washbasins and hip baths. Wastewater was poured off into a bucket and carried out. Note the soap compartment on the rim of the tub. (Historic American Buildings Survey, Library of Congress.)

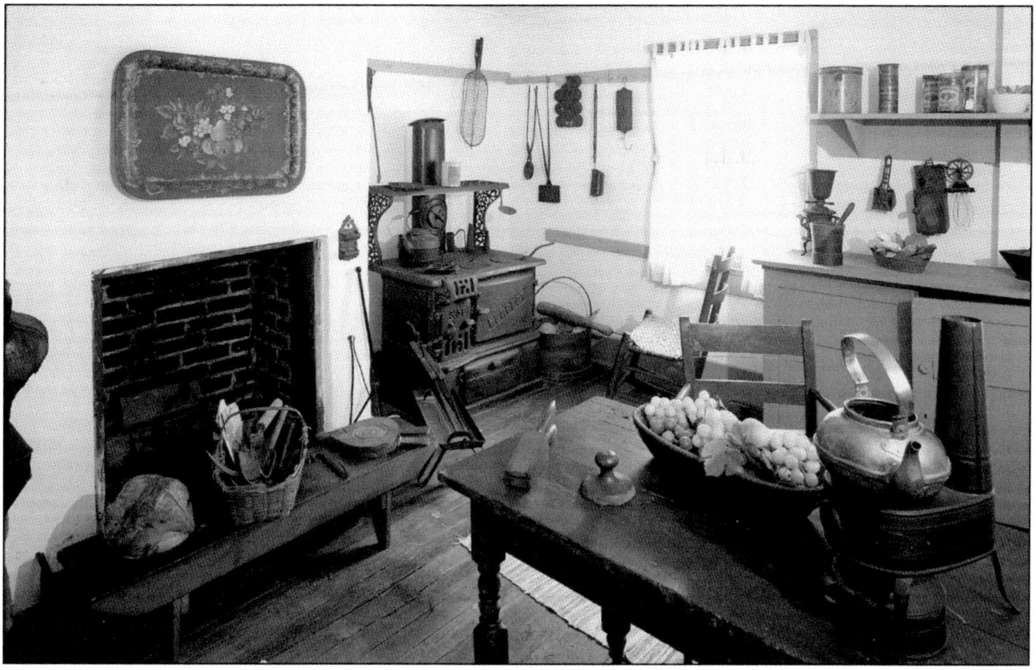

KITCHEN. The kitchen contains a variety of utensils reflecting 19th-century life such as a teakettle, lemon squeezer, corn popper, ladles, and mortar and pestle. On the bench at left are Anna's gardening tools. After 1868, the Warners' housekeeper, Bertha Buckner, generally cooked the meals, but both sisters were good bakers. Dinner was always at noon and supper at 6:00 p.m. (Historic American Buildings Survey, Library of Congress.)

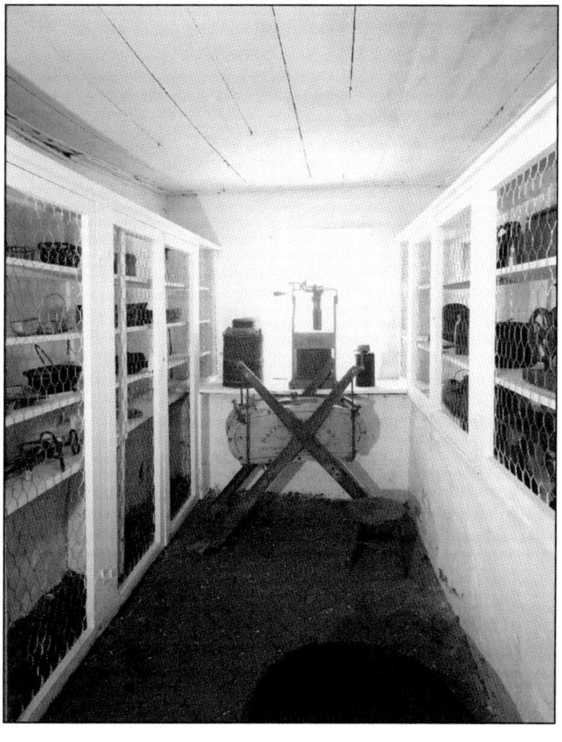

BUTTERY. The buttery or milk room was dug partially into the ground. Its relatively low temperatures kept milk and root vegetables from spoiling. At center is a Davis Swinging Churn made by the Vermont Farm Machine Company. On the window shelf are a milk pail, kneading machine, and a grinder. Wall shelves hold baskets and cooking utensils. (Historic American Buildings Survey, Library of Congress.)

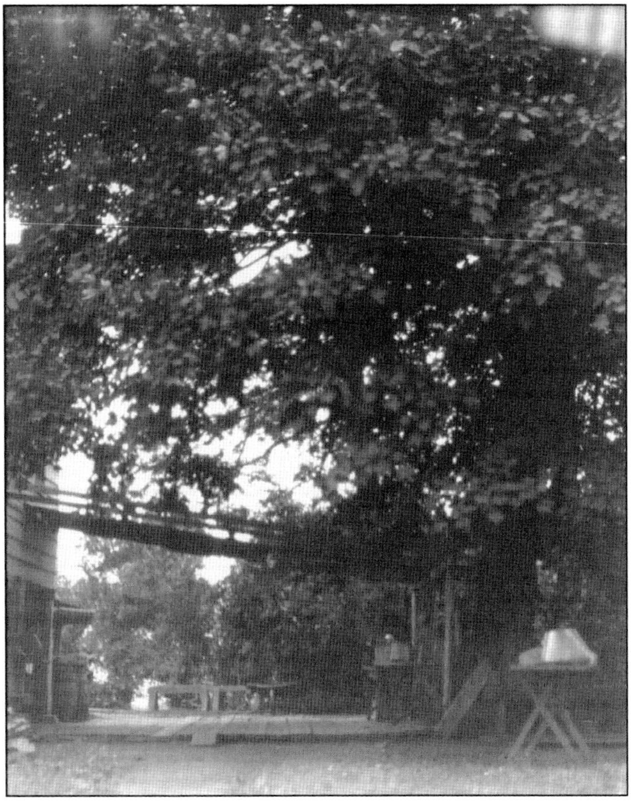

LEAN-TO. Off the kitchen area, this lean-to was used for household chores in the warm months. Washing, churning, skimming milk, and cooking could be done here. Among Warner documents are recipes for puddings, gingerbread, fritters, pumpkin pie, and ice cream. Bertha Buckner was known for her cakes and Aunt Fanny for her piecrusts. Anna and Susan Warner prided themselves on their breads and pies.

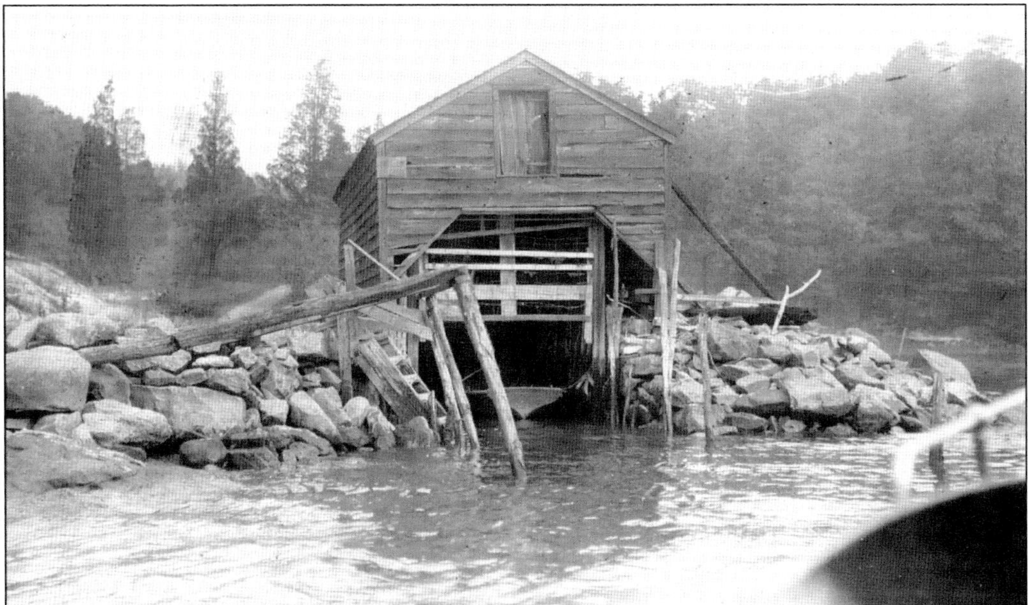

BOATHOUSE. Down the long curving path from the house, the boathouse at the water's edge sheltered the Warner family rowboat. Both Susan and Anna enjoyed rowing in the early morning. West Point's professional ferryman once exclaimed to Anna that he never saw a woman row as well as Susan.

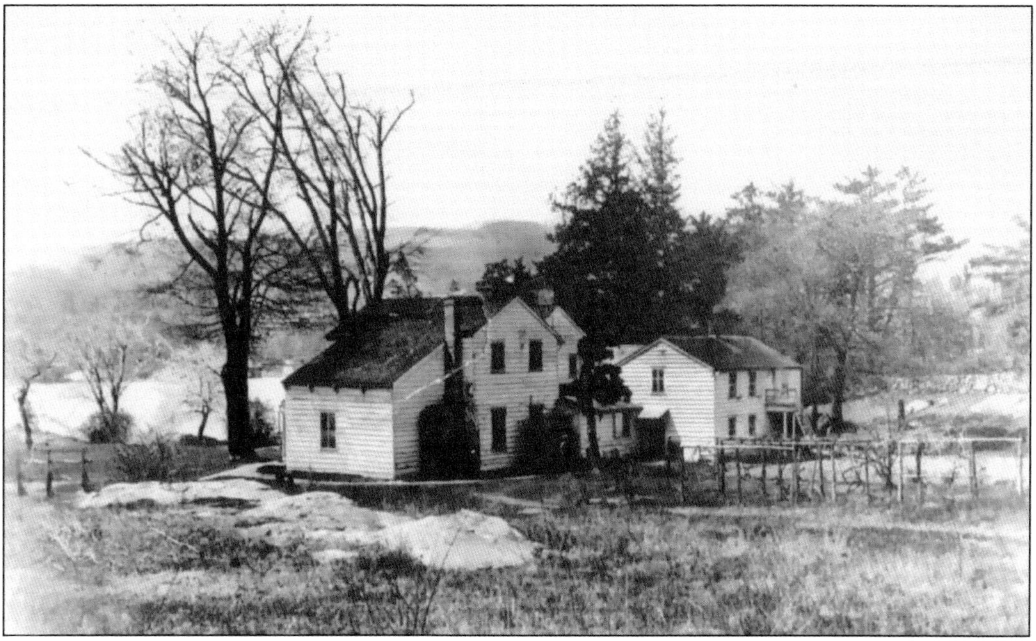

FARM. In the early 1840s, the home on Constitution Island became a true farm with chickens, pigs, cows, a bull, dogs, horses, and cats. Unfortunately debts began to mount. Henry Warner borrowed from friends to make mortgage payments. As money got scarce, the Warner women assumed the responsibility for chopping firewood, churning butter, tending a large garden, cooking, laundry, and making all the family clothing.

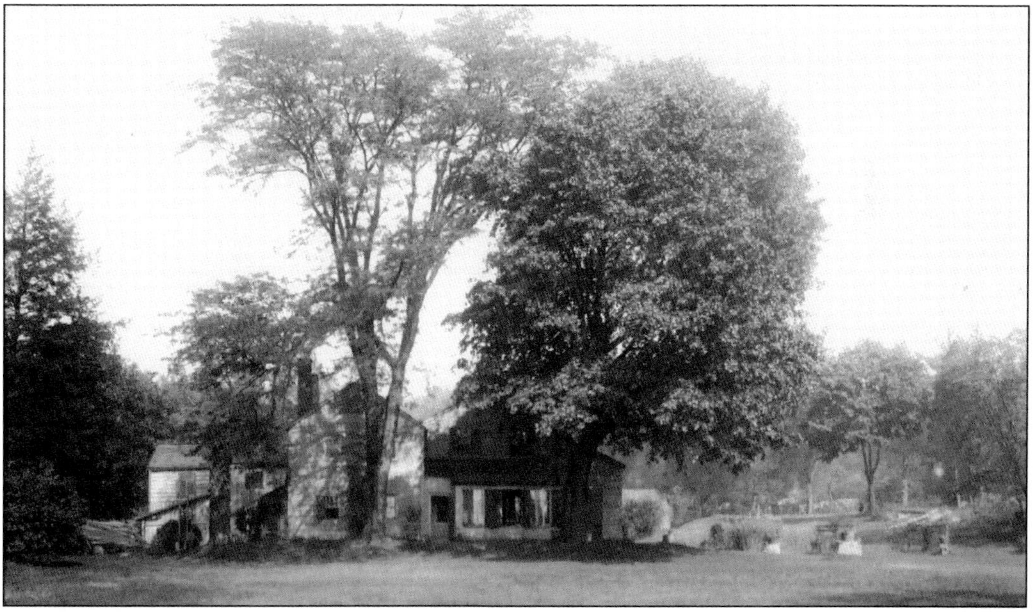

THE WARNER HOUSE. "You think truly," wrote Susan to her cousin in 1841, "That our island home is a delightful, retired quiet place; it is so . . . but whoever betakes himself to any island and thinks to leave all cares behind him will find it, I believe, a vain hope." The family's monetary situation became increasingly difficult, made worse by Henry's time-consuming and expensive lawsuits regarding land access and water rights to Constitution Island.

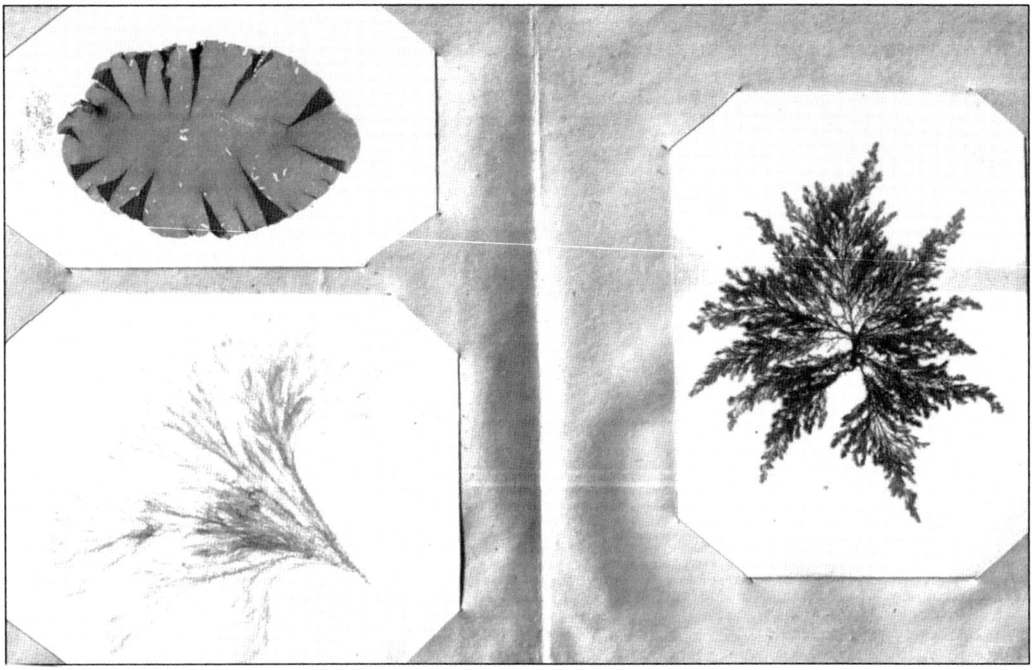

FLOWERS. Both Susan and Anna Warner shared a lifelong love of flowers. From her youth, Susan was fond of studying flowers and pressing them into album pages like the one above. It was a popular Victorian hobby at which she excelled. Her father had made her a fine flower press. Anna loved to garden, especially in her border garden, seen below. She took pleasure in finding interesting blossoms for Susan to press. Even as a child, wherever she traveled, she tried to find specimens for Susan's "botanizing." This was a strong bond between the two sisters. Upon Susan's death, Anna turned away mourning bouquets that were sent to her. Later she wrote to friends, explaining that she could not endure seeing flowers at that time, "I was bearing all that I could bear." (Below, USMA Library.)

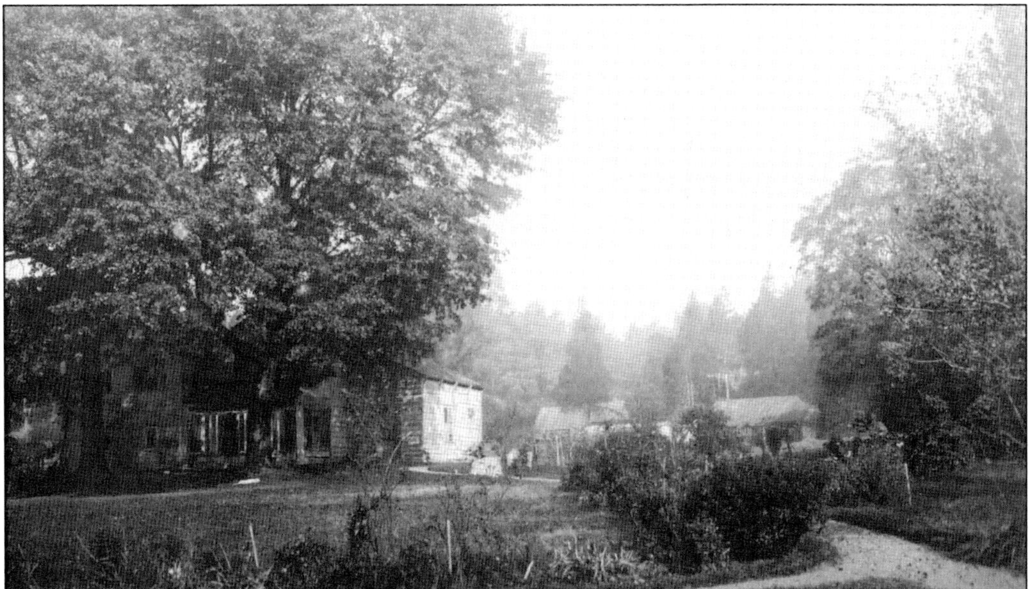

Four

SUSAN AND ANNA

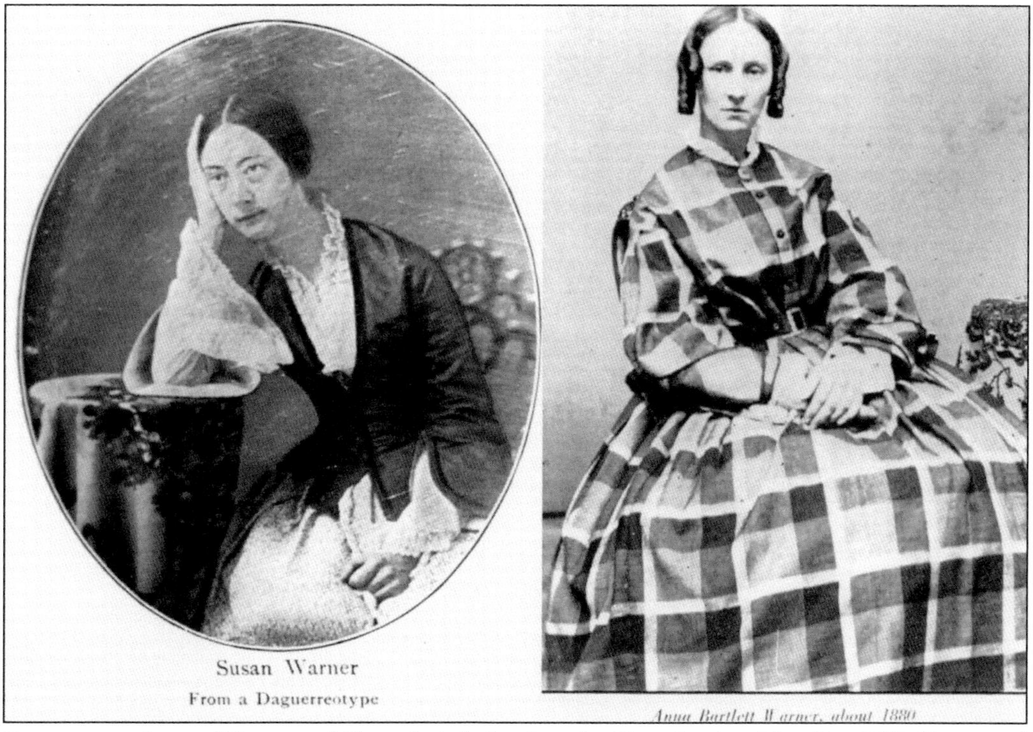

SUSAN AND ANNA WARNER. When their father bought Constitution Island in 1836, Susan and Anna had no idea that it would become their permanent home. A financial crisis led to their move from the bustling upper-middle-class social whirl of the city to the life of farmers struggling to find money for food and mortgage payments. They solved their problem by writing for a living. Theirs is a story of resourcefulness, devotion, and two very busy pens.

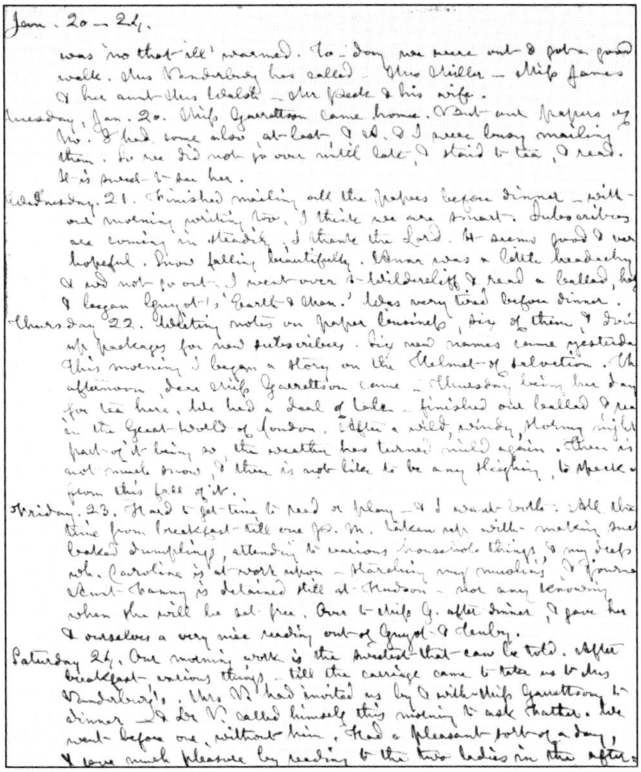

Jan. 20 – 24.

was "no that 'ill' warmed. To-day we were out & got a good walk. Mrs Vanderburgh has called – Mrs Miller – Miss James & her aunt Mrs Walsh – Mr Peale & his wife.

Tuesday, Jan. 20. Miss Garretson came home. Sent out papers of No. 8 had come also at last & A. & I were busy mailing them. So we did not go over until late, & staid to tea, & read. It is sweet to see her.

Wednesday. 21. Finished mailing all the papers before dinner – with our morning writing too, I think we are smart. Subscribers are coming in steadily, I thank the Lord. It seems good & very hopeful. Snow falling beautifully. Anna was a little headachy & did not go out – I went over to Wildercliff & read a ballad, & I began Guyot's 'Earth & Man.' Was very tired before dinner.

Thursday 22. Writing notes on paper business, six of them, & doing up packages for new subscribers. Six new names came yesterday. This morning I began a story on the Helmet of Salvation. The afternoon dear Miss Garretson came – Thursday being her day for tea here, we had a deal of talk – finished our ballad & read in the Great World of London. After a wild, windy, stormy night part of it being so, the weather has turned mild again. There is not much snow, & there is not like to be any sleighing, to speak of, from this fall of it.

Friday. 23. Hard to get time to read or play – & I want both. All the time from breakfast till one P. M. taken up with making suet baked dumplings, attending to various household things, & my desk work. Caroline is at work upon – starching my muslins & [illegible] Aunt Fanny is detained still at Hudson – not any knowing when she will be set free. Over to Miss G. after dinner, & gave her & ourselves a very nice reading out of Guyot & Stanley.

Saturday 24. Our morning work is the sweetest that can be told. After breakfast various things – till the carriage came to take us to Mrs Vanderburgh's. Mrs V. had invited us by & with Miss Garretson to dinner – & Dr V. called himself this morning to ask Father. We went before one, without him. Had a pleasant sort of a day, & gave much pleasure by reading to the two ladies in the after-

JOURNAL PAGE. Many details about the life of the Warner family come from the journals Susan Warner kept throughout her life. In 1838, Henry Warner had to sell his townhouse and move the family to Constitution Island. At age 18, it was a difficult move for Susan. She wrote poignantly of "leaving our crimson cushions and tall mirrors; with greenhouse, carriage and a corps of servants . . . to the greatly changed life of the Highlands."

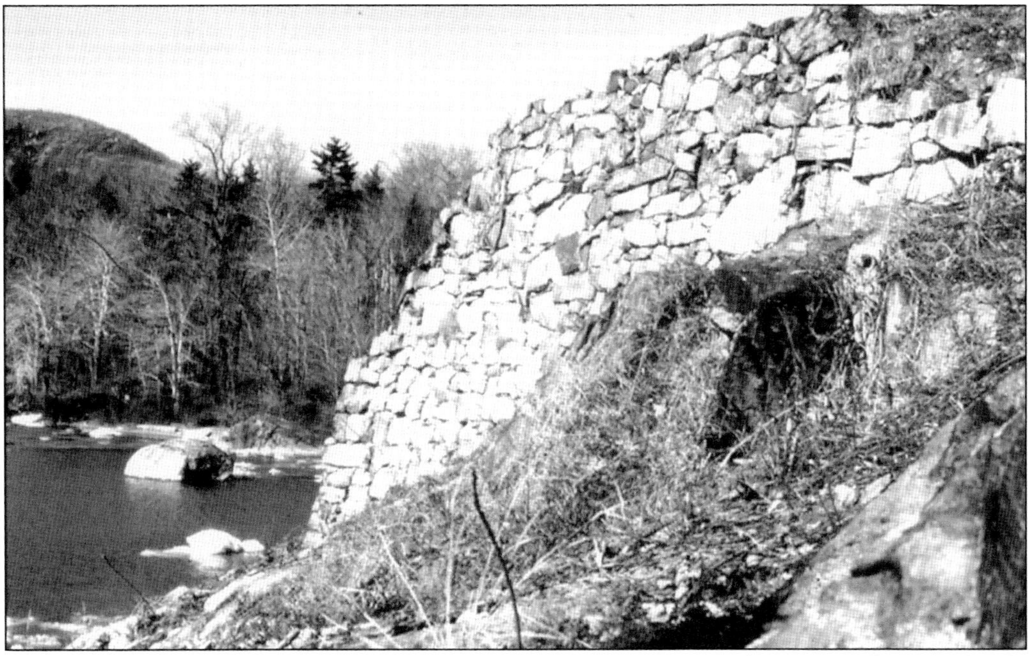

EXPLORATION. Anna Warner was the more active of the two sisters. She was 13 when the family moved to the island, a young, energetic teenager, who enjoyed exploring the woods and rocky hills. She loved climbing the old forts and the magazine pictured here, discovering unusual wild flowers, "roaming everywhere and fearing nothing," she later wrote.

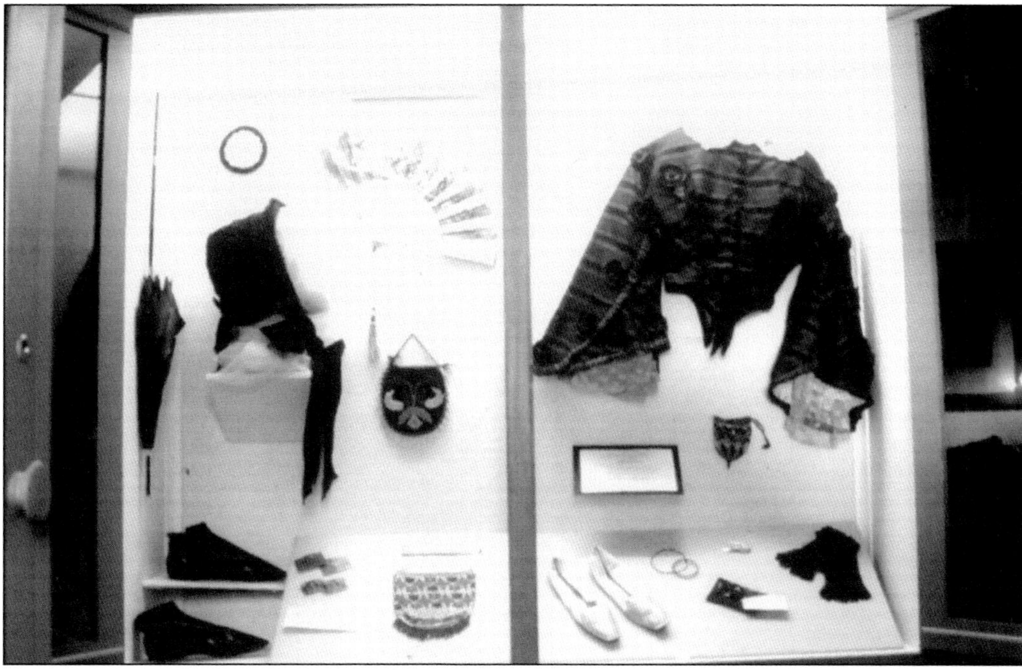

CLOTHING EXHIBIT. Garments and accessories on display at the Warner House belonged to Susan, Anna, and their mother. Clothing was the outward sign of social class in 19th-century society. Visiting and entertaining required proper attire. As their silk dresses wore out and were replaced with their homemade calicoes, they socialized less and less. "If you have nothing to wear," wrote Anna, "few want you."

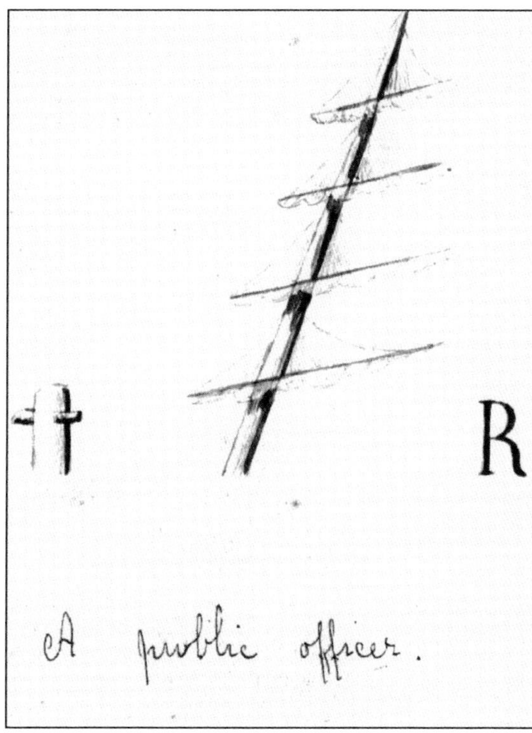

PUZZLE. Artistic and well read, Susan and Anna enjoyed creating their own entertainments. This card is from a collection of word picture puzzles drawn in pencil. Under the visual clue, a phrase is given as a hint. The answer is postmaster.

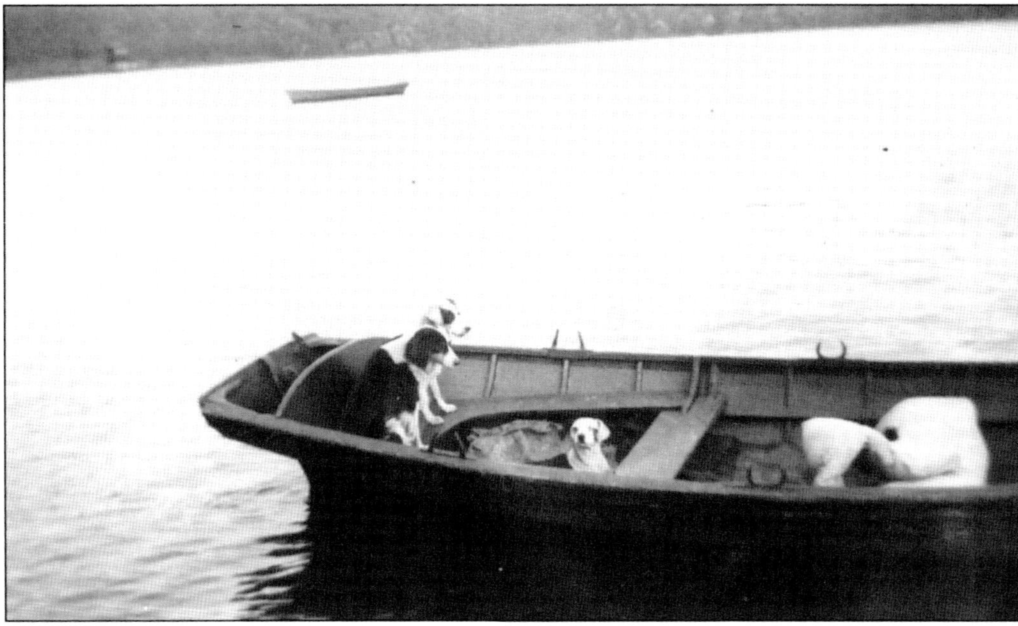

ROWING. Rowing was an important means of transportation for the Warners. Susan and Anna Warner became adept at handling their sturdy rowboat, seen here with three canine passengers. They rowed to West Point, Cold Spring, Garrison, and Highland Falls, sometimes just for pleasure. Often the sisters went fishing and crabbing in their boat.

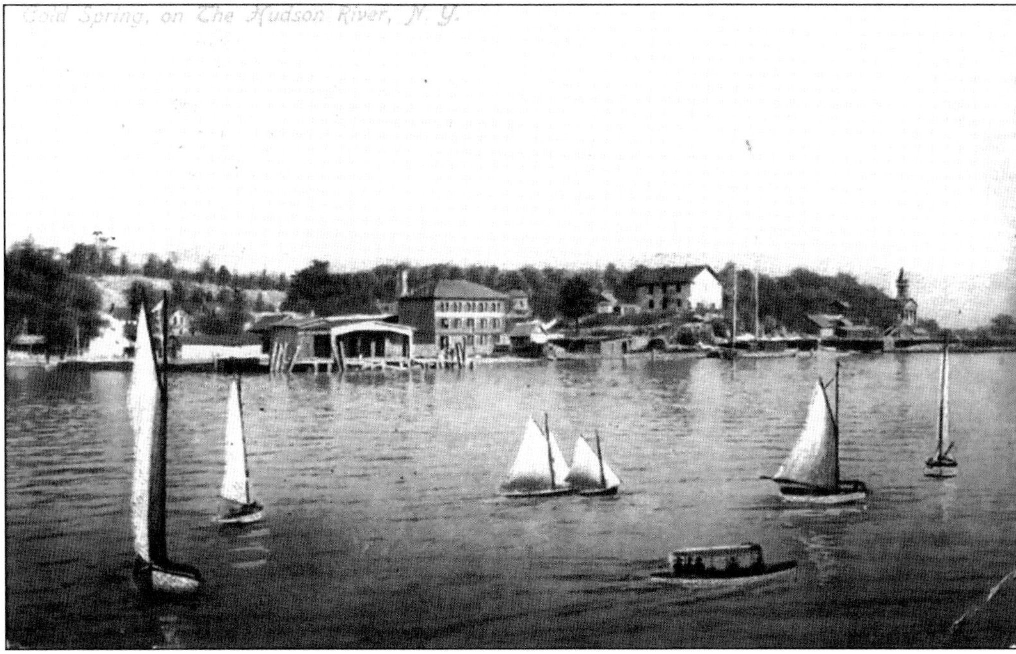

COLD SPRING. The Warner sisters frequently rowed Henry Warner to Cold Spring for business or legal matters. Henry had built dikes along the 50-acre swamp between the island and the mainland to make it habitable. Hot disputes with neighbors erupted regarding land use and water rights. Henry's resources, both financial and emotional, were drained after 10 years of expensive litigation. (Donnery collection.)

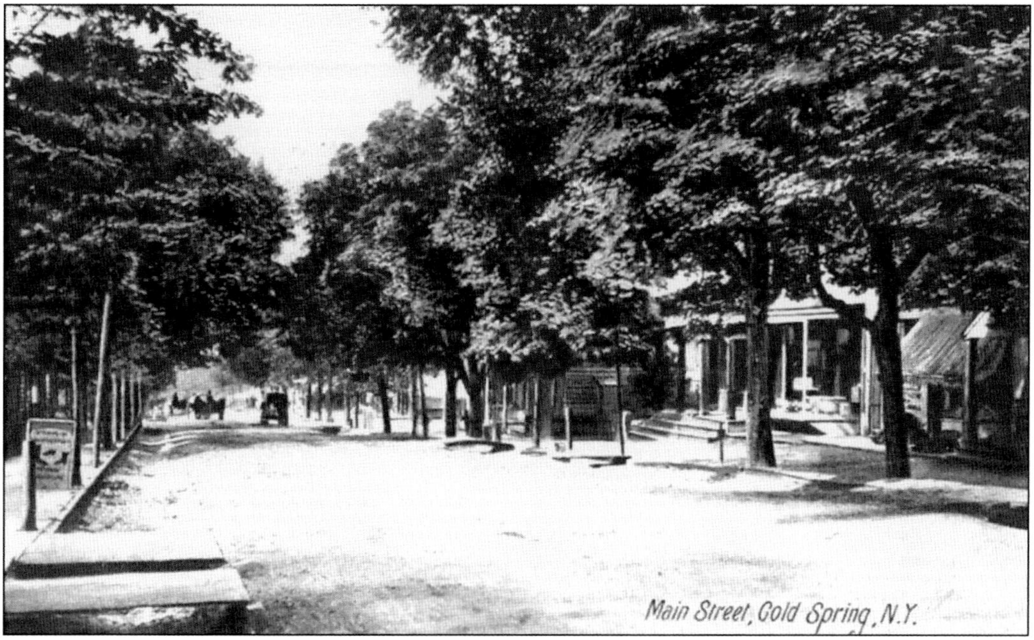

MAIN STREET, COLD SPRING. The Warners received their mail at the Cold Spring and West Point post offices. In October 1838, Anna was visiting cousins in Hudson, New York. Susan's journal entry states that after she churned eight pounds of butter, "We rowed to Cold Spring and back and there Father found a letter for me from Anna which gave me some pleasure, of course." (Donnery collection.)

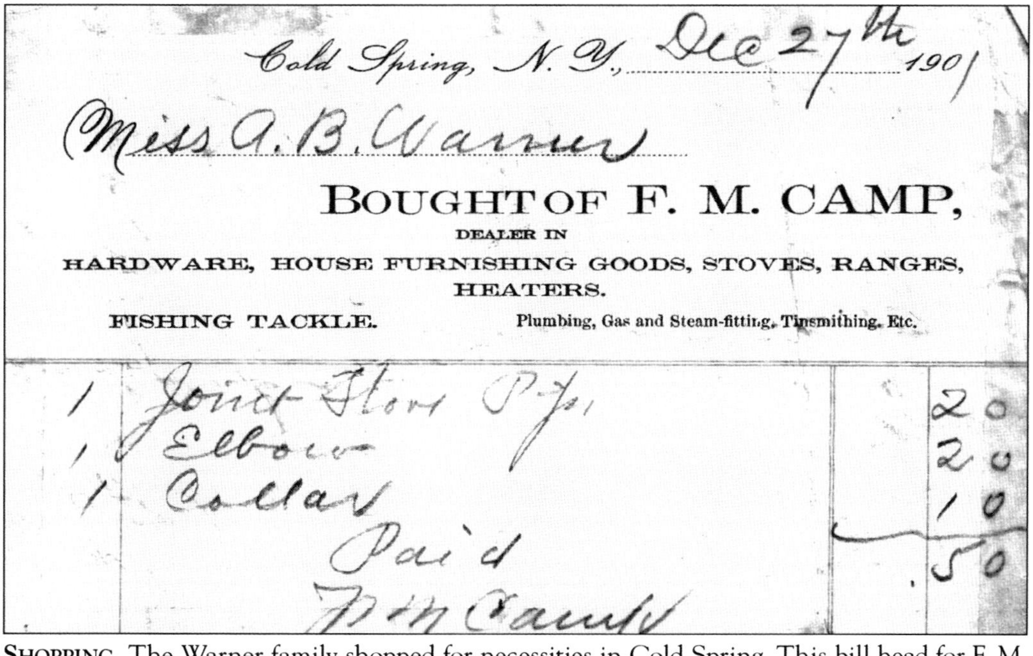

Cold Spring, N. Y., Dec 27th 1901

Miss A. B. Warner

BOUGHT OF F. M. CAMP,

DEALER IN

HARDWARE, HOUSE FURNISHING GOODS, STOVES, RANGES, HEATERS.

FISHING TACKLE. Plumbing, Gas and Steam-fitting, Tinsmithing, Etc.

1	Joint Stove P.	20
1	Elbow	20
1	Collar	10
	Paid	50
	F M Camp	

SHOPPING. The Warner family shopped for necessities in Cold Spring. This bill head for F. M. Camp dated 1901 indicates that Anna's stove needed repair. The family physician Dr. Richard Giles was a resident of Cold Spring. In later years, Warner employees Bertha and Willis Buckner did most of the errands and shopping and were well known in the community.

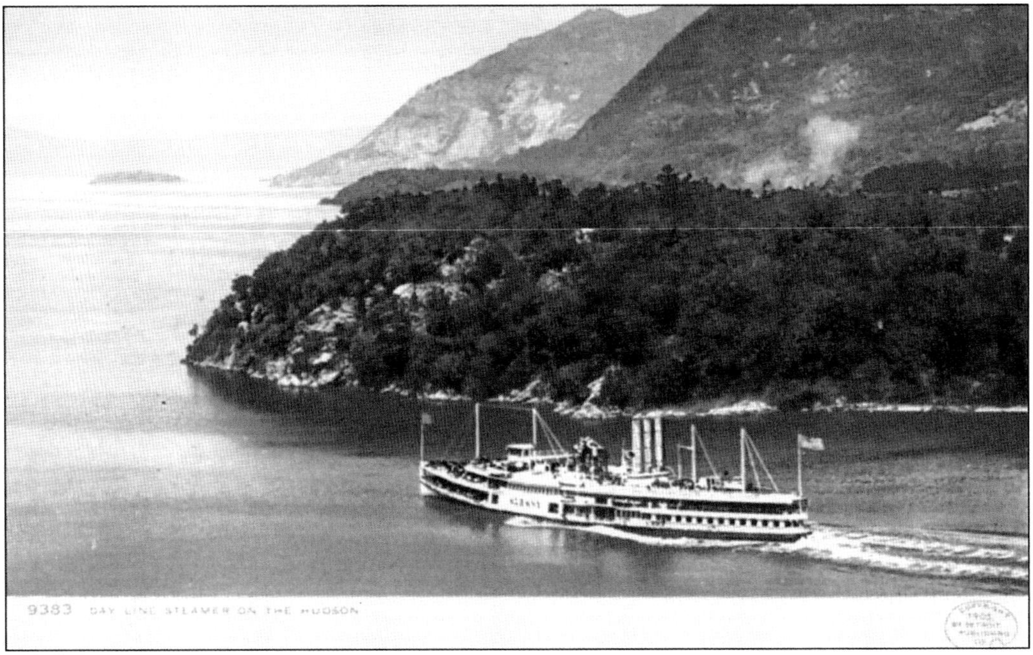

STEAMBOATS. Heading for Newburgh and points north, the *Albany* rounds Constitution Island, above. Pollopel's, or Bannerman's, Island can be seen in the distance. Steamboats were the best choice for transportation between river towns during the first half of the 19th century. Family trips and Henry Warner's business commutes to Albany and New York City required the Warners to travel frequently by boat. Susan Warner's journals make mention of trips on the *Albany*, *Superior*, *James Madison*, and *Highlander*. In the 1830s, boats docking at West Point used a floating dock that stretched into the river. "With a north wind and a down tide," wrote Anna, "it was not unheard of thing for the big steamer to miss her landing and try again." The sisters often rowed their father to the academy's North Dock. In later years, the South Dock, below, became the West Point Landing. (Above, Donnery collection; below, Gunza collection.)

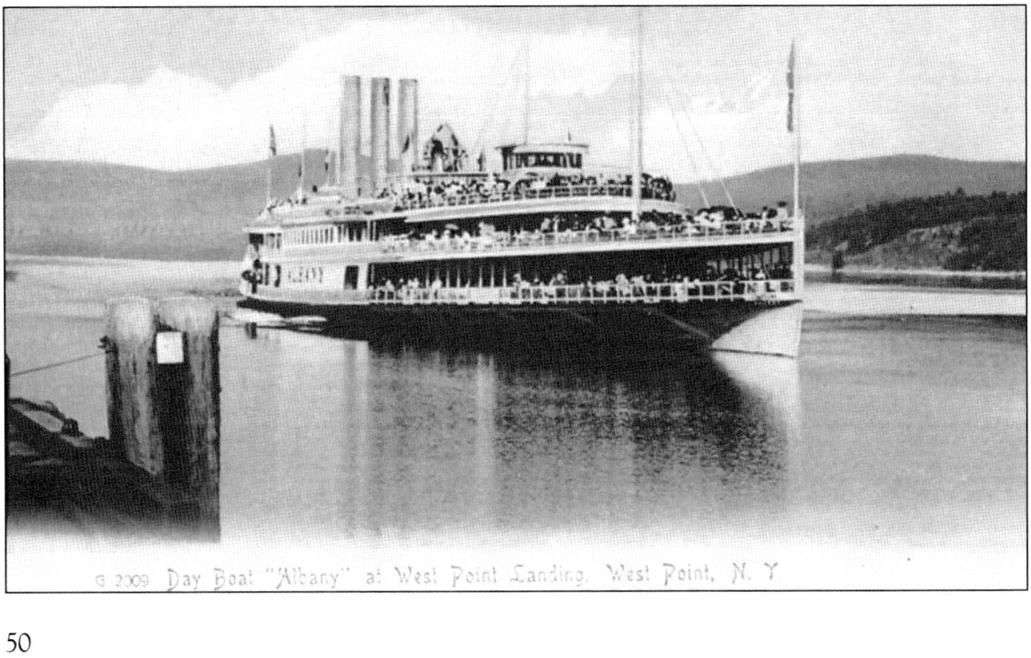

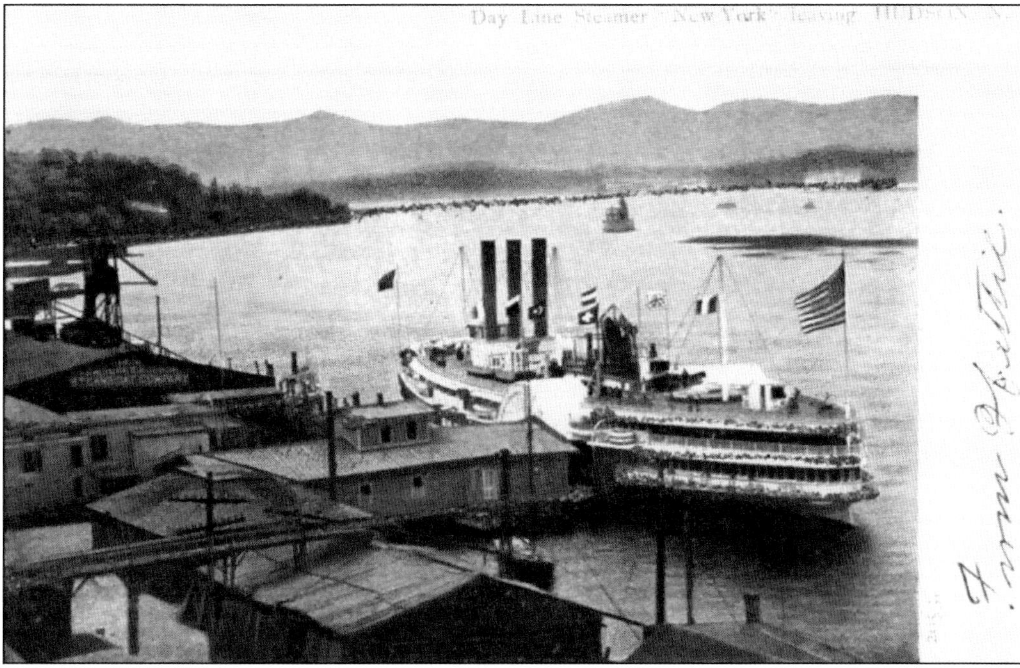

HUDSON. Henry had a second sister, Nancy Warner Frary, who lived in Hudson, New York. When he, Aunt Fanny, and the girls visited her, they traveled to Hudson by steamboat. Here the Day Line steamer *New York* leaves Hudson on a trip south. The Warners had close ties to their relatives in Canaan, New York, as well. (Gunza collection.)

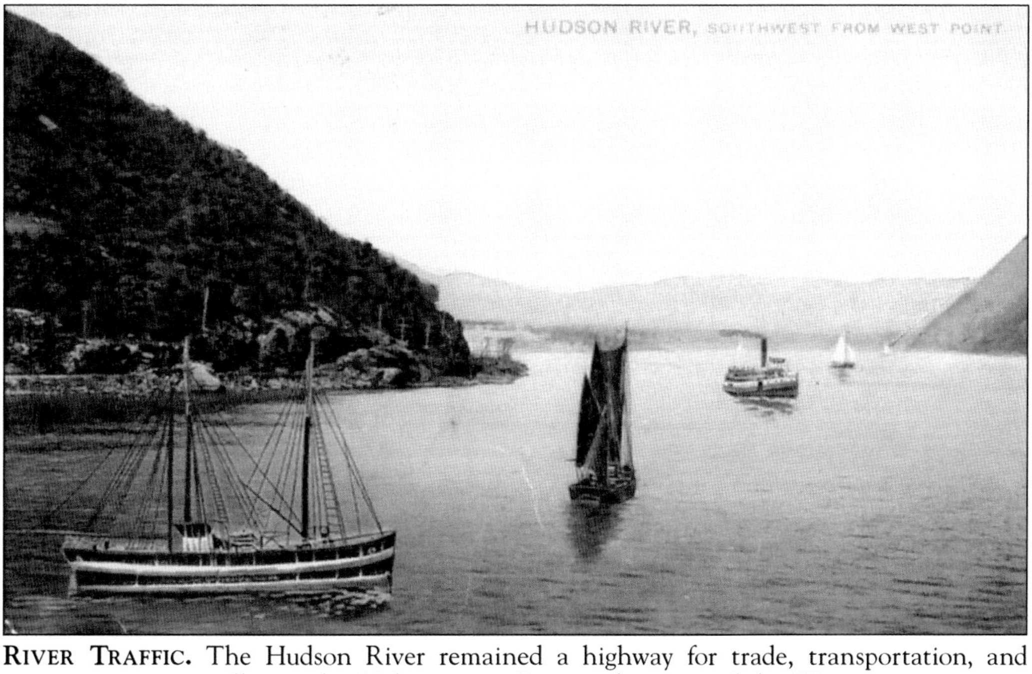

RIVER TRAFFIC. The Hudson River remained a highway for trade, transportation, and passenger service well into the 20th century. During the years of the Warner occupancy, a constant parade of steamboats, sloops, ferries, and sailing vessels passed Constitution Island. (Gunza collection.)

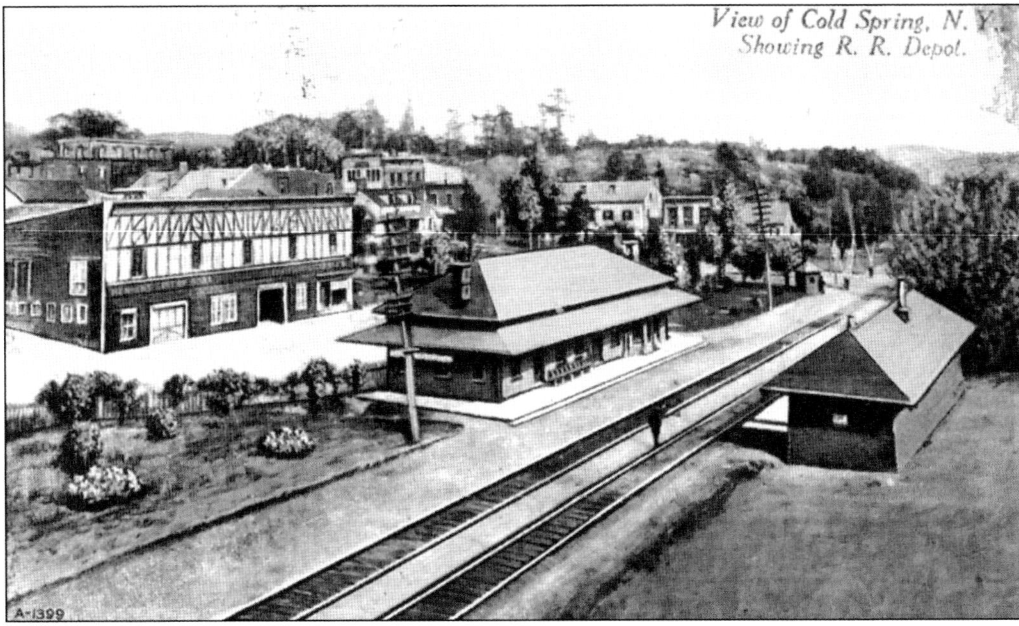

HUDSON RIVER RAILROAD. After 1849, Henry Warner often commuted to the city by the Hudson River Railroad. Susan and Anna Warner traveled occasionally by rail as well. They boarded the train at the Cold Spring railroad station, above. Actually a portion of track was on Warner property crossing the marsh at Constitution Island by means of a pile bridge. In 1869, the Hudson River Railroad merged with the New York Central Railroad. Their fastest train was the *20th Century Limited*, seen in the vintage image below. (Donnery collection.)

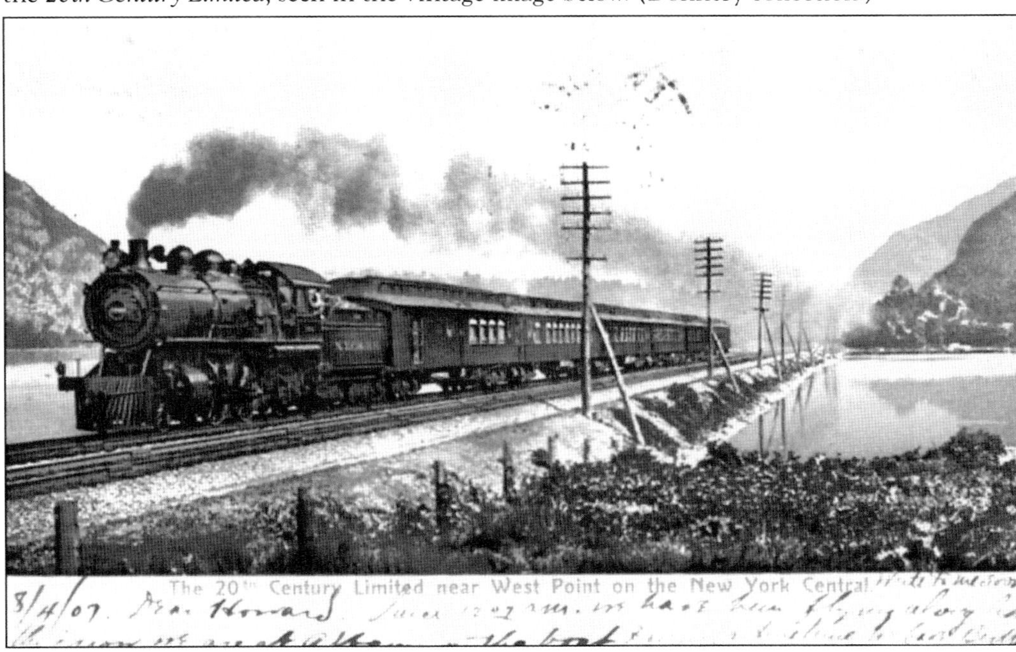

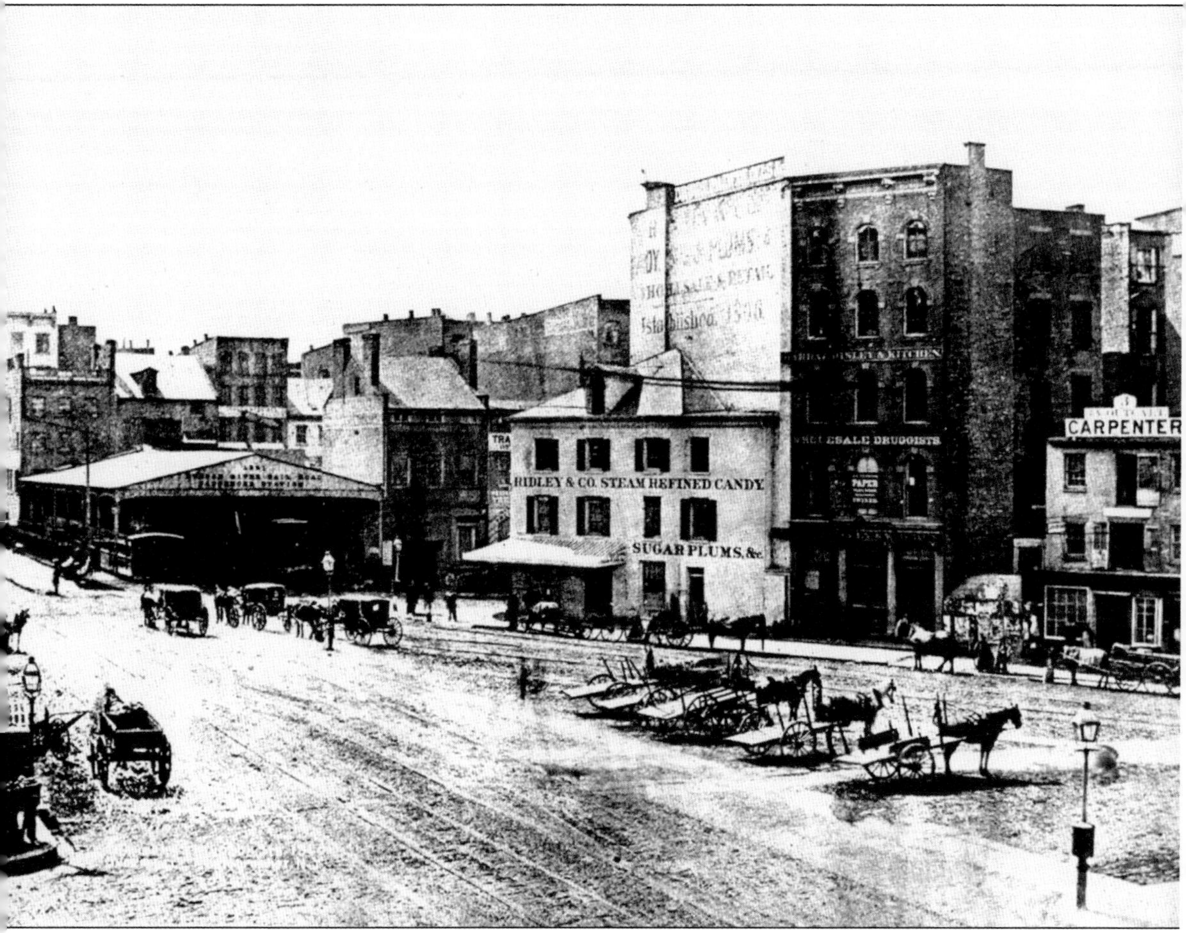

PASSENGER STATION, C. 1852. The passenger station of the Hudson River Railroad was built in 1851 at the intersection of Chambers and Hudson Streets. The Warners arrived at this station when they came to the city to visit or shop. Carriages were available for hire. After the Civil War, the horse-drawn omnibus became popular. Susan's journal mentions taking a "bus ride" from the train station to her destination in New York. (The New York Historical Society.)

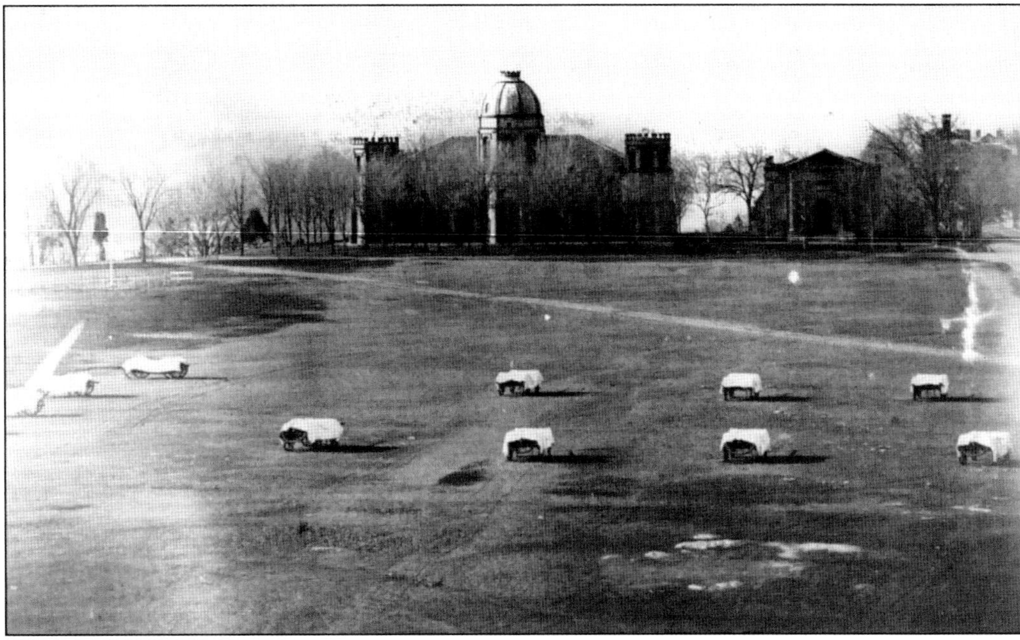

THOMAS DEPARTS. The last time Thomas Warner walked across this plain to his chapel was in 1839. Accused of violations, including visiting a hospitalized cadet without permission, he incurred the wrath of USMA superintendent René De Russy and was dismissed. He moved to France, intending to start a private school in Paris, but no record of it exists. Thomas accrued debts and was sent to a French prison where he died of cholera. (USMA Library.)

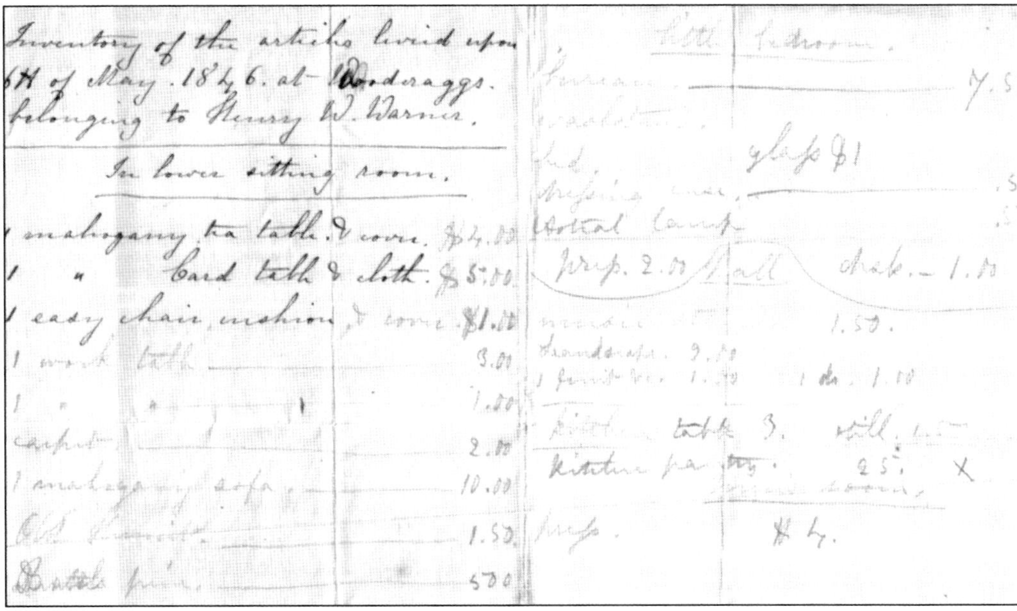

Inventory of the articles levied upon
6th of May. 1846. at Woodcraggs.
belonging to Henry W. Warner.

In lower sitting room.

1 mahogany tea table & cover. $4.00
1 " Card table & cloth. $5.00
1 easy chair, cushion, & cover $1.00
1 work table 3.00
1 " 1.00
carpet 2.00
1 mahogany sofa 10.00
1.50
5.00

AUCTION. Throughout the 1840s, the family sank deeper into poverty. They rented out the attic rooms above the kitchen to earn money. By 1846, a sheriff's auction was held to pay debts. Among the items on this "inventory of the articles levied upon" were paintings, carpeting, washstands, and furniture. The Warners watched as their possessions were sold. Anna compared her family's experience to being like mice in a room full of snakes.

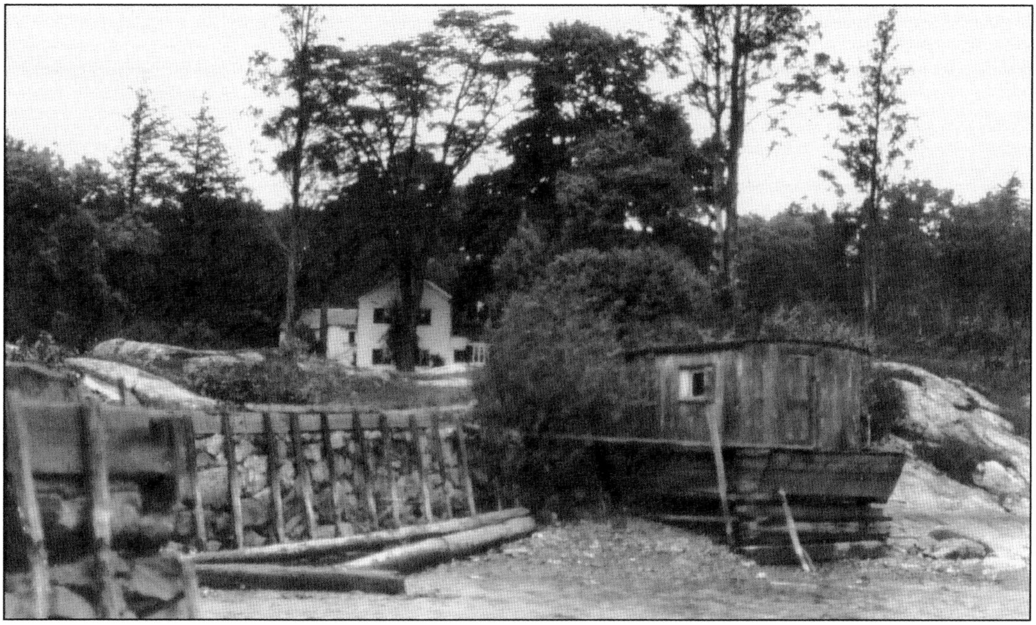

HARD TIMES. During the 1840s, the family had experienced lack of food, candles, warm winter clothing, and the death of their cow. At one point, a burning rag set in lard served as a light. One evening, after a walk down to the river, Susan Warner reflected in her diary about, "the bare old house . . . exactly like a place where poor people live . . . with a cut-loose-from-the world air, it is just like us."

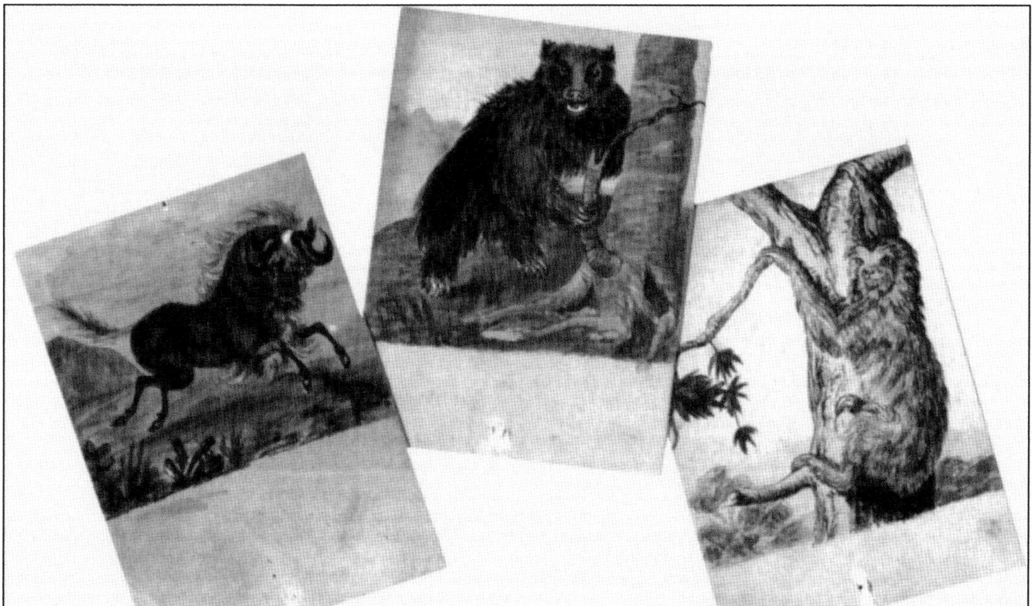

ANIMAL CARD. Hard times led Anna to be the first member of the family to earn money as a creative writer. In 1847, she invented Robinson Crusoe's Farmyard, an educational game played with colored cards of animals. The manufacturer printed the cards, which Anna and Susan colored by hand. Anna could color 12 packs of 24 cards per day at a penny per pack.

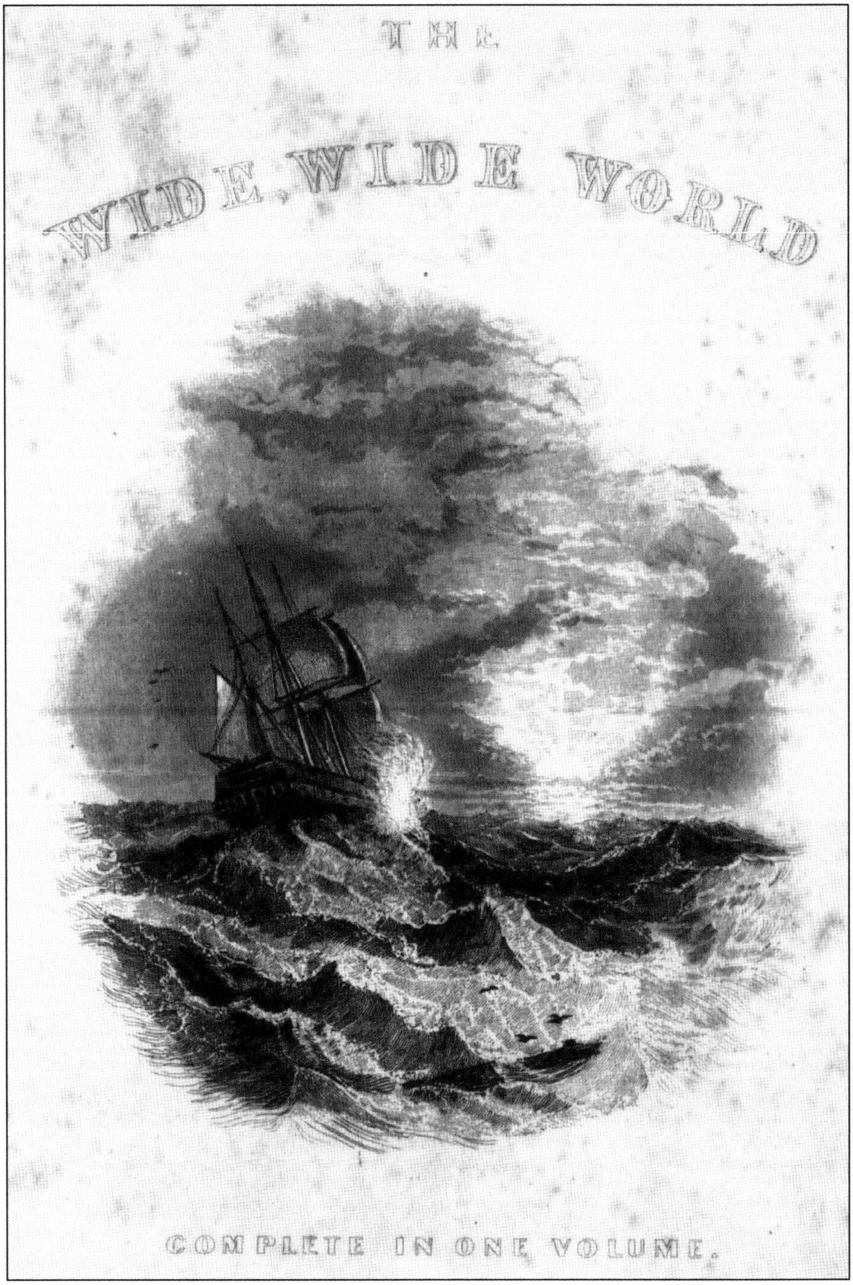

THE WIDE, WIDE WORLD. In 1848, Aunt Fanny suggested to Susan Warner that she write a novel. Susan began immediately and wrote steadily for one year completing her first book, *The Wide, Wide World*, in the summer of 1849. That fall, Henry Warner brought the manuscript to several publishers, all of whom rejected it. Finally he tried George Putnam, who gave it to his mother to critique. Days later she told her son, "If you never publish another book, publish this." Written under the pseudonym Elizabeth Wetherell, it is an inspirational tale of humility and self-sacrifice about an orphan named Ellen Montgomery. Published in December 1850, the novel became immensely popular. It remained in print for 80 years in more than 100 editions and was translated into at least seven languages. In its day, it was outsold only by *Uncle Tom's Cabin*.

QUEECHY. Susan began her second novel before the first one was published. *Queechy* was set in a rural town modeled on Canaan, New York. Published in 1852, it received excellent reviews. Susan wrote over 30 other well-received novels and children's books before her death in 1885. She is known for detailed descriptions of 19th-century rural life.

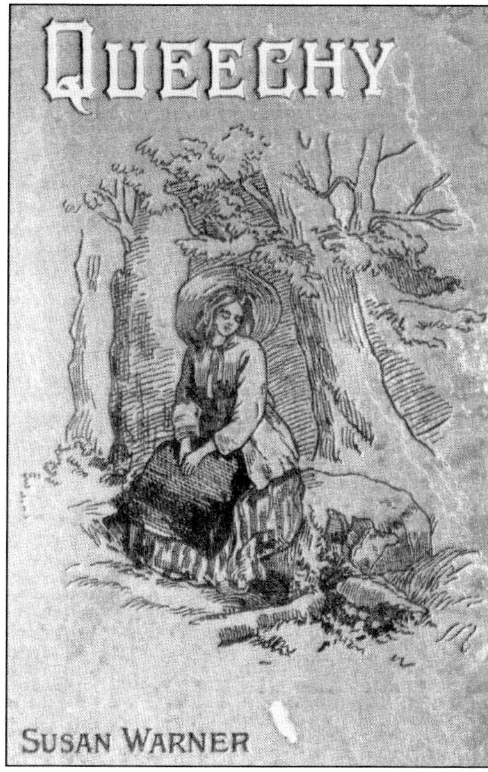

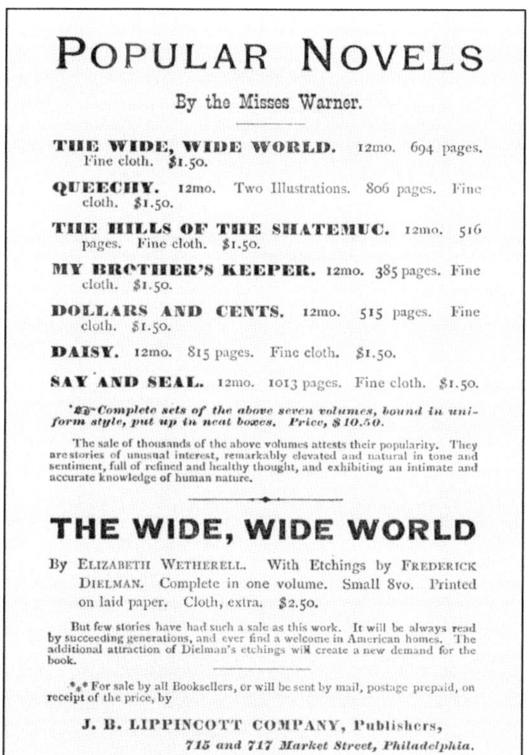

POPULAR NOVELS

By the Misses Warner.

THE WIDE, WIDE WORLD. 12mo. 694 pages. Fine cloth. $1.50.

QUEECHY. 12mo. Two Illustrations. 806 pages. Fine cloth. $1.50.

THE HILLS OF THE SHATEMUC. 12mo. 516 pages. Fine cloth. $1.50.

MY BROTHER'S KEEPER. 12mo. 385 pages. Fine cloth. $1.50.

DOLLARS AND CENTS. 12mo. 515 pages. Fine cloth. $1.50.

DAISY. 12mo. 815 pages. Fine cloth. $1.50.

SAY AND SEAL. 12mo. 1013 pages. Fine cloth. $1.50.

Complete sets of the above seven volumes, bound in uniform style, put up in neat boxes. Price, $10.50.

The sale of thousands of the above volumes attests their popularity. They are stories of unusual interest, remarkably elevated and natural in tone and sentiment, full of refined and healthy thought, and exhibiting an intimate and accurate knowledge of human nature.

THE WIDE, WIDE WORLD

By ELIZABETH WETHERELL. With Etchings by FREDERICK DIELMAN. Complete in one volume. Small 8vo. Printed on laid paper. Cloth, extra. $2.50.

But few stories have had such a sale as this work. It will be always read by succeeding generations, and ever find a welcome in American homes. The additional attraction of Dielman's etchings will create a new demand for the book.

*** For sale by all Booksellers, or will be sent by mail, postage prepaid, on receipt of the price, by

J. B. LIPPINCOTT COMPANY, Publishers,
715 and 717 Market Street, Philadelphia.

ADVERTISEMENT. After the great success of *The Wide, Wide World*, Susan went on to write other books alone and in collaboration with Anna. This contemporary advertisement for Warner books claims the "stories are of unusual interest, remarkably elevated and natural in tone and sentiment, full of refined and healthy thought, and exhibiting an intimate and accurate knowledge of human nature." A fine cloth edition of a Warner novel cost $1.50.

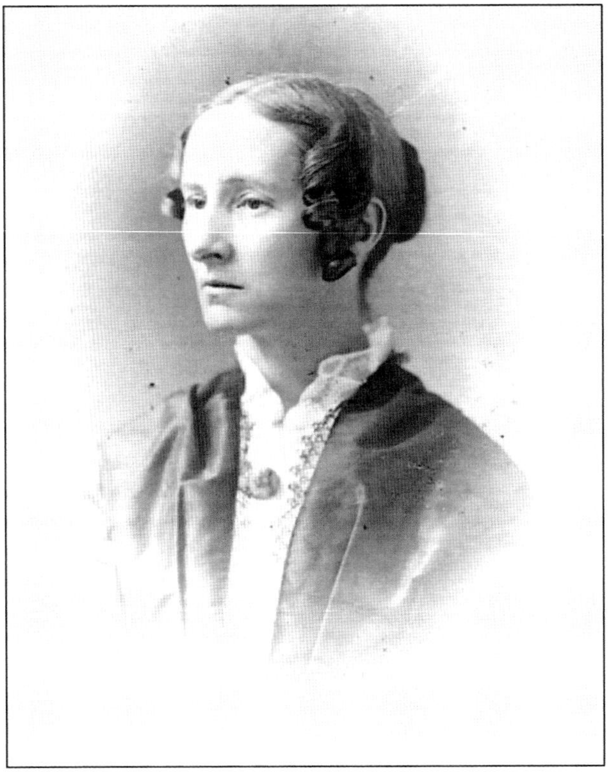

AMY LOTHROP. After her sister's success, Anna Warner decided to try her hand at writing a novel. *Dollars and Cents*, written under the pseudonym of Amy Lothrop, was the first of many books from her pen. Among others were *West Point Colors*, *Hymns of the Church Militant*, and *Susan Warner*, a biography of her sister.

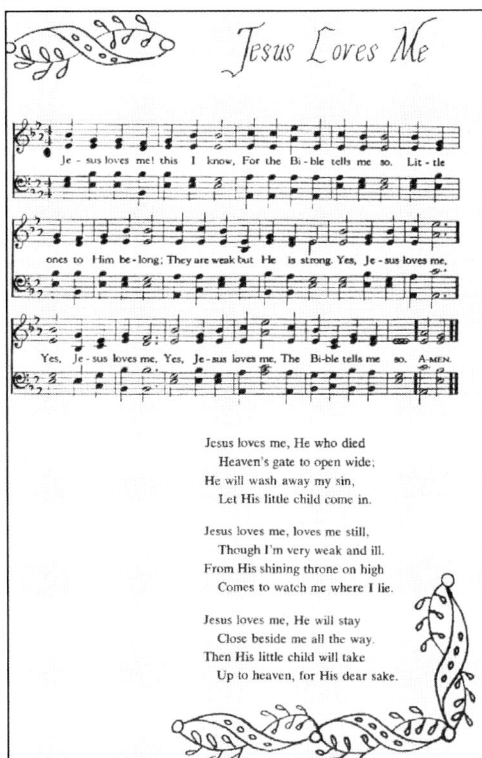

JESUS LOVES ME. During the winter of 1858–1859, the Warner sisters wrote *Say and Seal*, their first collaboration. Anna later recalled the fun that they had being busy on the same piece of work. The words to *Jesus Loves Me* were written by Anna and appear in that book as a verse spoken by a teacher to a dying child.

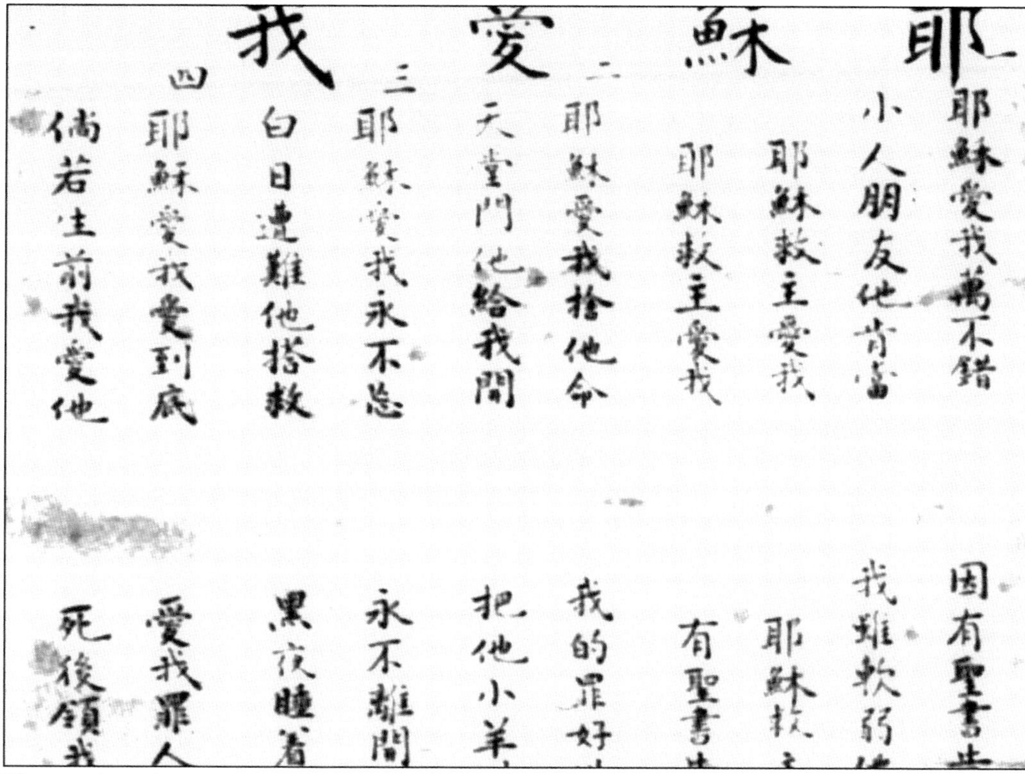

HYMN. Anna's poem was set to music by William Bradbury, a musician and teacher, in 1862. *Jesus Loves Me* became immediately popular and spread around the world through the work of missionaries. Anna received this Chinese translation as a gift from a grateful missionary in China. It hangs today in the Warner House.

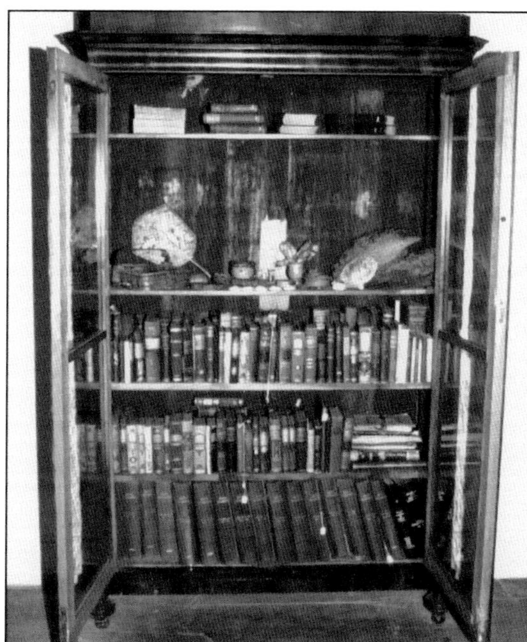

BOOKCASE. The Warner sisters kept a special bookcase in their parlor to store their published works. About 100 books were written by the Warner sisters, separately or in collaboration, including novels, religious treatises, children's books, and a gardening manual.

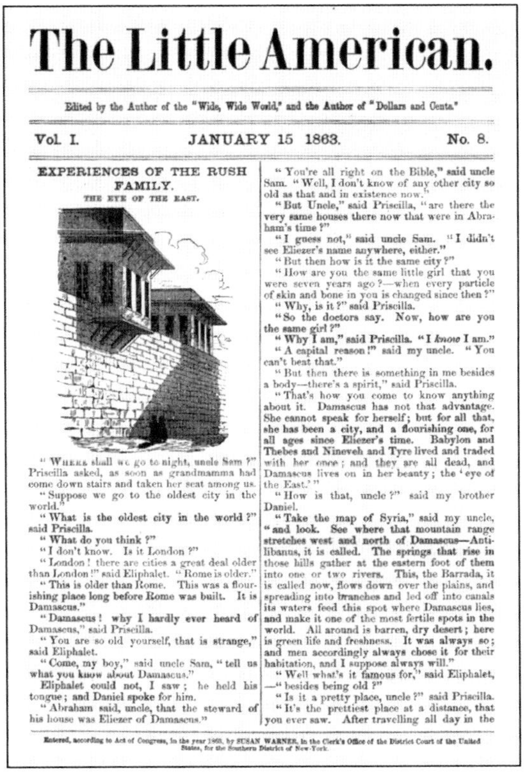

The Little American.

Edited by the Author of the "Wide, Wide World," and the Author of "Dollars and Cents."

Vol. I. JANUARY 15 1863. No. 8.

EXPERIENCES OF THE RUSH FAMILY.

THE EYE OF THE EAST.

"Where shall we go to-night, uncle Sam?" Priscilla asked, as soon as grandmamma had come down stairs and taken her seat among us.

"Suppose we go to the oldest city in the world."

"What is the oldest city in the world?" said Priscilla.

"What do you think?"

"I don't know. Is it London?"

"London! there are cities a great deal older than London!" said Eliphalet. "Rome is older."

"This is older than Rome. This was a flourishing place long before Rome was built. It is Damascus."

"Damascus! why I hardly ever heard of Damascus," said Priscilla.

"You are so old yourself, that is strange," said Eliphalet.

"Come, my boy," said uncle Sam, "tell us what you know about Damascus."

Eliphalet could not, I saw; he held his tongue; and Daniel spoke for him.

"Abraham said, uncle, that the steward of his house was Eliezer of Damascus."

"You're all right on the Bible," said uncle Sam. "Well, I don't know of any other city so old as that and in existence now."

"But Uncle," said Priscilla, "are there the very same houses there now that were in Abraham's time?"

"I guess not," said uncle Sam. "I didn't see Eliezer's name anywhere, either."

"But then how is it the same city?"

"How are you the same little girl that you were seven years ago?—when every particle of skin and bone in you is changed since then?"

"Why, is it?" said Priscilla.

"So the doctors say. Now, how are you the same girl?"

"Why I am," said Priscilla. "I *know* I am."

"A capital reason!" said my uncle. "You can't beat that."

"But then there is something in me besides a body—there's a spirit," said Priscilla.

"That's how you come to know anything about it. Damascus has not that advantage. She cannot speak for herself; but for all that, she has been a city, and a flourishing one, for all ages since Eliezer's time. Babylon and Thebes and Nineveh and Tyre lived and traded with her once; and they are all dead, and Damascus lives on in her beauty; the 'eye of the East.'"

"How is that, uncle?" said my brother Daniel.

"Take the map of Syria," said my uncle, "and look. See where that mountain range stretches west and north of Damascus—Anti-libanus, it is called. The springs that rise in those hills gather at the eastern foot of them into one or two rivers. This, the Barrada, it is called now, flows down over the plains, and spreading into branches and led off into canals its waters feed this spot where Damascus lies, and make it one of the most fertile spots in the world. All around is barren, dry desert; here is green life and freshness. It was always so; and men accordingly always chose it for their habitation, and I suppose always will."

"Well what's it famous for," said Eliphalet, —"besides being old?"

"Is it a pretty place, uncle?" said Priscilla.

"It's the prettiest place at a distance, that you ever saw. After travelling all day in the

Entered, according to Act of Congress, in the year 1863, by SUSAN WARNER, in the Clerk's Office of the District Court of the United States, for the Southern District of New-York.

The Little American. In 1862 and 1863, Susan and Anna Warner produced this magazine for children. It contained articles on history, geography, poetry, natural history, and serialized fiction. This particular issue, dated November 15, 1862, had an article on grasses as well as a continuing story called "The Breakfast Table." A subscription cost $1.50 per year plus 6¢ in advance for postage. The venture broke even financially.

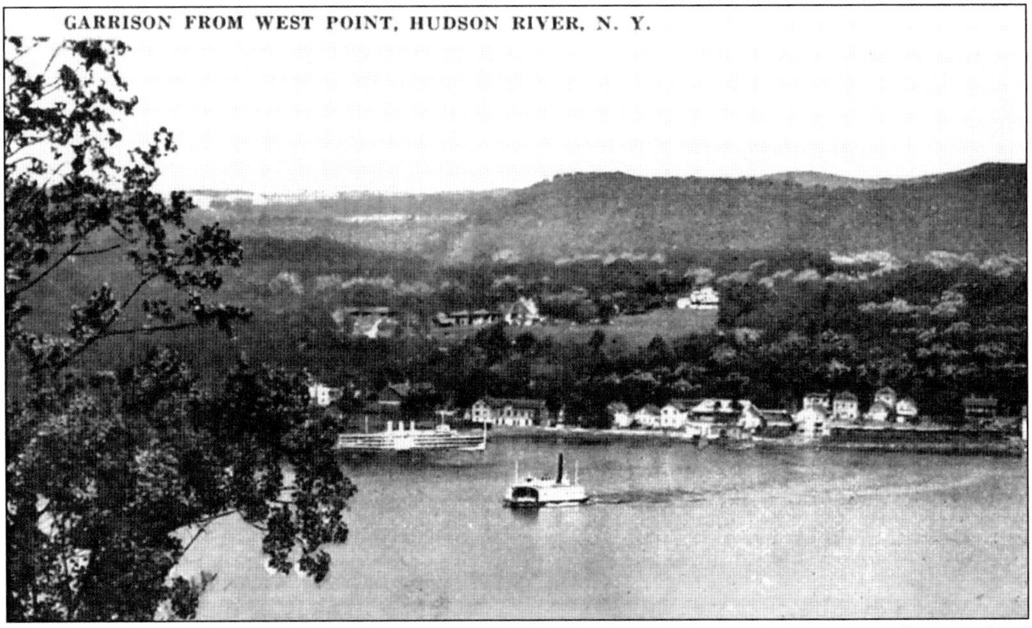

Missionary Work. Three years after the move to Constitution Island, Susan and Anna had formally joined the Presbyterian church. They devoted time to the distribution of religious tracts among local farmers. This entailed rowing to Garrison, climbing the hills to visit homes, and offering literature. When invited, Susan stayed to talk about religion. In this way, she became acquainted with several Garrison families. (Donnery collection.)

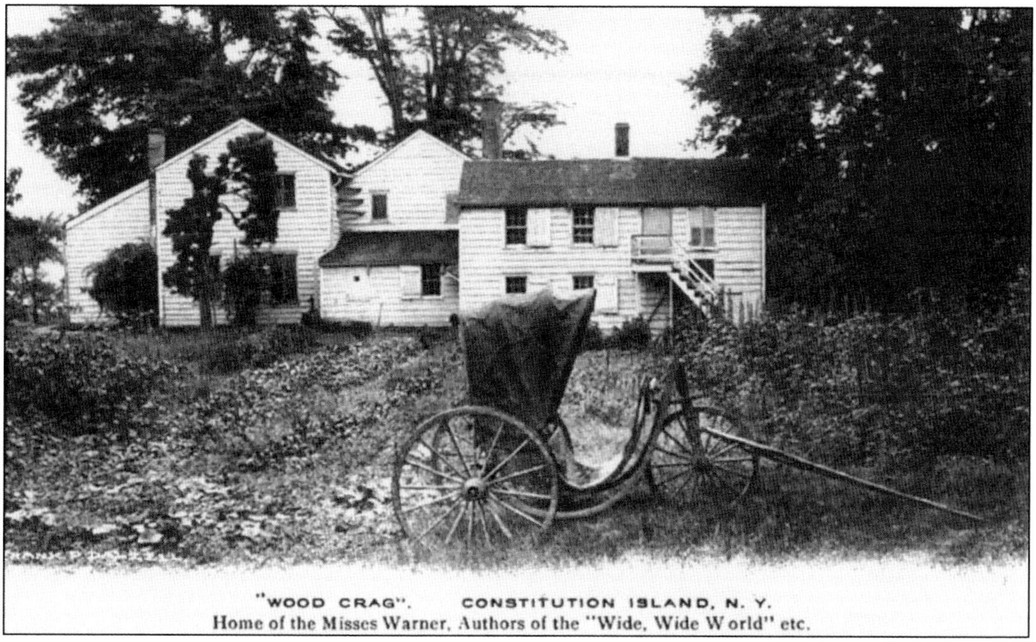

CELEBRITY. After 1850, the Warner sisters wrote constantly. By the 1860s, they had achieved celebrity status. Their house was the subject of postcards. Despite their success, the Warners' prolific literary output never made them rich due to lax copyright laws and pirated editions. Their situation improved, however, and they were able to hire help and spend winters away from the island. (Gunza collection.)

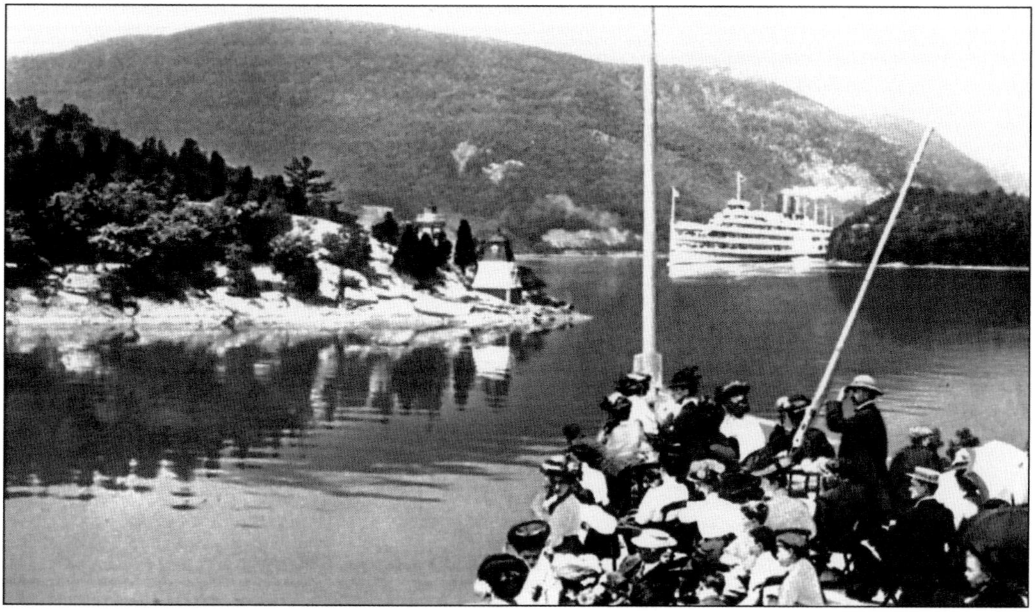

DAY LINE. In the late 19th century, a scenic ride on a Day Line steamer was a pleasant sightseeing adventure as seen in this vintage postcard. Two popular attractions in the Highlands were the military academy and the home of the Warner sisters. This steamboat approaches the Gee's Point lighthouses on West Point. The large steamer in the distance is just passing Constitution Island at right. (Donnery collection.)

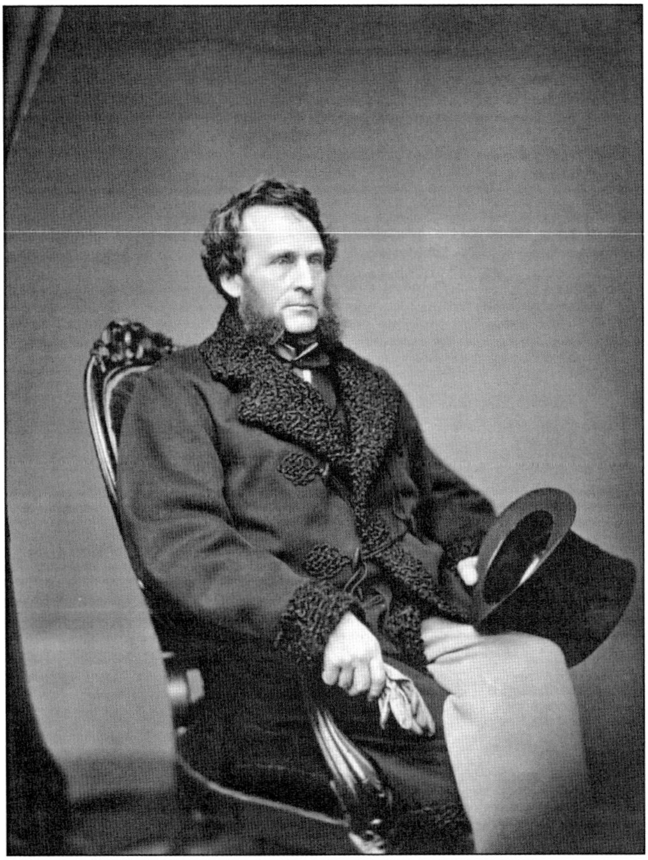

The Squirrels. Whenever possible, the Warners spent winters away from the cold isolation of the island, closing the house, and taking rooms elsewhere. They often wintered in Highland Falls at accommodations belonging to their family friend, John Bigelow, left, publisher and statesman who owned the *New York Post* and served as minister to France under Abraham Lincoln. On occasion, they occupied rooms in the main estate house, the Squirrels, pictured below. (Left, Sidamon-Eristoff collection; below, photograph by Kevin Coffey.)

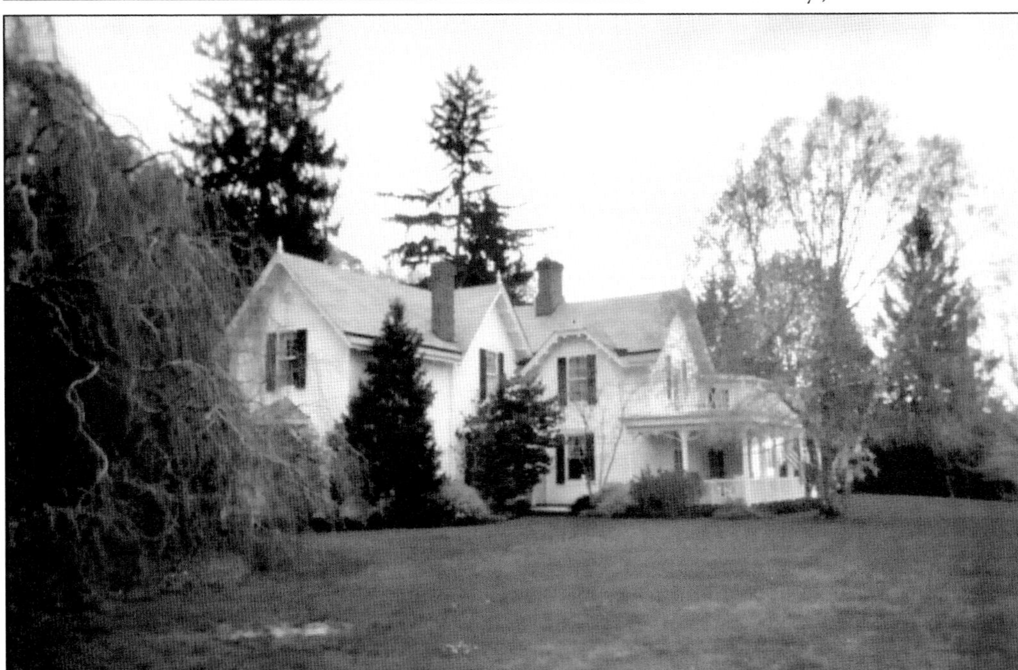

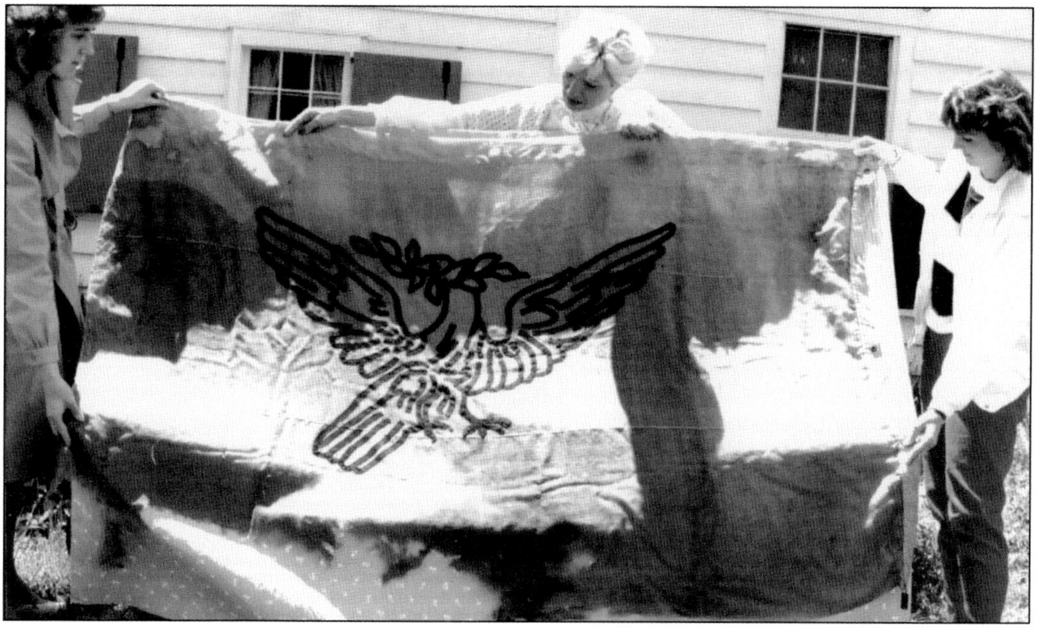

MEMORIAL FLAG. The Warner sisters followed the Civil War closely through newspaper accounts. The outcome was a source of happiness and relief. Upon the death of Lincoln, they expressed their deep sorrow by making the memorial flag shown here after some 20th-century conservation work. As Lincoln's funeral train passed their island, the sisters stood alongside the tracks and displayed this flag.

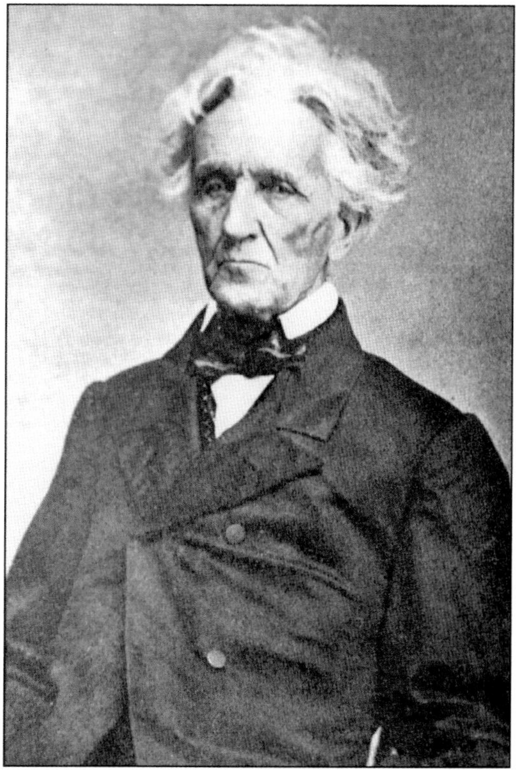

FATHER. Henry Warner died in 1875. "It was an untold blessing," wrote Anna Warner, "in those years of many privations that my father was what he was. The clearest mind, the most ardent lover of books and study . . . in his busiest and most troubled years, he always found time to talk with his children. He read to us in the evening, poetry, history, fiction. Our mealtimes were delightful seasons of talk, and discussion."

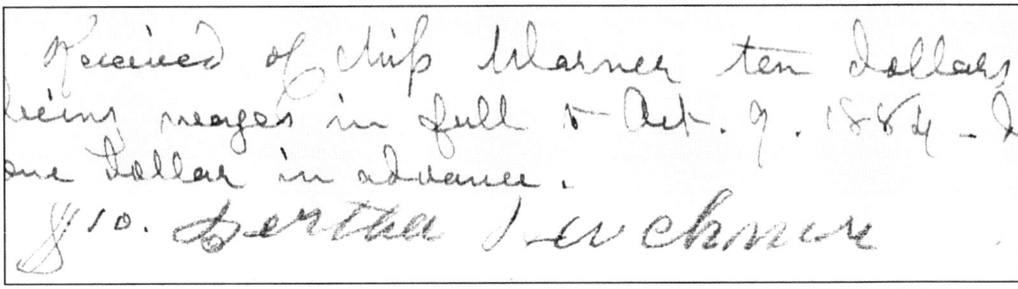

Received of Miss Warner ten dollars
being wages in full to Oct. 9. 1884 – &
one dollar in advance.
$10. Bertha Buckner

BERTHA AND WILLIS BUCKNER. This receipt reads, "Received of Miss Warner ten dollars being wages in full to Oct. 9, 1884 and one dollar in advance. $10." It is signed Bertha Buckner. Born in Virginia, Buckner began working for the Warners in 1868, when she was about 17. A tall, handsome, woman with tawny complexion and dignified posture, she remained with the Warners for 47 years. Over time, she became more of a companion than a servant. Bertha married Willis Buckner, below, a former slave who was hired by the Warners in 1865 as a caretaker, boatman, butler, and coachman. He is pictured beside a three-wheel chaise in elegant livery, which he reportedly enjoyed wearing. Willis died in 1907. Bertha moved to Schneider Avenue in Highland Falls after Anna's death in 1915. Bertha died in 1921.

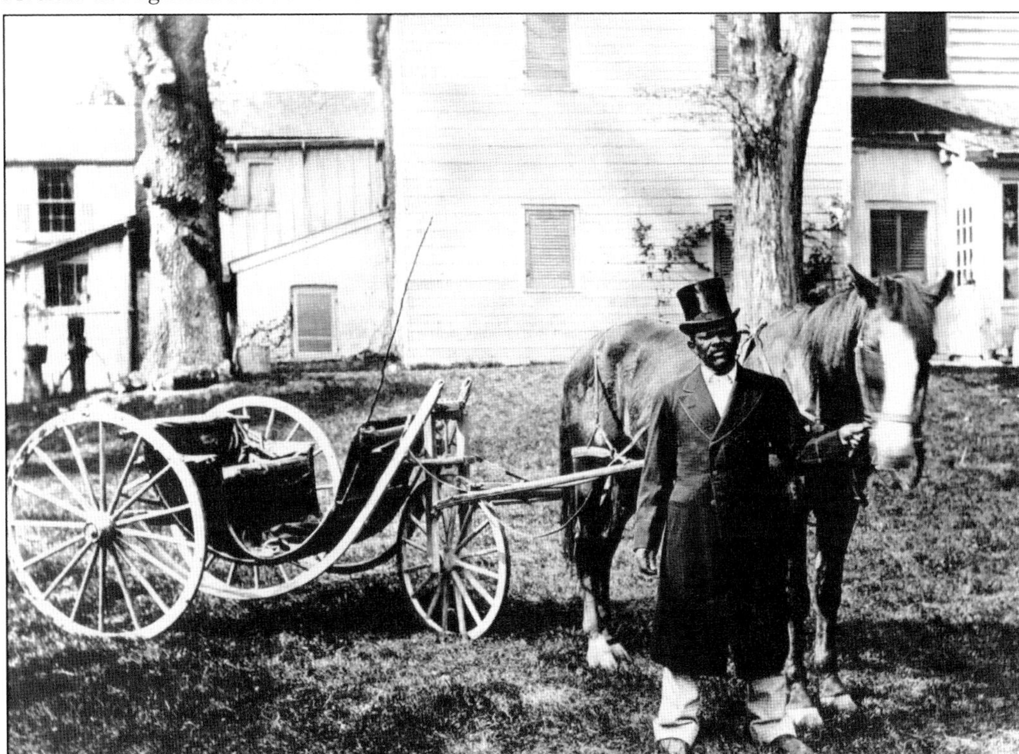

Five

CADET STUDENTS

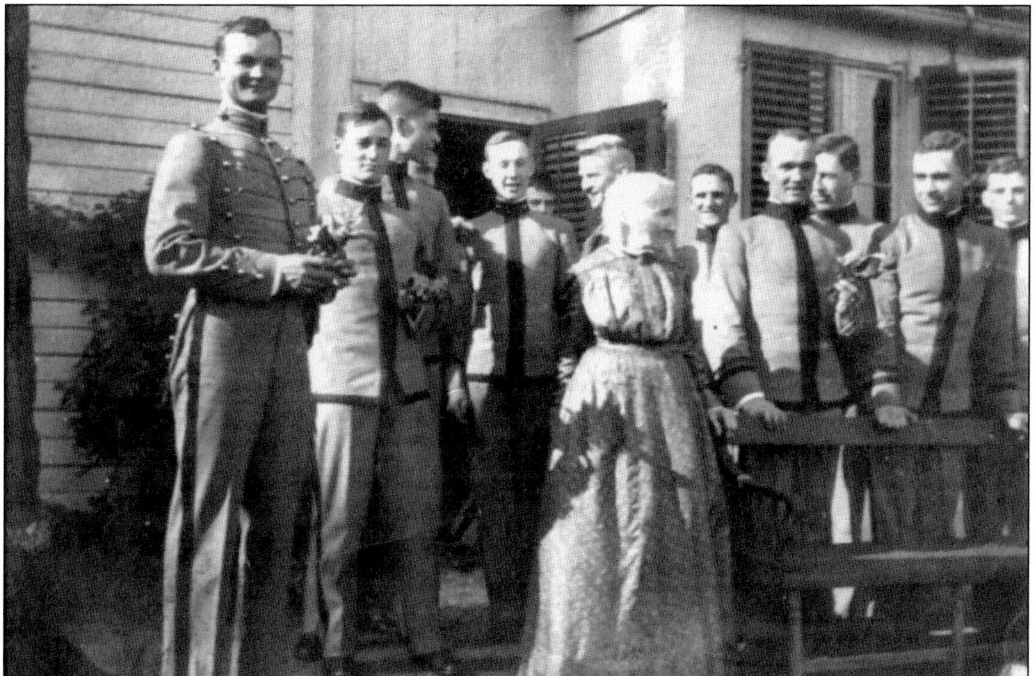

BIBLE CLASS. Surrounded by her cadet Bible students, Anna Warner stands in front of her home about 1914. It was Susan who began teaching Bible classes at West Point in 1875. Anna carried on for 30 more years after Susan's death in 1885. In summer, the classes were held on the island. Long-lasting friendships developed from these classes. Over the years, the sisters received countless letters and visits from graduates who were inspired by their kindness, spirituality, and patriotism.

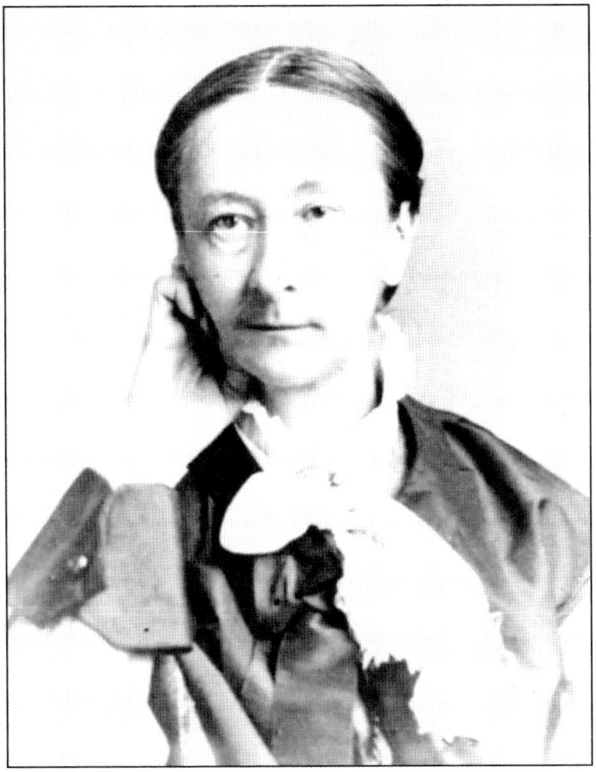

BIBLE TEACHER. After Henry Warner's death in 1875, Susan Warner began giving Bible classes to officers' wives at West Point. She was 56 years old. Her reputation as an excellent teacher spread, and soon, the cadets requested that she teach them too. Uncertain at first, she found the cadets to be interested students.

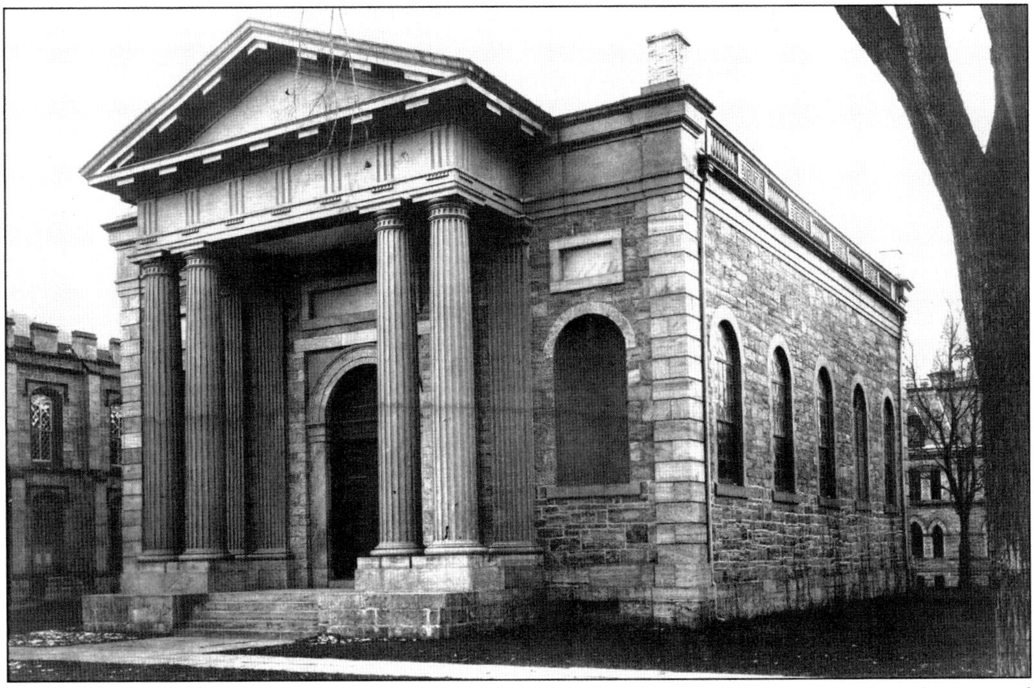

BIBLE LESSONS. Susan held Bible class every Sunday afternoon at the Cadet Chapel, pictured here in its original site near the plain. In 1911, the chapel was moved to its current site at the West Point Cemetery. It is now referred to as the Old Cadet Chapel. (USMA Library.)

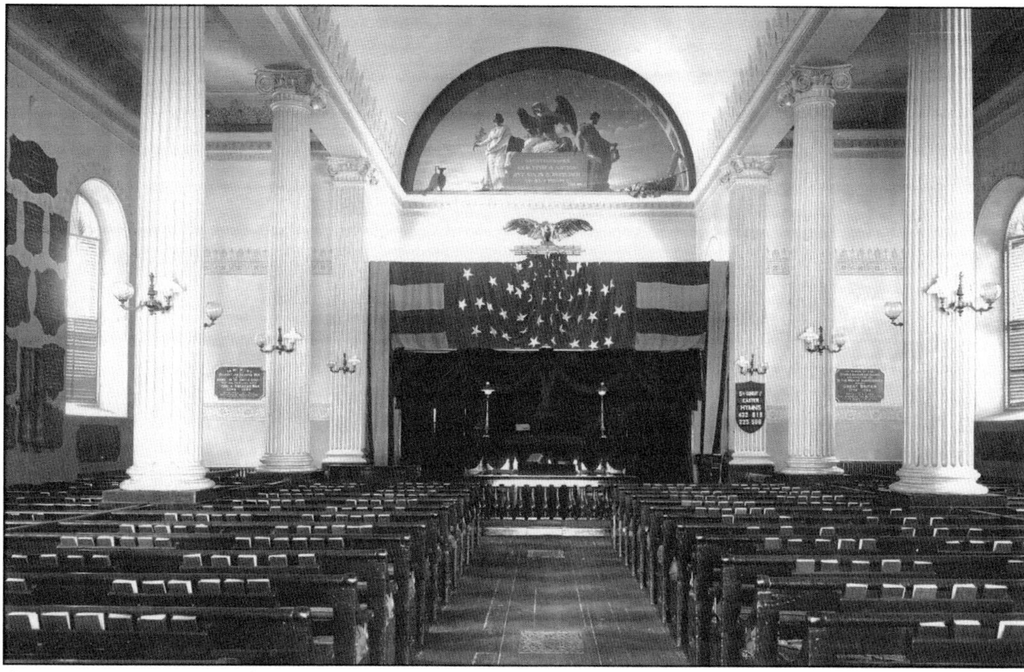

CHAPEL INTERIOR. The stately interior of the Old Cadet Chapel was the perfect place for the Bible classes. In winter, classes were held here. In warm weather, the cadets were allowed the unusual privilege of rowing out to Constitution Island for their lessons. This was a special opportunity since the cadets were normally confined to the post. (USMA Library.)

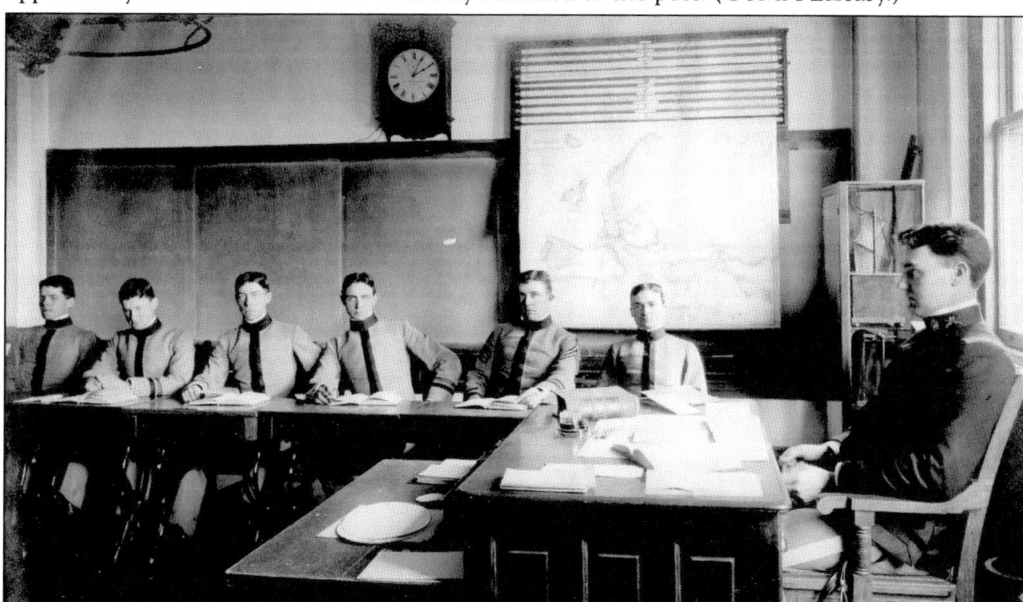

HISTORY CLASS. Cadets and their instructor sit in a small group recitation class in the Department of Law and History in 1903. Academic rigor left little time for diversion. Bible classes on Constitution Island were particularly popular with plebes, or new cadets. As one remembered, "The relaxation from the hard and trying existence of a first-year man at West Point made us appreciate the wholesome home atmosphere of Miss Warner's environment." (USMA Library.)

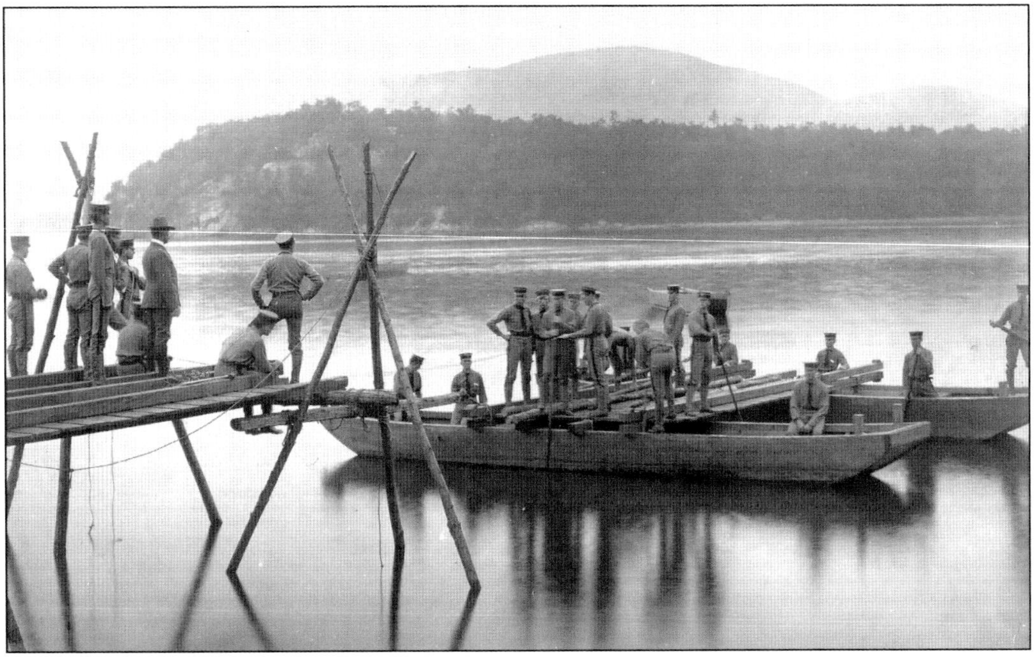

Bridge Building. Part of the cadet training in military engineering involved construction of temporary bridges on the Hudson River. With Constitution Island as a backdrop, cadets extend a bridge out from the North Dock by means of pontoon boats. Although it is only a quarter-mile away, cadets were not permitted to go to the island unless they were members of the Bible class. (USMA Library.)

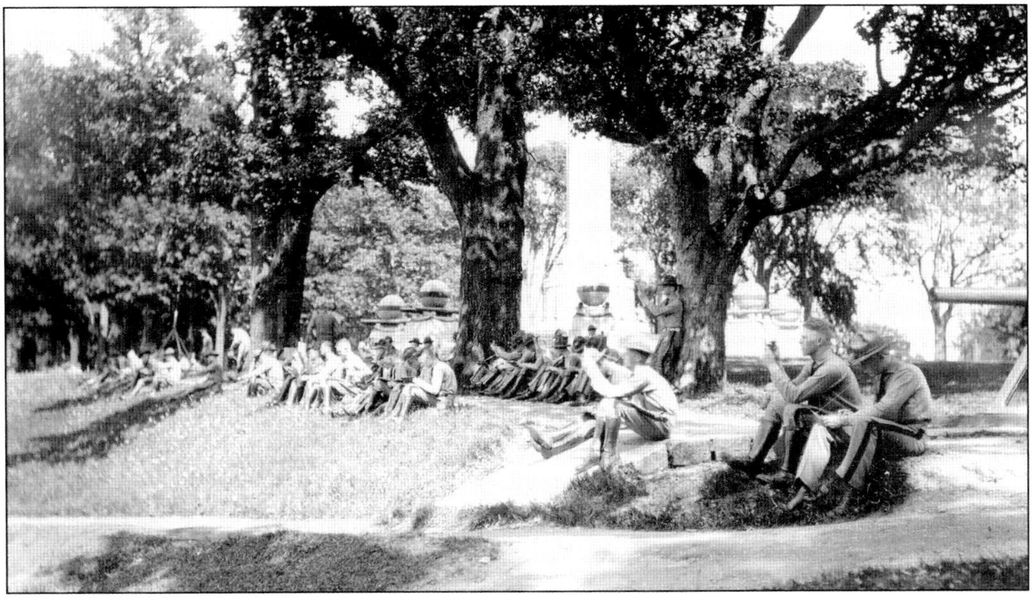

Drawing Class. This drawing class at Trophy Point sits sketching Constitution Island and the northern Highlands. What looks like a leisurely activity actually was not. All cadets had to learn to draw in order to give accurate representations of a battlefield. It was a coveted privilege to actually visit the island they were drawing, attend Bible class, stay for tea, and briefly escape military supervision. (USMA Library.)

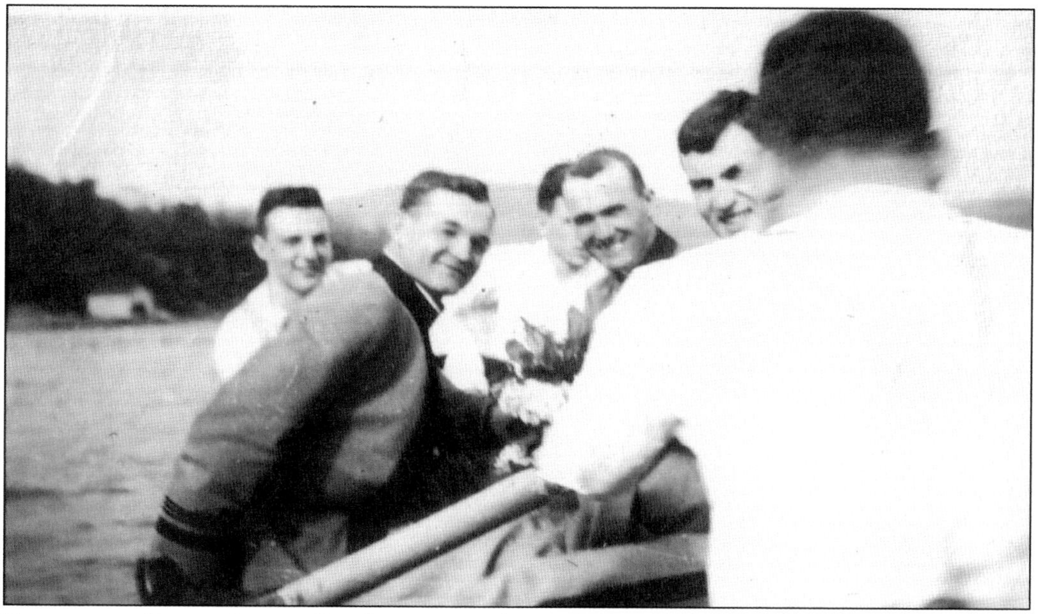

ROWING TO BIBLE CLASS. Clearly enjoying their outing, members of the Bible class row over to Constitution Island. Cadets had to apply for and be granted permission to attend Bible class on the island in the summer months. After arriving on the island, they would have class in the Warner house or in a large white tent on the lawn. After class, they enjoyed lemonade and gingerbread or cake, a bit of home for the young men who often did not see their own families for years.

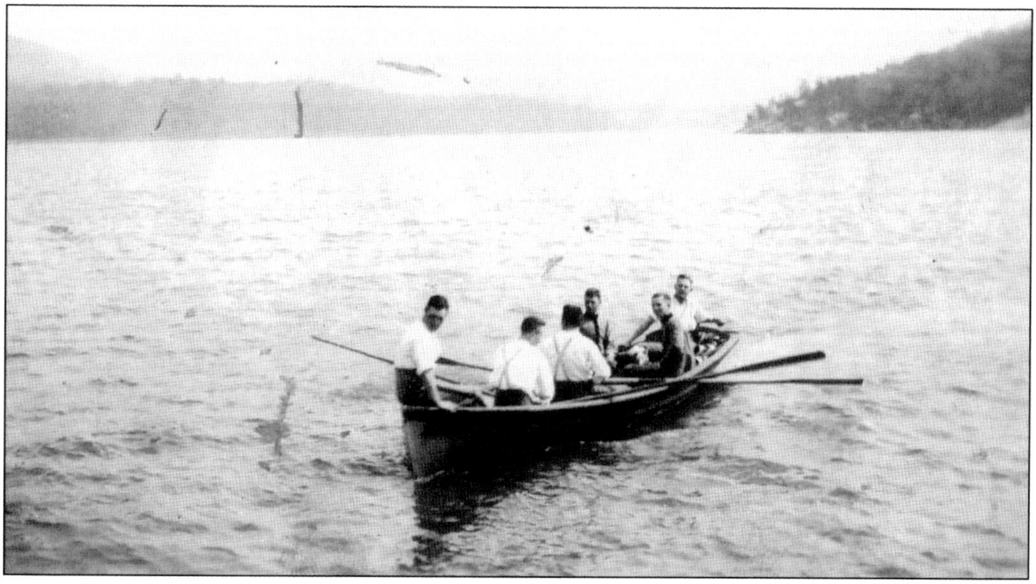

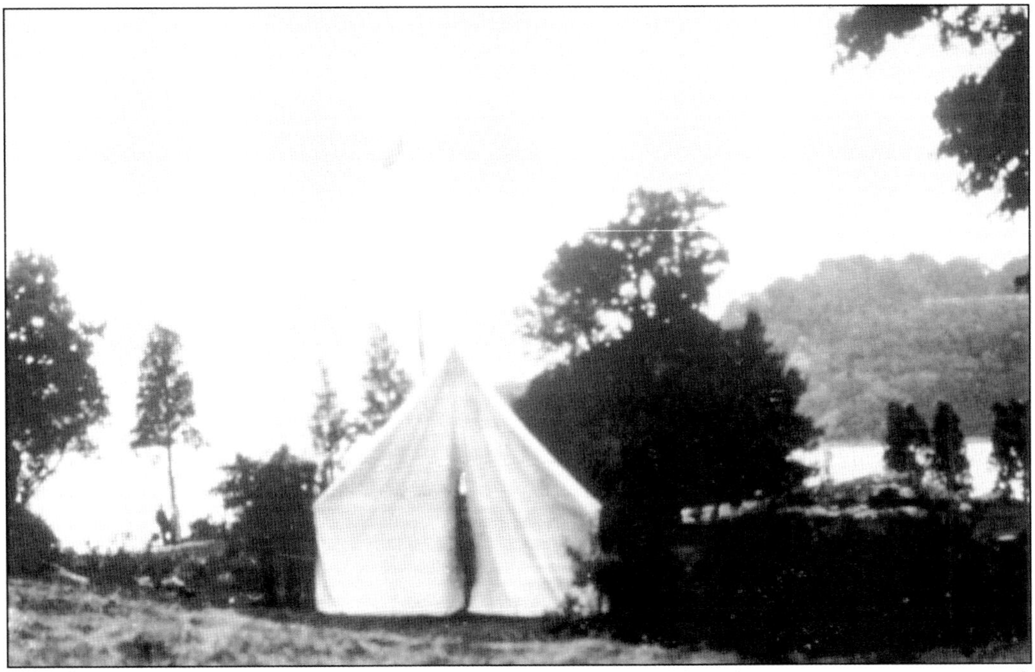

SUMMER SCHOOL. In summer, the Bible classes were often held in this tent. An 1898 *New York Times* retrospective on Susan Warner offered this noteworthy observation: "It is doubtful if any where in the world's history this spectacle can be duplicated, of successive classes of young men, being trained at the hands of a great government in the arts of war, sitting each week at the feet of a woman to study the gospel of peace."

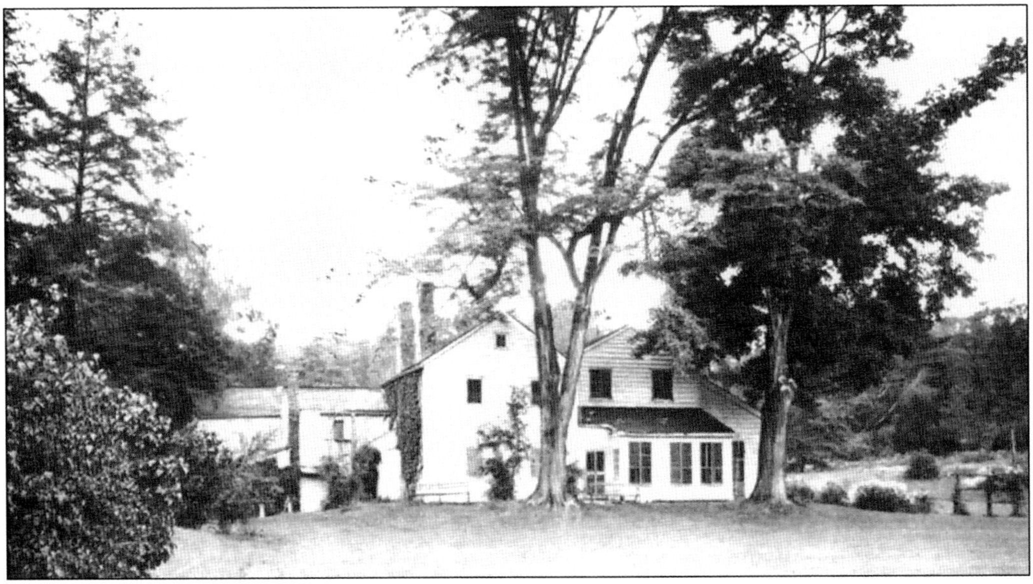

RECOLLECTION. Crampton Jones, a member of Anna Warner's last Bible class, recalled the happiness of rowing to the island. After securing the boat, "we would stroll across the greensward covered with trees and flowers to the quaint colonial house set in the bower of trees. This heavenly scene would have brought repose to anyone but it was like the Elysian fields to the hard driven cadet." (MacLeod collection.)

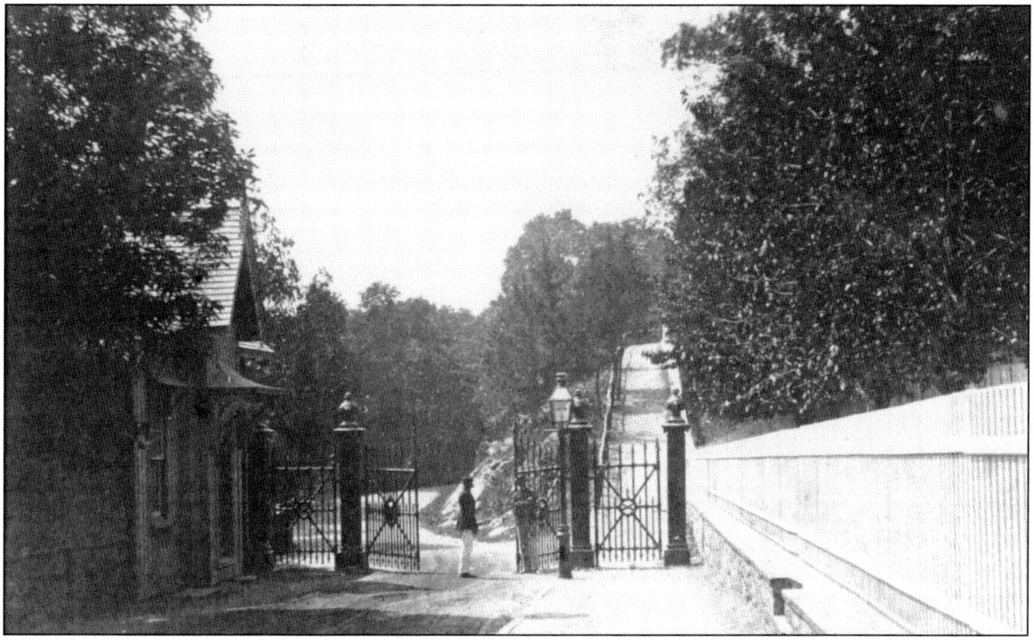

SOUTH GATE. This wrought iron gate marked the boundary of West Point in the 1880s. During their years as Bible teachers, Susan and Anna often spent winters in the village of Highland Falls, two miles south of this gate. In the late 1880s, the superintendent occasionally loaned his carriage to bring Anna from the village to the Cadet Chapel. (USMA Library.)

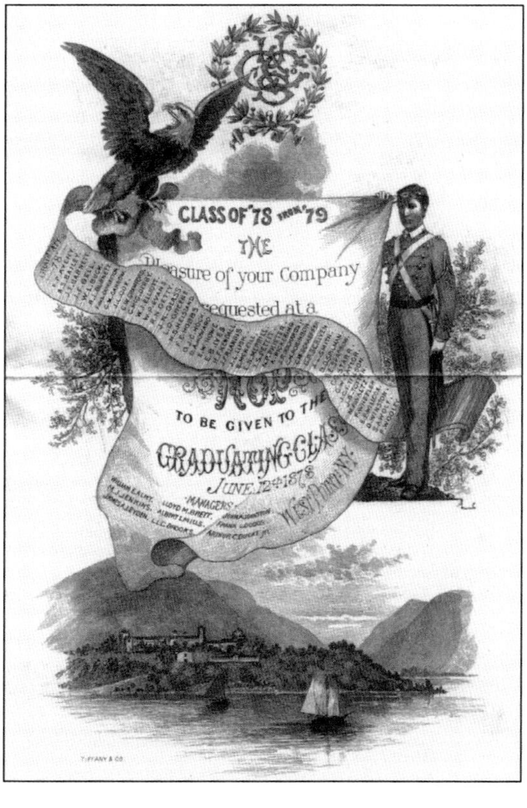

INVITATION. Susan and Anna frequently received invitations from the Bible students to events at West Point such as this farewell hop. They were also on the guest list for graduations, parades, and other events. One year, braving a severe storm, Anna attended a Hundredth Night celebration so she would not disappoint her students. In a letter written about 1900, she remarked to a friend that some of her "boys" who had graduated did not want to get married unless she attended the ceremony.

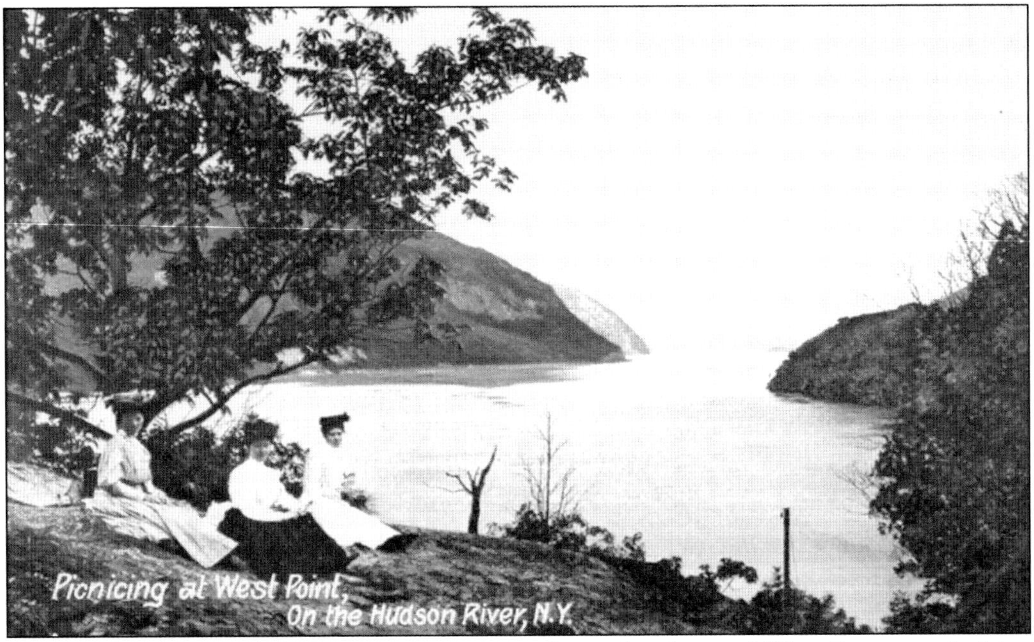

PICNIC. Three young ladies enjoy a picnic on the rocky shore of West Point overlooking Constitution Island. During the early 1900s, cadet Bible students were allowed to accept invitations from Anna Warner to attend Saturday tea or dinner. She invited their girlfriends as well. As years passed, Anna was invited to many weddings of former students, and several brought their brides long distances to meet her. (Donnery collection.)

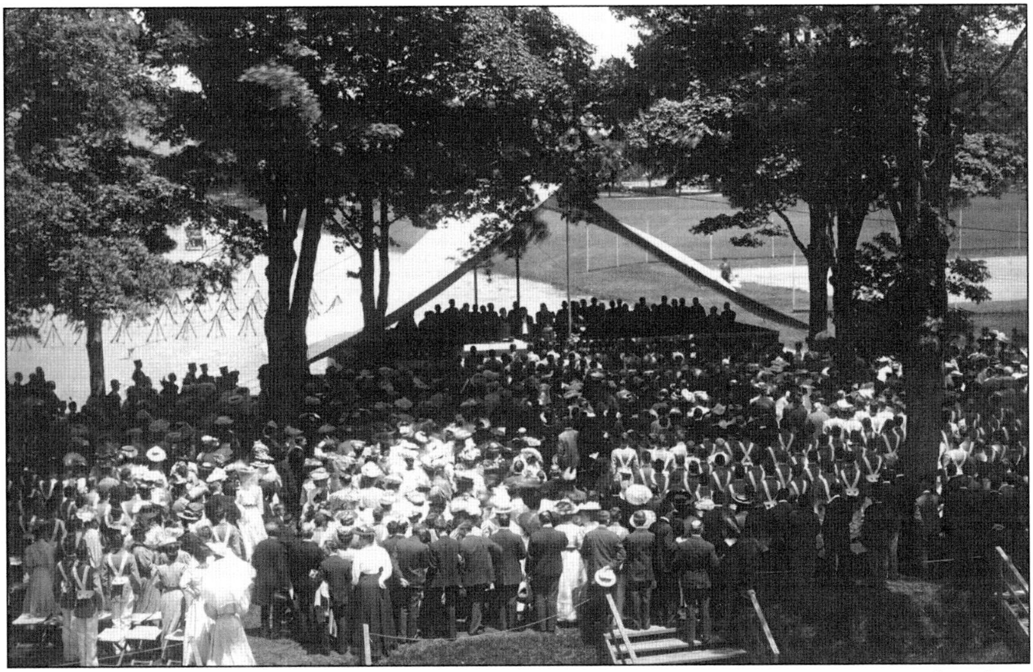

USMA GRADUATION. Highly respected by the cadets, the Warner sisters were invited to their students' graduations in June. The 1906 graduation exercises pictured here was held in front of the library. Secretary of War William Howard Taft presented the diplomas. (USMA Library.)

SUPERINTENDENT'S QUARTERS. In a move to tighten discipline, cadets were forbidden to attend Bible lessons at Constitution Island in 1882. USMA superintendent Maj. Wesley Merritt offered the use of his historic home for the summer classes. Susan Warner declined, but by 1883, permission to row to the island was restored. Anna was a guest here in 1887 when the Merritts invited her to hear Mark Twain speak to the cadets. (USMA Library.)

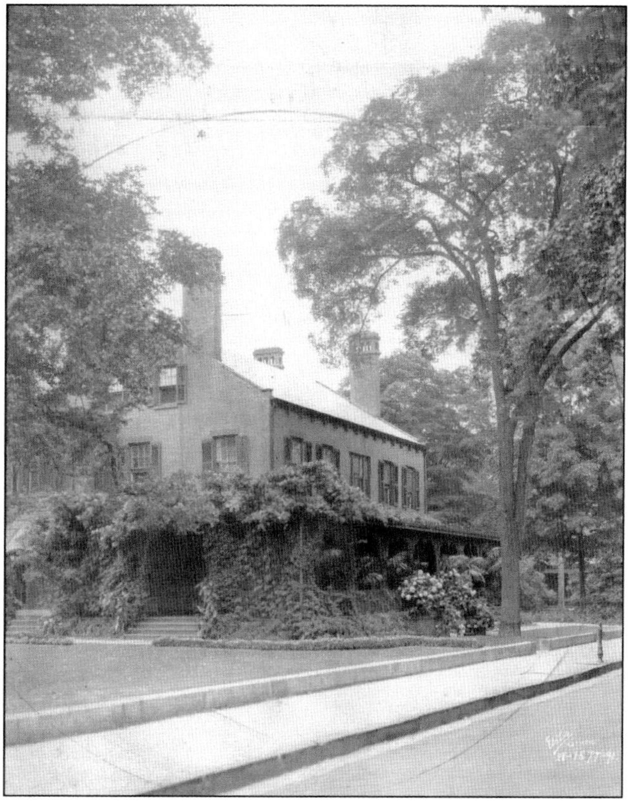

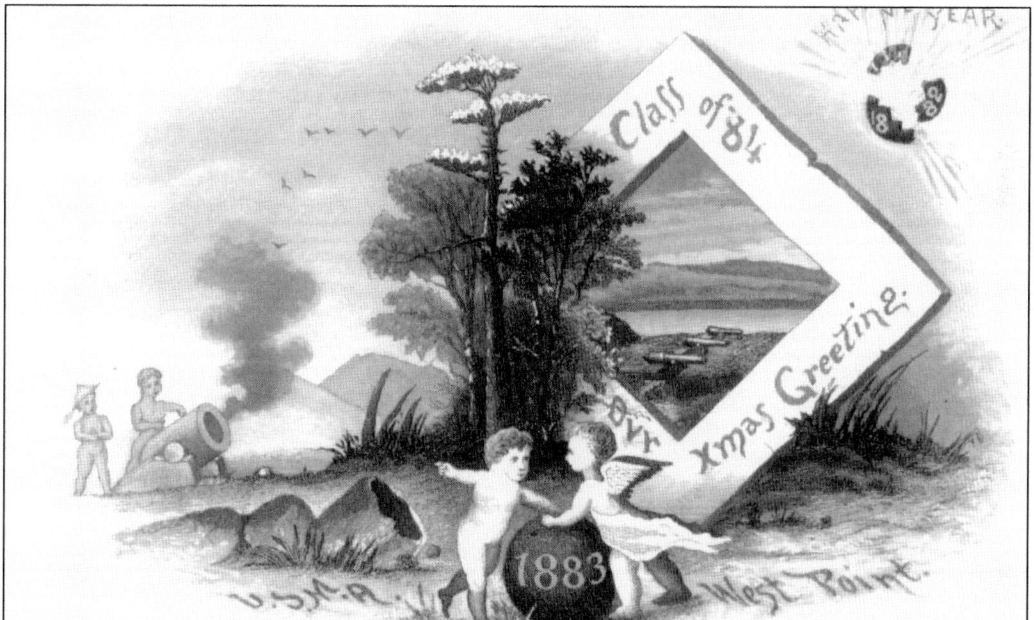

CHRISTMAS CARD. In this charming holiday greeting, the cannonball of 1882 bursts apart to welcome the new year of 1883. Susan received this unique Christmas card from a cadet student in the class of 1884.

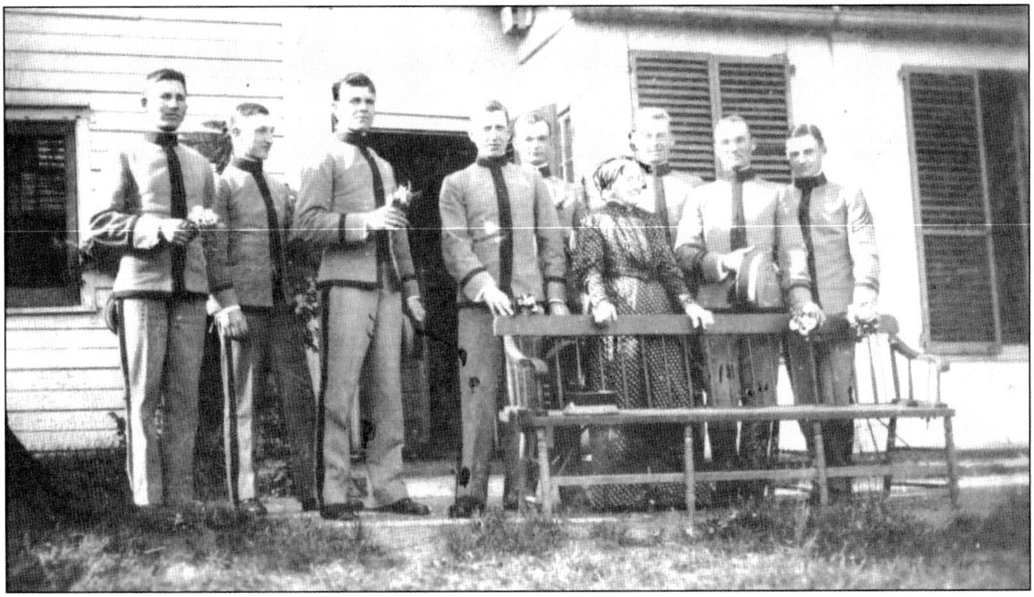

ANNA AS TEACHER. After Susan Warner's death in 1885, Anna Warner continued the Bible classes. In this photograph, eight Bible students surround their diminutive teacher in front of the Warner house about 1913. Each holds a nosegay of flowers prepared by Anna for them. Her cadets had special permission to keep this nonmilitary item in their rooms.

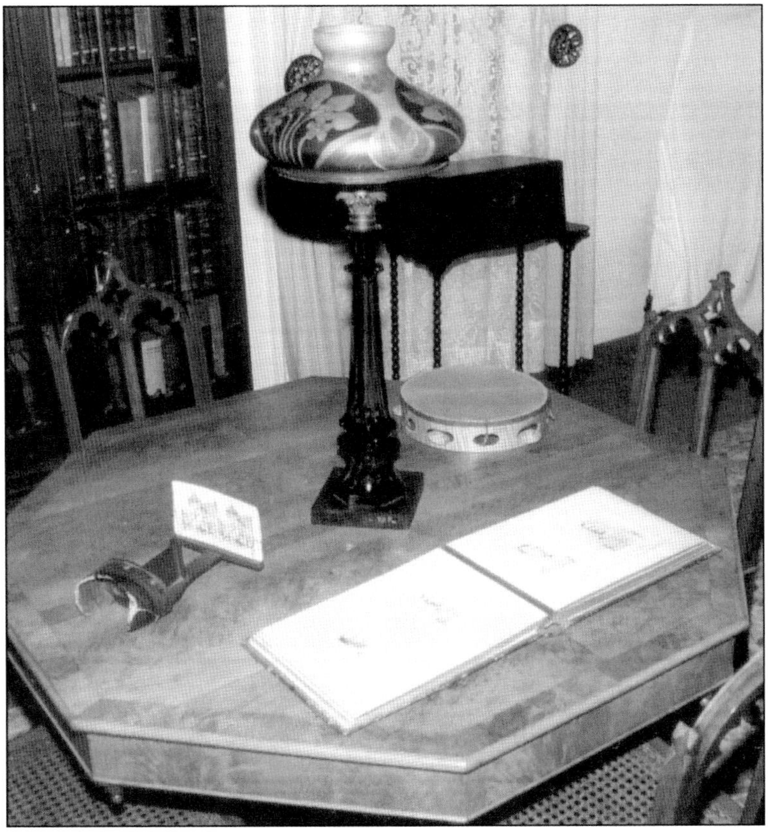

PHOTO ALBUM. On several tables in the Warner House, cadet photograph albums are displayed. These were gifts given to Susan and Anna by graduating classes of Bible students. To the left of this album is a stereopticon for three-dimensional postcard viewing. It was a gift from Susan to Anna in 1862. The sisters enjoyed shopping for inexpensive images of foreign places to describe in their books.

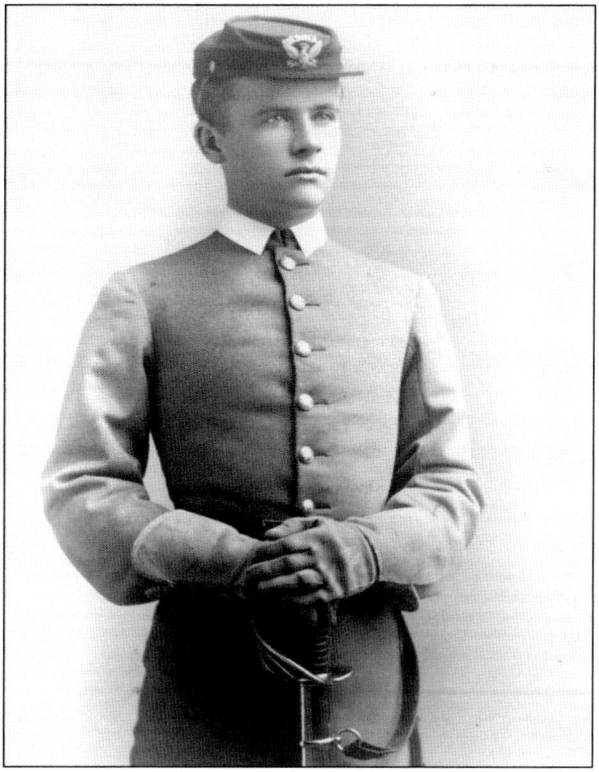

WILLIAM S. BIDDLE. The words of their students are the most eloquent testimony to the effect the Warner sisters had on their pupils. William Biddle, class of 1885, wrote that Susan was "a sincere and gifted teacher . . . my mind often dwells in gratitude and affection upon the deeds of this noble woman." (USMA Library.)

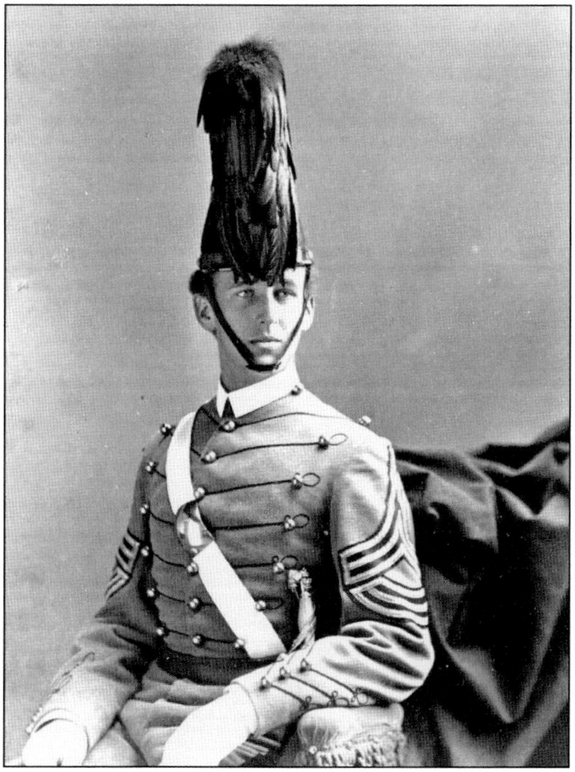

WILLIAM M. BLACK. William Black, class of 1877, had known both Warner ladies as teachers. In a memoir written in 1915, he spoke of Susan as "intensely interested and interesting in her work with cadets." Of Anna he said, "The influence of Miss Anna's life and teachings must be felt and must remain a factor for good wherever the Army goes." (USMA Library.)

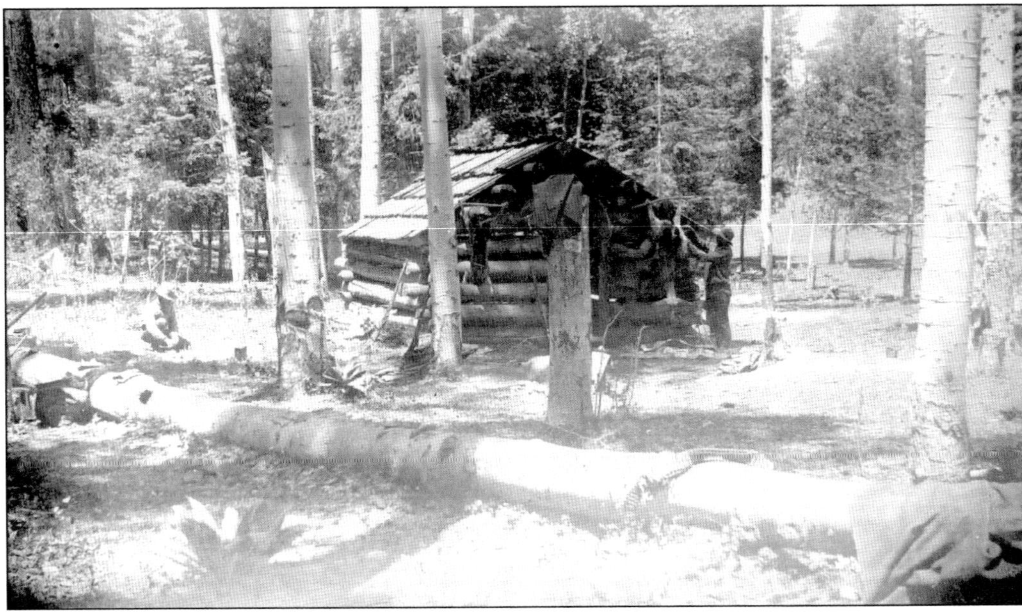

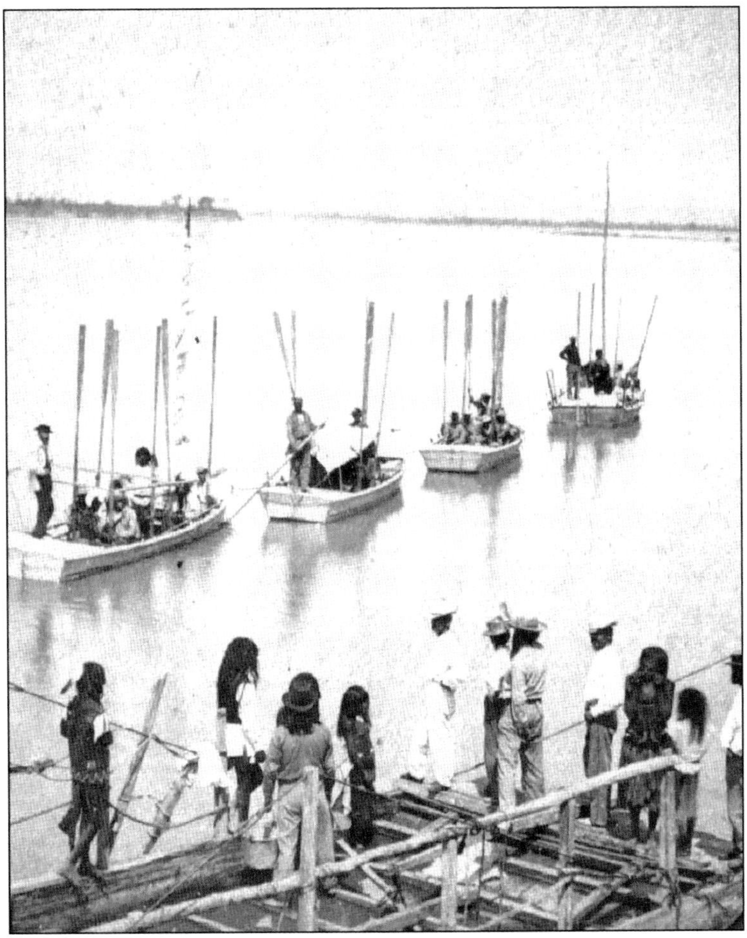

CORRESPONDENCE. One of the Warner sisters' greatest joys was corresponding with former students, now young officers at distant army posts. Return letters often included photographs that Susan and Anna Warner saved. Above a young officer snapped this shot of his log cabin at the foot of San Francisco Mountain in Arizona in 1887. The image at left is an 1871 stereoscopic view of an expedition down the Colorado River. Forty years of classes meant hundreds of students across the country. "Your class extends from the Atlantic to the Pacific," wrote Mark Hersey, class of 1887. "Hardly an Army Post but what has some officer who has been under your tuition."

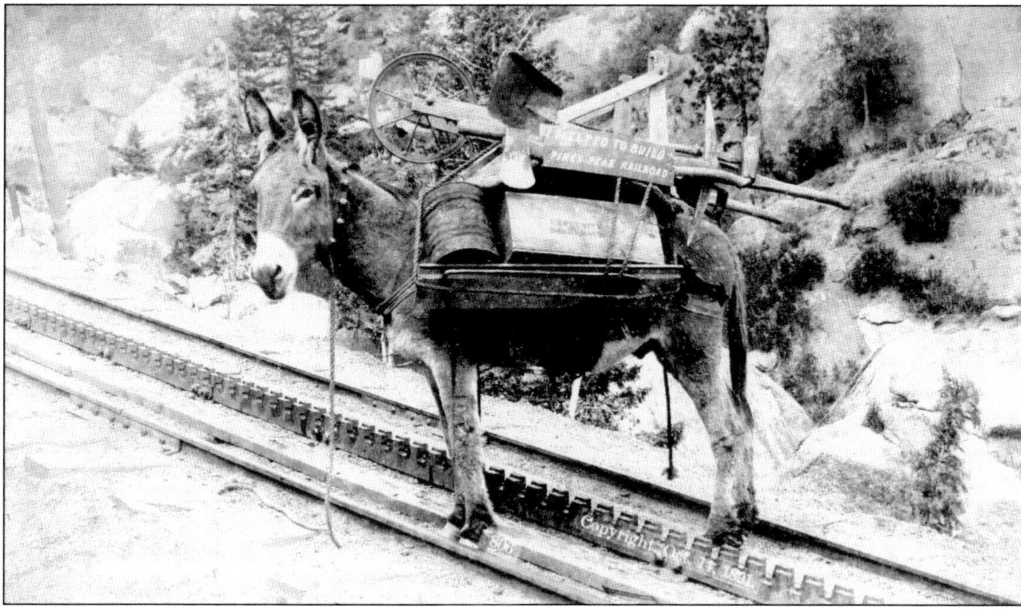

PHOTOGRAPHS FROM AFAR. The mule above helped to build Pike's Peak Railroad, as did the former Bible student who took the photograph. The Warners undoubtedly gave moral and spiritual support to their friends far away. Return letters were filled with heartwarming thoughts, which must have been very gratifying. Ernest Hinds, class of 1887, sent this sentiment from Arkansas: "Miss Warner, you never can know in this world the good you are doing." The image below of a young lieutenant and his wife was sent from Fort Barrancas in Pensacola, Florida, in 1892.

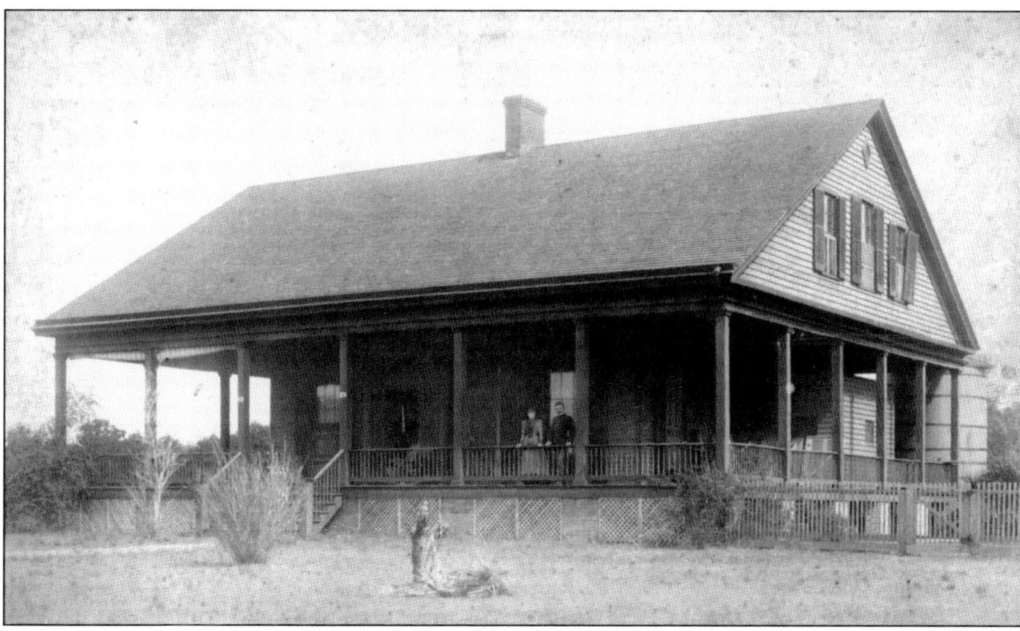

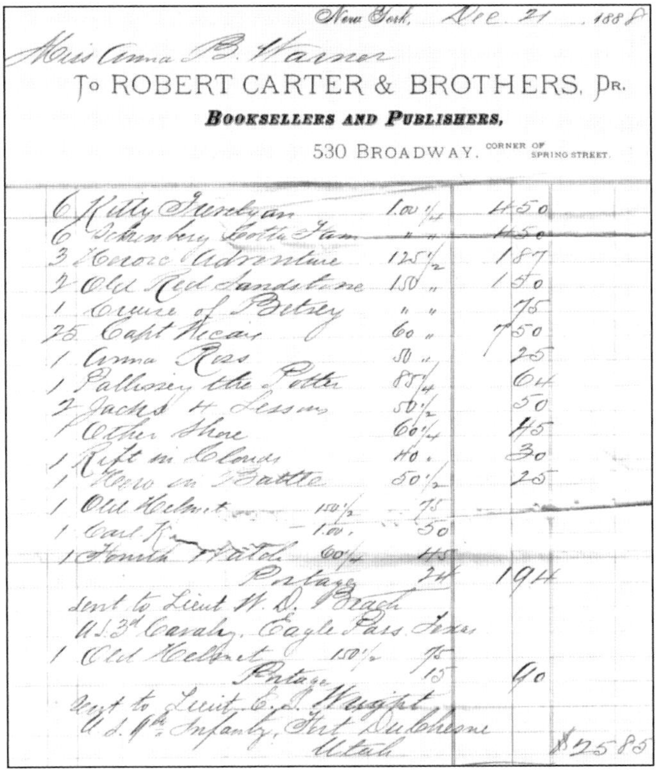

New York, Dec. 21 1888

Miss Anna B. Warner

To ROBERT CARTER & BROTHERS, Dr.

BOOKSELLERS AND PUBLISHERS,

530 BROADWAY, CORNER OF SPRING STREET.

6 Kitty Trevelyan 1.00 ¾ 4 50
6 Schonberg Cotta Fam " " 4 50
3 Heroic Adventure 125 ½ 1 87
2 Old Red Sandstone 150 " 1 50
1 Cruise of Betsey " " 75
25 Capt Hecar 60 " 7 50
1 Anna Ross 50 " 25
1 Palissy the Potter 85 ¾ 64
2 Jacks & Lessons 50 ½ 50
1 Other Shore 60 ¾ 45
1 Rift in Clouds 40 . 30
1 Hero in Battle 50 ½ 25
1 Old Helmet 150 ½ 75
1 Carl K 1.00 . 50
1 Fourth Watch 60 ¾ 45
Postage 24 19 4
Sent to Lieut W. D. Beach
U.S. 3rd Cavalry, Eagle Pass, Texas
1 Old Helmet 150 ½ 75
Postage 15 90
Sent to Lieut C. S. Wright
U.S. 9th Infantry, Fort DuChesne
Utah
$25 85

CARTER BILL. The Warner sisters often sent gifts of books to their former students who were stationed at distant army posts. This bill dated 1888 contains two such orders. Most of the books, including Warner novels *The Old Helmet*, *Carl Krinken*, and *The Fourth Watch*, were sent to Lt. W. D. Beach in Eagle Pass, Texas. A single copy of *The Old Helmet* went to Lt. C. S. Wright of Fort DuChesne, Utah.

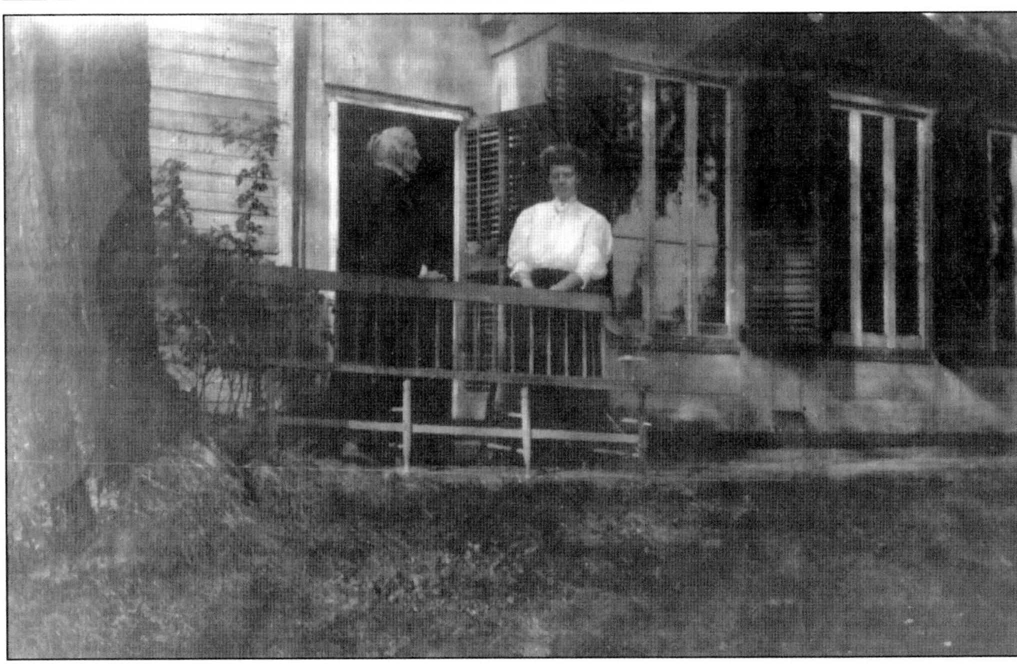

MRS. MCKELL, C. 1907. Former students often returned to Constitution Island with their wives or sweethearts. Here Anna Warner poses with Mrs. David McKell, whose husband, a member of the class of 1904, wrote a memoir about Anna. He was impressed with her love of birds, her passion for gardening, and her commitment to physical exercise to keep herself strong.

Six

GARDENING BY HERSELF

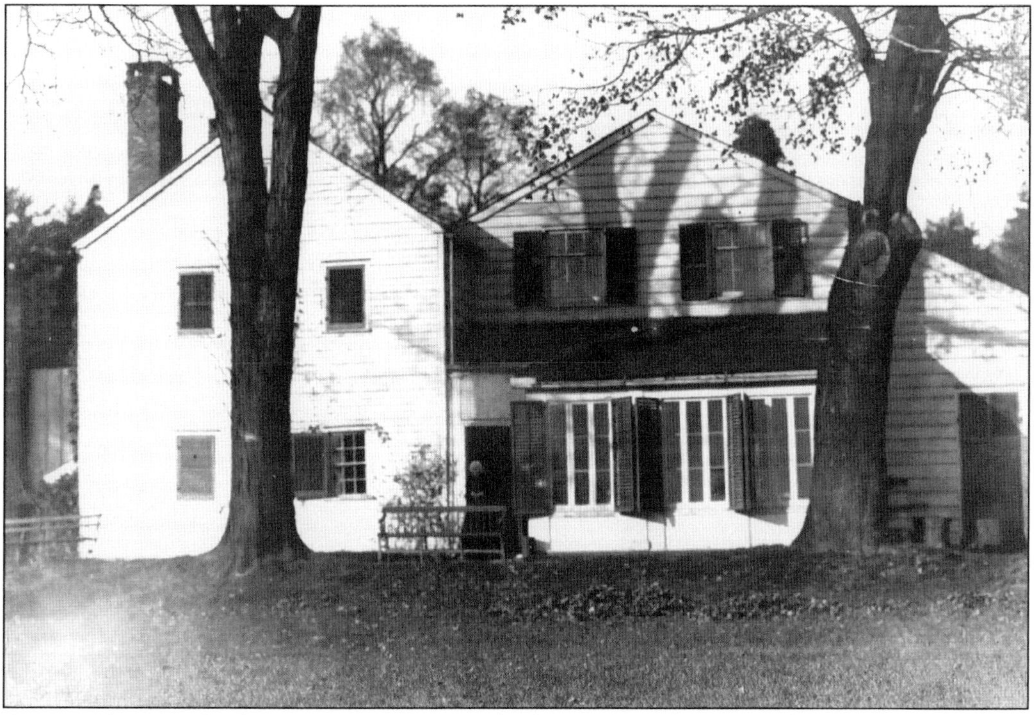

ANNA. Alone in the doorway, Anna Warner looks out from the piazza about 1908. Anna lived another 30 years after the death of Susan Warner. She continued writing until 1909. Her final book was a biography of her sister called simply *Susan Warner*. Each morning she rowed on the river, often listening to the 5:45 a.m. sound of reveille as she passed West Point.

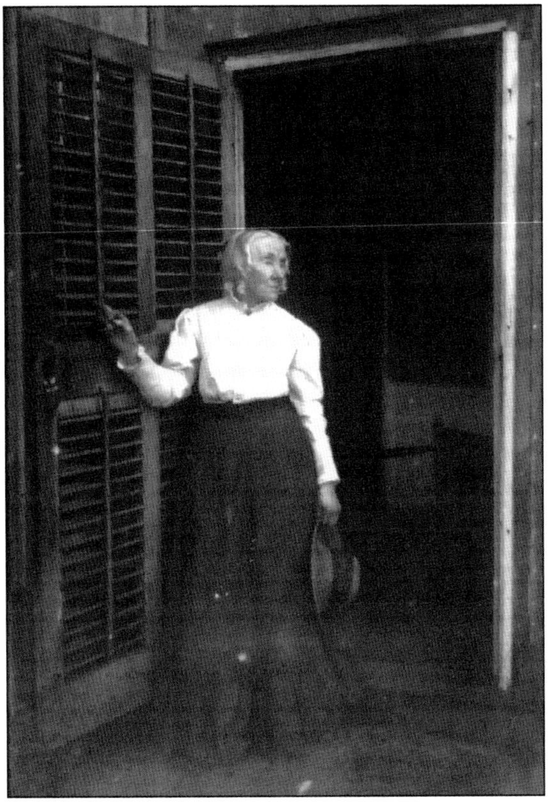

Looking Beyond. Garden hat in hand, Anna Warner looks out toward her wide lawn and the river beyond. After Susan Warner's death in 1885, with the help of Bertha and Willis Buckner, she lovingly maintained her gardens and continued the Bible classes.

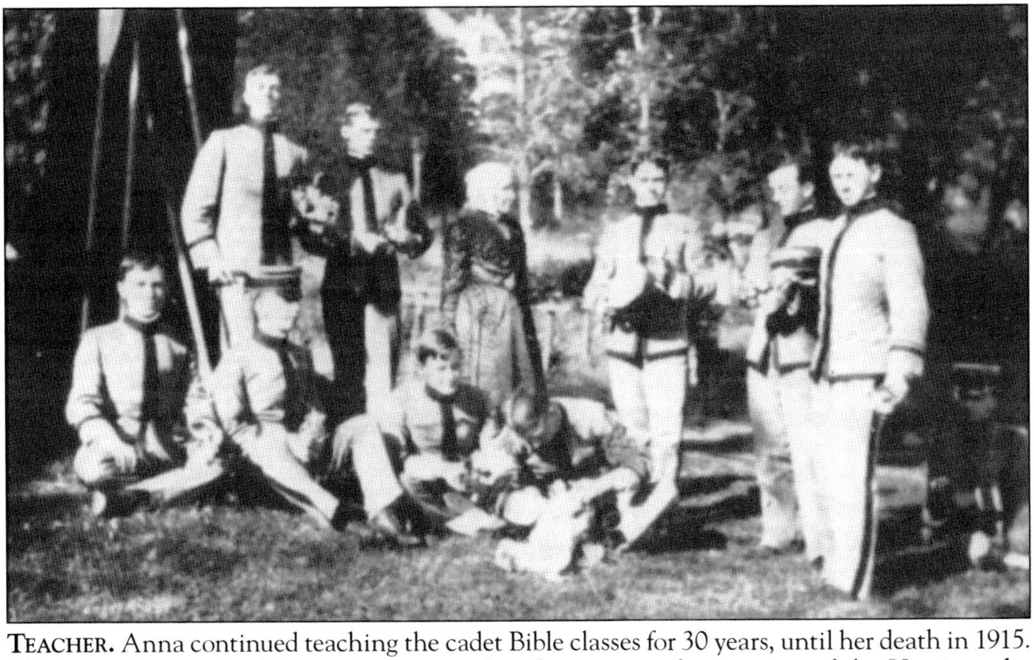

Teacher. Anna continued teaching the cadet Bible classes for 30 years, until her death in 1915. This rare photograph of her with a group of students comes from a copy of the *Howitzer*, the USMA yearbook, about 1908. The informal pose captures five of the boys seated on the grass. The young gentleman in the foreground plays with Anna's dog. (USMA Library.)

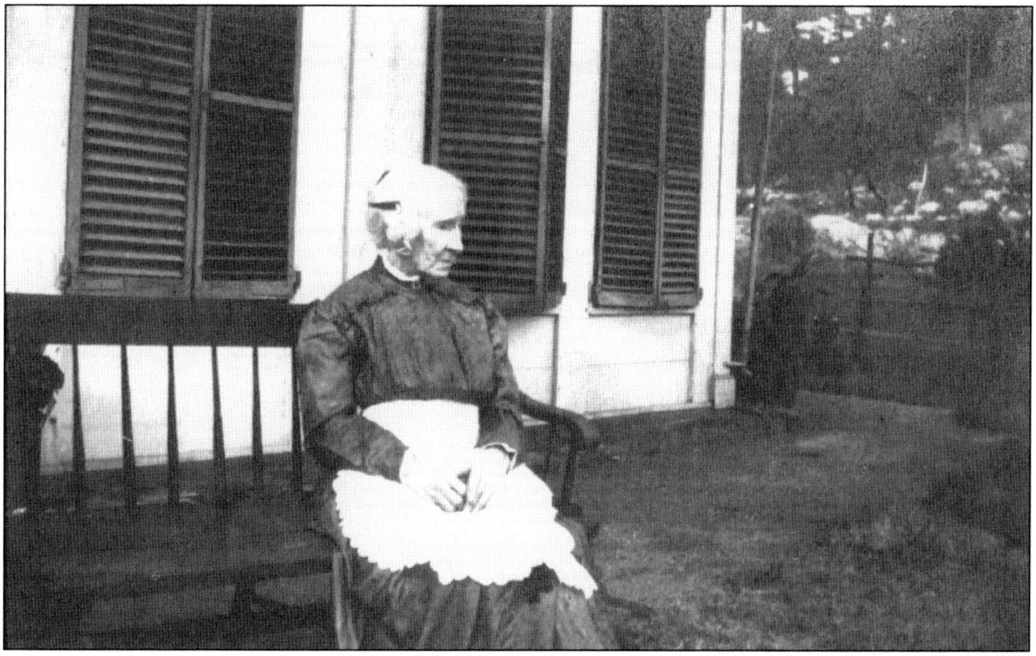

OLD FASHIONED. Throughout her life, Anna maintained a hairstyle and manner of dressing popular in her youth. Olivia Phelps Stokes, a longtime friend, compiled a memoir that contained this recollection of Anna: "As time went on, it became difficult to have clothes made. My mother had a seamstress . . . who consented to go to the island to make full gathered skirts, white ruffled undersleeves for the full oversleeves, and ruffled necks."

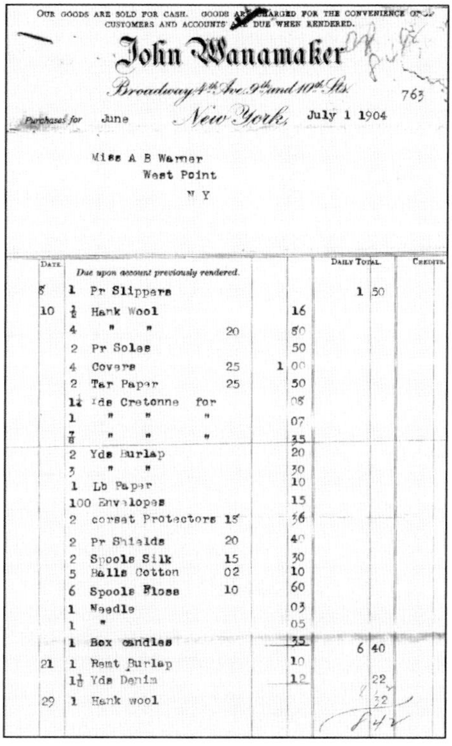

OUR GOODS ARE SOLD FOR CASH. GOODS ARE CHARGED FOR THE CONVENIENCE OF CUSTOMERS AND ACCOUNTS ARE DUE WHEN RENDERED.

John Wanamaker

Broadway 4th Ave. 9th and 10th Sts. 763

Purchases for June New York, July 1 1904

Miss A B Warner
West Point
N Y

DATE					DAILY TOTAL	CREDITS
	Due upon account previously rendered.					
8	1 Pr Slippers				1 50	
10	½ Hank Wool			16		
	4 " "	20		80		
	2 Pr Soles			50		
	4 Covers	25	1	00		
	2 Tar Paper	25		50		
	1¼ Yds Cretonne for			08		
	1 " " "			07		
	⅞ " " "			35		
	2 Yds Burlap			20		
	3 " "			30		
	1 Lb Paper			10		
	100 Envelopes			15		
	2 corset Protectors	15		36		
	2 Pr Shields	20		40		
	2 Spools Silk	15		30		
	5 Balls Cotton	02		10		
	6 Spools Floss	10		60		
	1 Needle			03		
	1 "			05		
	1 Box candles			35	6 40	
21	1 Remt Burlap			10		
	1⅛ Yds Denim			12	22	
29	1 Hank wool				32	

WANAMAKER BILL. Anna occasionally purchased items from New York City shops, which were shipped up by train. This bill, from the John Wanamaker store on Broadway at Nineth Avenue, is for household and personal necessities for living on her island at the age of 80. Included are slippers, wool, shoe soles, sewing goods, candles, paper, envelopes, and, in keeping with her old-fashioned style, two corset protectors.

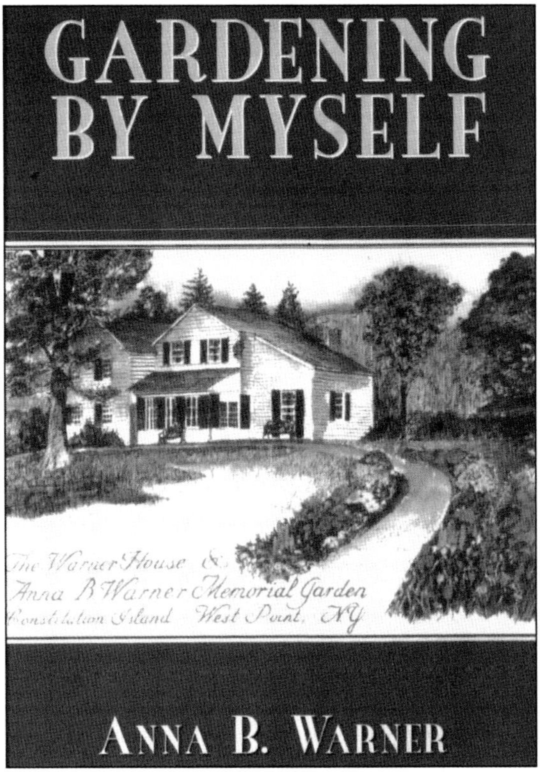

GARDENING. "Gardening by oneself is so lovely, and so easy a thing, I would fain have everybody try it." So Anna Warner began her book *Gardening by Myself*, originally published in 1872. It was a month-by-month manual full of practical advice including the care of bulbs, plants, seeds, roses, and vines. A labor of love, this was the first book by an American woman explaining how to do the actual work of tending a garden.

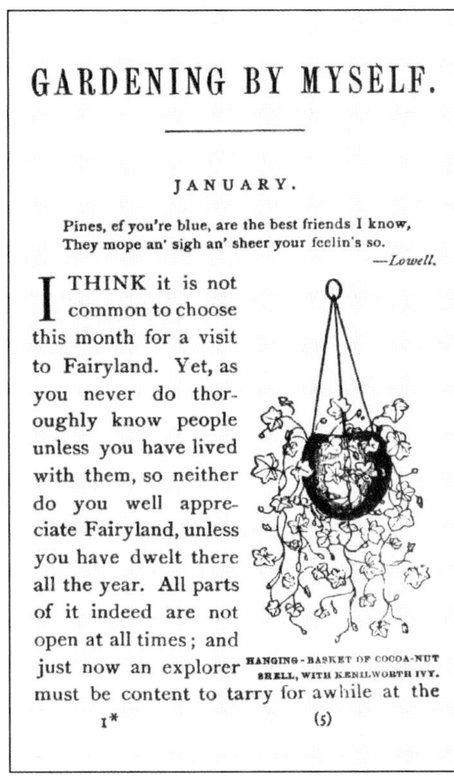
GARDENING BY MYSELF.

JANUARY.

Pines, ef you're blue, are the best friends I know,
They mope an' sigh an' sheer your feelin's so.
—*Lowell.*

I THINK it is not common to choose this month for a visit to Fairyland. Yet, as you never do thoroughly know people unless you have lived with them, so neither do you well appreciate Fairyland, unless you have dwelt there all the year. All parts of it indeed are not open at all times; and just now an explorer must be content to tarry for awhile at the

HANGING-BASKET OF COCOA-NUT SHELL, WITH KENILWORTH IVY.

1* (5)

ILLUSTRATIONS. Illustrated with her own artwork, *Gardening by Myself* was a success. The first chapter, titled "January," begins with this drawing of a hanging basket of cocoa-nut shell with Kenilworth ivy. Other illustrations include the cell structure of a maple root, a set of ladies' garden tools, vine supports, and pruning techniques.

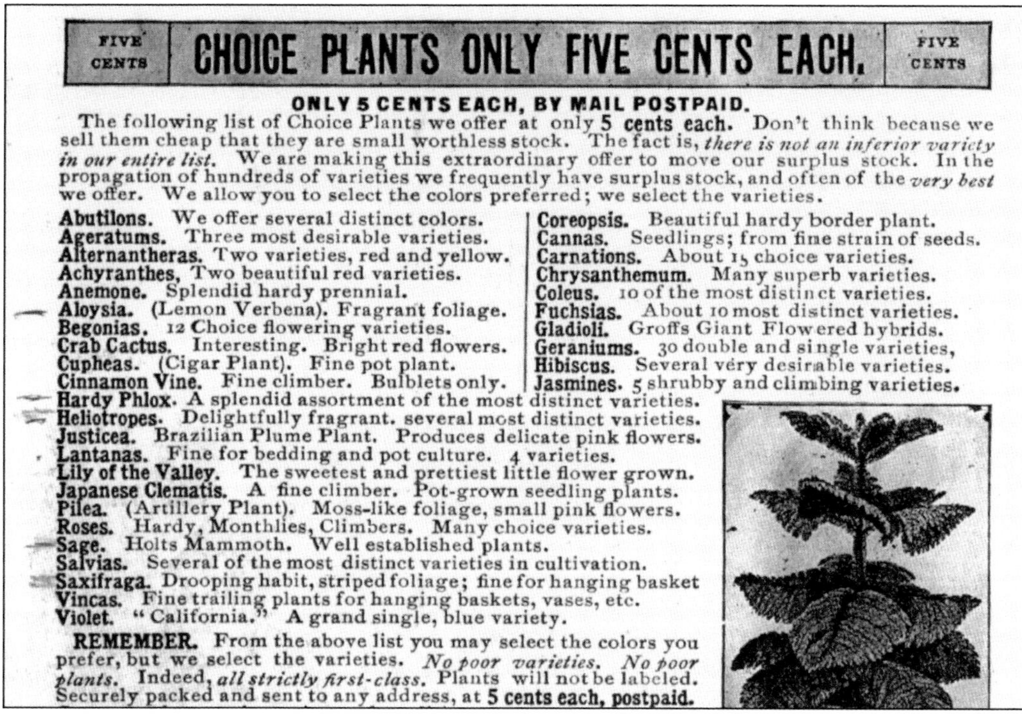

FIVE CENTS **CHOICE PLANTS ONLY FIVE CENTS EACH.** FIVE CENTS

ONLY 5 CENTS EACH, BY MAIL POSTPAID.

The following list of Choice Plants we offer at only **5 cents each.** Don't think because we sell them cheap that they are small worthless stock. The fact is, *there is not an inferior variety in our entire list.* We are making this extraordinary offer to move our surplus stock. In the propagation of hundreds of varieties we frequently have surplus stock, and often of the *very best* we offer. We allow you to select the colors preferred; we select the varieties.

Abutilons. We offer several distinct colors.
Ageratums. Three most desirable varieties.
Alternantheras. Two varieties, red and yellow.
Achyranthes. Two beautiful red varieties.
Anemone. Splendid hardy prennial.
Aloysia. (Lemon Verbena). Fragrant foliage.
Begonias. 12 Choice flowering varieties.
Crab Cactus. Interesting. Bright red flowers.
Cupheas. (Cigar Plant). Fine pot plant.
Cinnamon Vine. Fine climber. Bulblets only.
Coreopsis. Beautiful hardy border plant.
Cannas. Seedlings; from fine strain of seeds.
Carnations. About 15 choice varieties.
Chrysanthemum. Many superb varieties.
Coleus. 10 of the most distinct varieties.
Fuchsias. About 10 most distinct varieties.
Gladioli. Groffs Giant Flowered hybrids.
Geraniums. 30 double and single varieties,
Hibiscus. Several very desirable varieties.
Jasmines. 5 shrubby and climbing varieties.
Hardy Phlox. A splendid assortment of the most distinct varieties.
Heliotropes. Delightfully fragrant. several most distinct varieties.
Justicea. Brazilian Plume Plant. Produces delicate pink flowers.
Lantanas. Fine for bedding and pot culture. 4 varieties.
Lily of the Valley. The sweetest and prettiest little flower grown.
Japanese Clematis. A fine climber. Pot-grown seedling plants.
Pilea. (Artillery Plant). Moss-like foliage, small pink flowers.
Roses. Hardy, Monthlies, Climbers. Many choice varieties.
Sage. Holts Mammoth. Well established plants.
Salvias. Several of the most distinct varieties in cultivation.
Saxifraga. Drooping habit, striped foliage; fine for hanging basket
Vincas. Fine trailing plants for hanging baskets, vases, etc.
Violet. "California." A grand single, blue variety.

REMEMBER. From the above list you may select the colors you prefer, but we select the varieties. *No poor varieties. No poor plants.* Indeed, *all strictly first-class.* Plants will not be labeled. Securely packed and sent to any address, at **5 cents each, postpaid.**

SEED CATALOGUE. Anna enjoyed spending cold winter days perusing seed catalogues, especially from the Templin and Henderson companies. She recommended to her readers that they acquire a good seed catalogue and choose wisely based on soil, climate, and their preference for color. On the page pictured above, Anna marked the plants she hoped to order. Elsewhere in the catalogue, she marked giant pansies, rosy pink geraniums, and double begonias. "There is a saying in the family that where others read novels, I study catalogues, and indeed it is so," she wrote. In February, the arrival of little packages of seeds was an occasion for excitement. "Each full of mystery, each rustling gently with promise." Below her border garden is brimming with flowers at the end of summer.

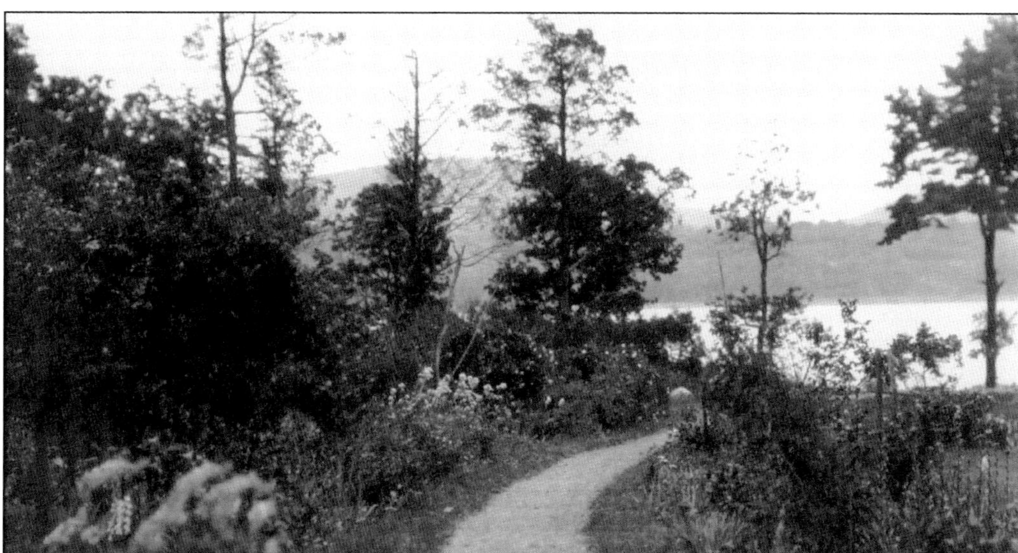

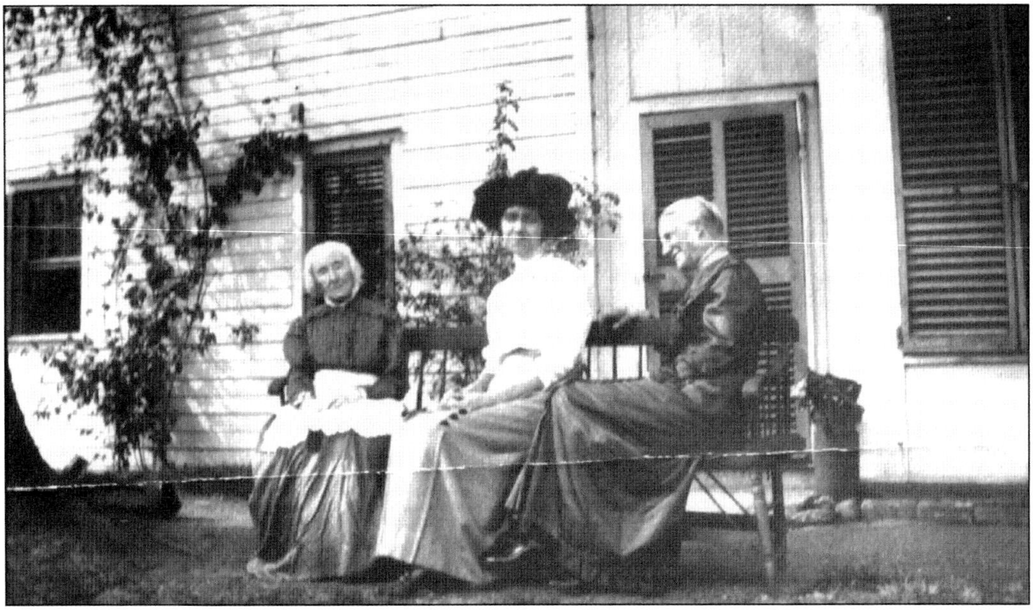

COUSINS CALLING. Many acquaintances, admirers, and fans visited Anna Warner at the island. Two of Anna's cousins came calling on a sunny afternoon in July 1913. Seated with Anna, left, on the bench in front of the Warner house are Amy Quackenbusch Hotchkiss, center, and Nina Frary.

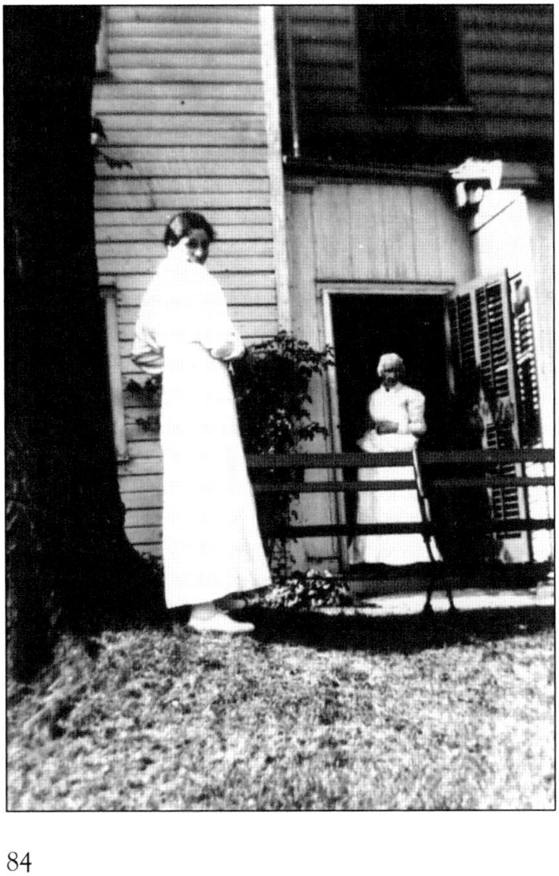

CHARLOTTE HARDING. Looking over her shoulder, Charlotte K. Harding smiles for a photograph in July 1912. Anna stands contemplatively in her doorway, a favorite rose bush on her right. (Sidamon-Eristoff collection.)

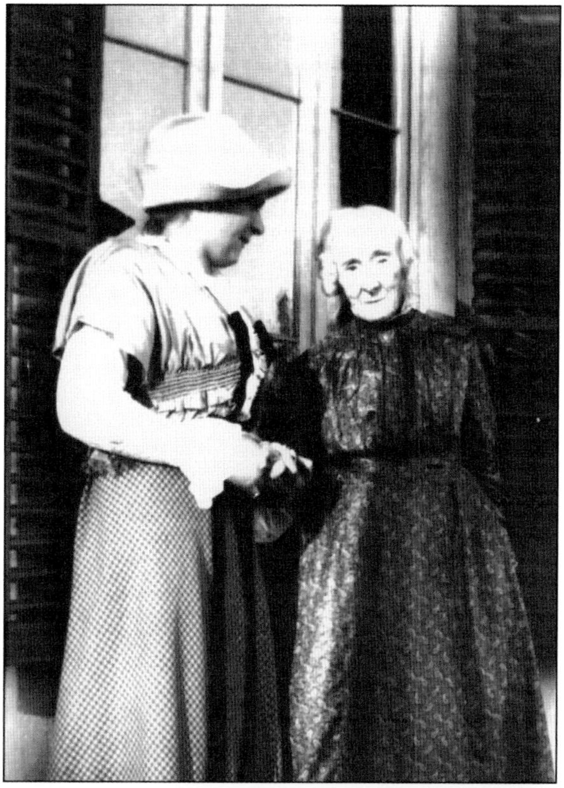

VISIT, OCTOBER 1913. Anna's friend Mrs. Charles E. Tracy, left, came to call in October 1913. After Anna's death, Mrs. Tracy served as the chairperson of the Martelaer's Rock Association, a group whose purpose was the preservation of the Warner House. (Sidamon-Eristoff collection.)

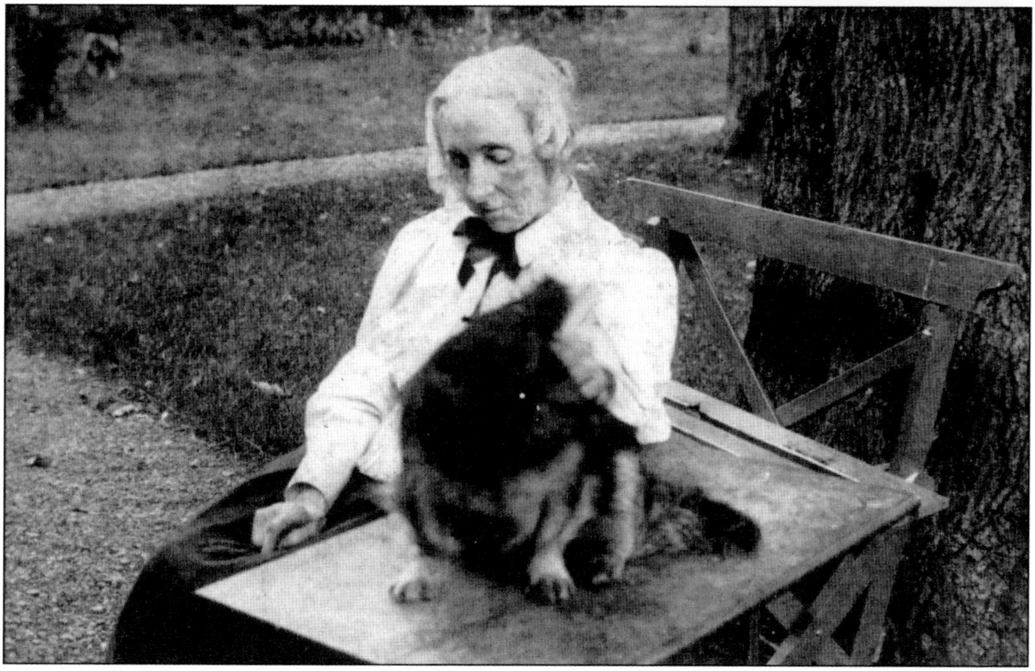

WARNER PET. In a quiet moment, Anna pets one of the many dogs she owned in her lifetime. They often accompanied her on walks over the island and while rowing on the river. Cadets recall being greeted by her dogs as they arrived at the island.

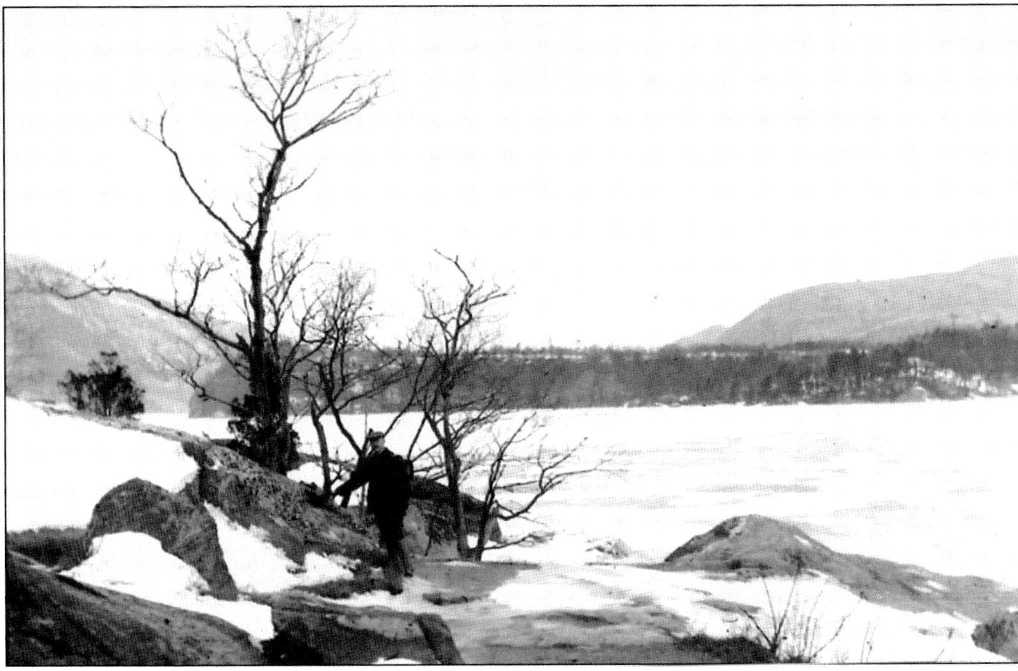

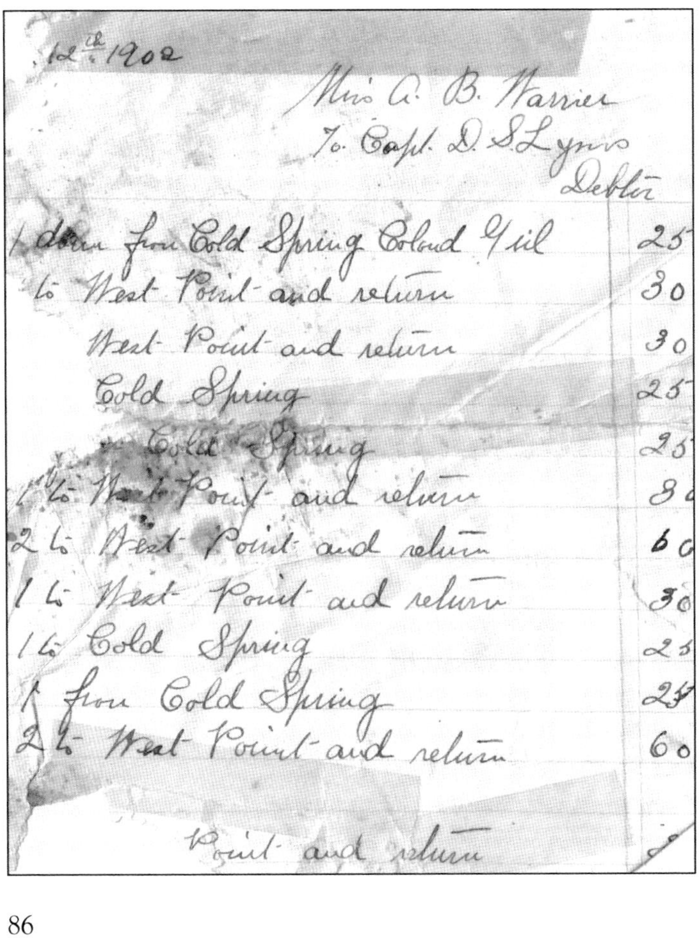

12th 1902

Mrs A. B. Warner
To Capt. D. S. Lyons
Debtor

1 down from Cold Spring Colored Girl 25
to West Point and return 30
West Point and return 30
Cold Spring 25
Cold Spring 25
1 to West Point and return 3[illegible]
2 to West Point and return 6[illegible]
1 to West Point and return 30
1 to Cold Spring 25
1 from Cold Spring 25
2 to West Point and return 60
Point and return

FERRIES. In 1909, writer William Howell photographed his friend "V.H.S," above, near the old ferry dock at Gee's Point. Historically most visitors to Constitution Island came and went by boat. The earliest ferry on record ran from Gee's Point, above, to the island. Mentioned frequently in Revolutionary War annals, it was owned jointly by Cornelius Gee and Mr. Nelson and was known as Nelson's Ferry. A century later, Capt. D. S. Lyons ran a ferry between West Point, Cold Spring, and Constitution Island. At left is a rare fragment of a handwritten bill written in 1902, listing charges for several trips Anna Warner made in May and June. (Above, PIPC Archives.)

FERRY TRAVELER. Lovely in her flowered hat and elegant white dress, an unidentified traveler on her way to Constitution Island had her picture snapped on a summer day. A notation on the back of the photograph says only "West Point Ferry, 1907."

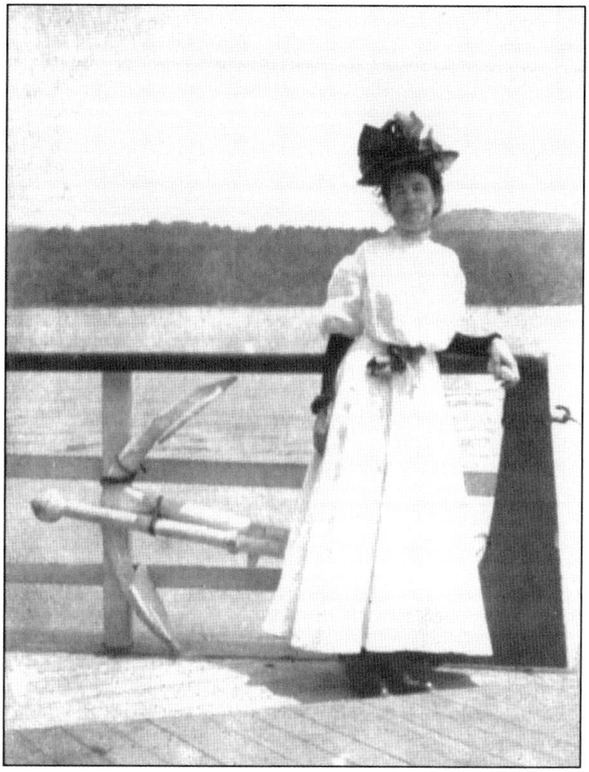

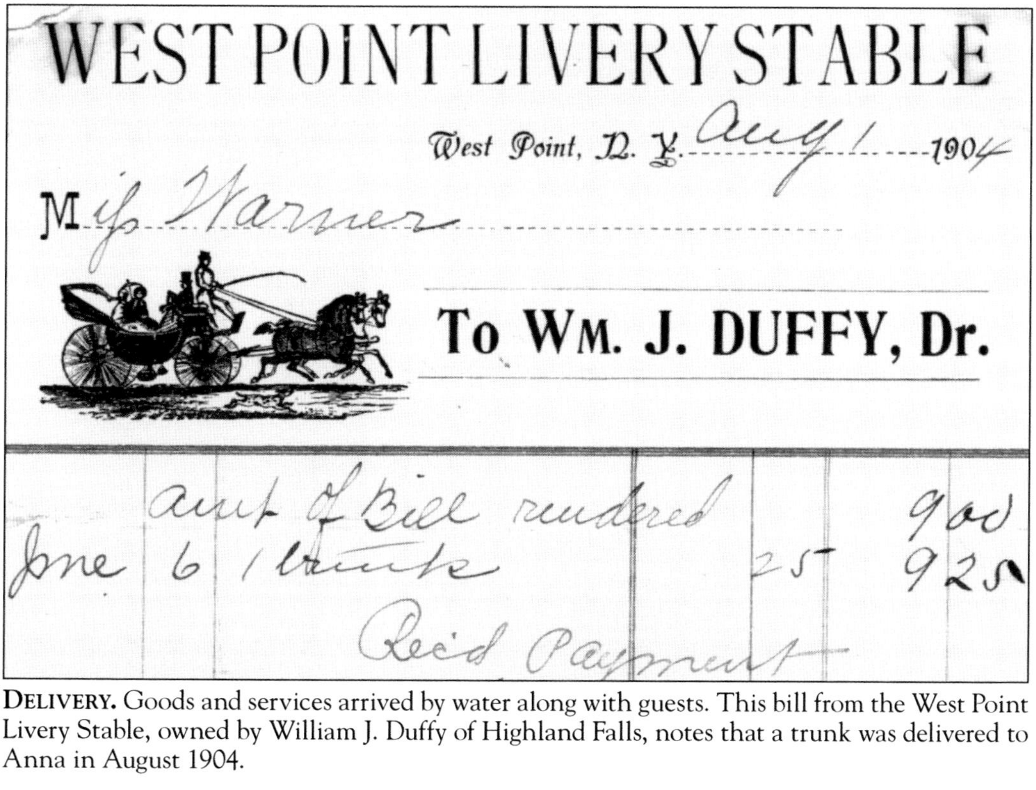

WEST POINT LIVERY STABLE

West Point, N. Y. Aug 1 1904

Miss Warner

To Wm. J. DUFFY, Dr.

		amt of Bill rendered		9 00
June	6	1 trunk	25	9 25

Rec'd Payment

DELIVERY. Goods and services arrived by water along with guests. This bill from the West Point Livery Stable, owned by William J. Duffy of Highland Falls, notes that a trunk was delivered to Anna in August 1904.

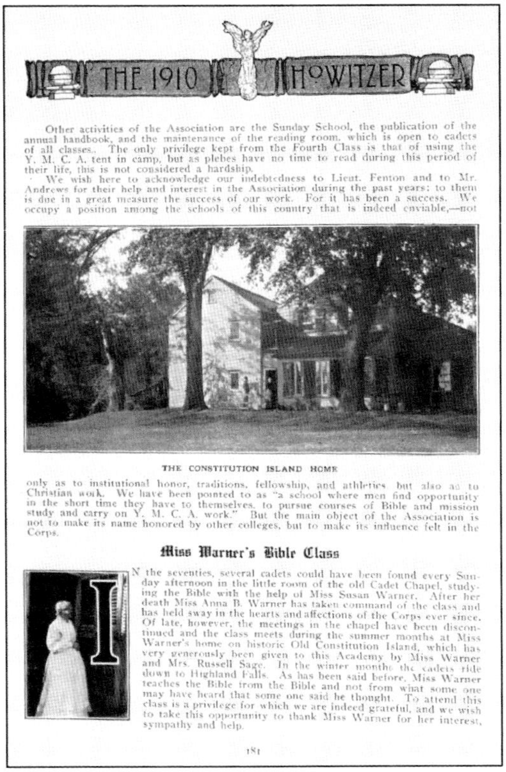

THE 1910 HOWITZER

Other activities of the Association are the Sunday School, the publication of the annual handbook, and the maintenance of the reading room, which is open to cadets of all classes. The only privilege kept from the Fourth Class is that of using the Y. M. C. A. tent in camp, but as plebes have no time to read during this period of their life, this is not considered a hardship.

We wish here to acknowledge our indebtedness to Lieut. Fenton and to Mr. Andrews for their help and interest in the Association during the past years; to them is due in a great measure the success of our work. For it has been a success. We occupy a position among the schools of this country that is indeed enviable,—not

THE CONSTITUTION ISLAND HOME

only as to institutional honor, traditions, fellowship, and athletics but also as to Christian work. We have been pointed to as "a school where men find opportunity in the short time they have to themselves, to pursue courses of Bible and mission study and carry on Y. M. C. A. work." But the main object of the Association is not to make its name honored by other colleges, but to make its influence felt in the Corps.

Miss Warner's Bible Class

IN the seventies, several cadets could have been found every Sunday afternoon in the little room of the old Cadet Chapel, studying the Bible with the help of Miss Susan Warner. After her death Miss Anna B. Warner has taken command of the class and has held sway in the hearts and affections of the Corps ever since. Of late, however, the meetings in the chapel have been discontinued and the class meets during the summer months at Miss Warner's home on historic Old Constitution Island, which has very generously been given to this Academy by Miss Warner and Mrs. Russell Sage. In the winter months the cadets ride down to Highland Falls. As has been said before, Miss Warner teaches the Bible from the Bible and not from what some one may have heard that some one said he thought. To attend this class is a privilege for which we are indeed grateful, and we wish to take this opportunity to thank Miss Warner for her interest, sympathy and help.

181

HOWITZER. Several editions of the USMA yearbook, *Howitzer*, contained tributes to Anna Warner. One such article praises her saying, "Under Miss Warner's guidance men have always found a happier understanding of their obligations to humanity and the way to a more complete and useful manhood . . . no mere words can adequately express the goodwill which the Army bears to Miss Warner." (USMA Library.)

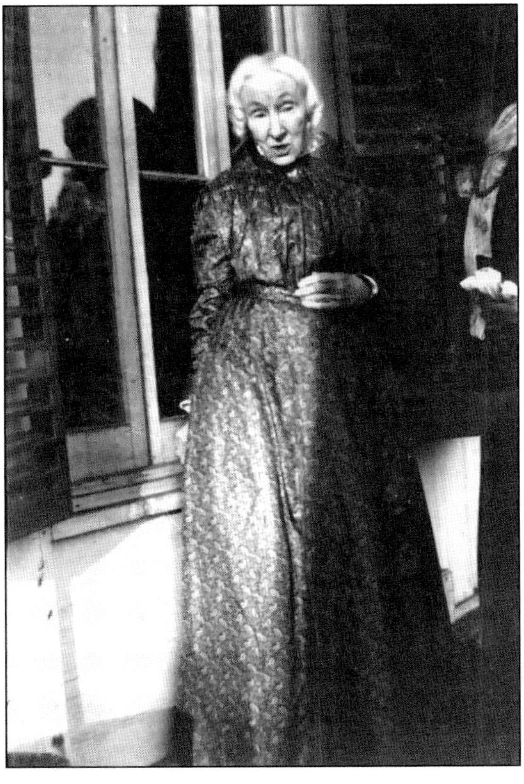

LIVELY CONVERSATION. Standing beside the piazza window, about 1910, Anna appears to be caught in a lively conversation. According to former student David McKell, "She had a fine sense of humor and was always ready for a good laugh."

WHITE DRESS. Olivia Phelps Stokes recalled that one morning, during a stay on the island, she looked out very early and "Miss Anna was at the flag pole, white dress, white curls flying in the breeze, white skirt and many petticoats blowing. She was hauling down the flag because the flag at West Point was at half mast. It was touching to see her anxiety . . . later Buckner told her that a cadet she knew had been killed."

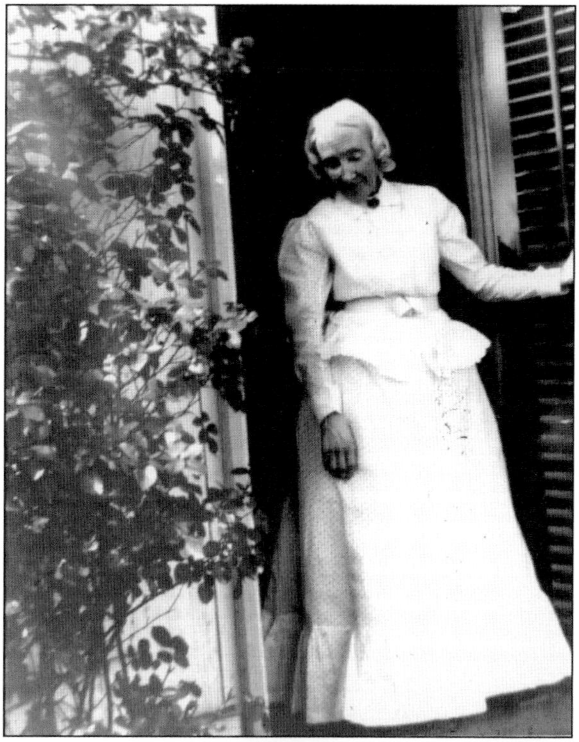

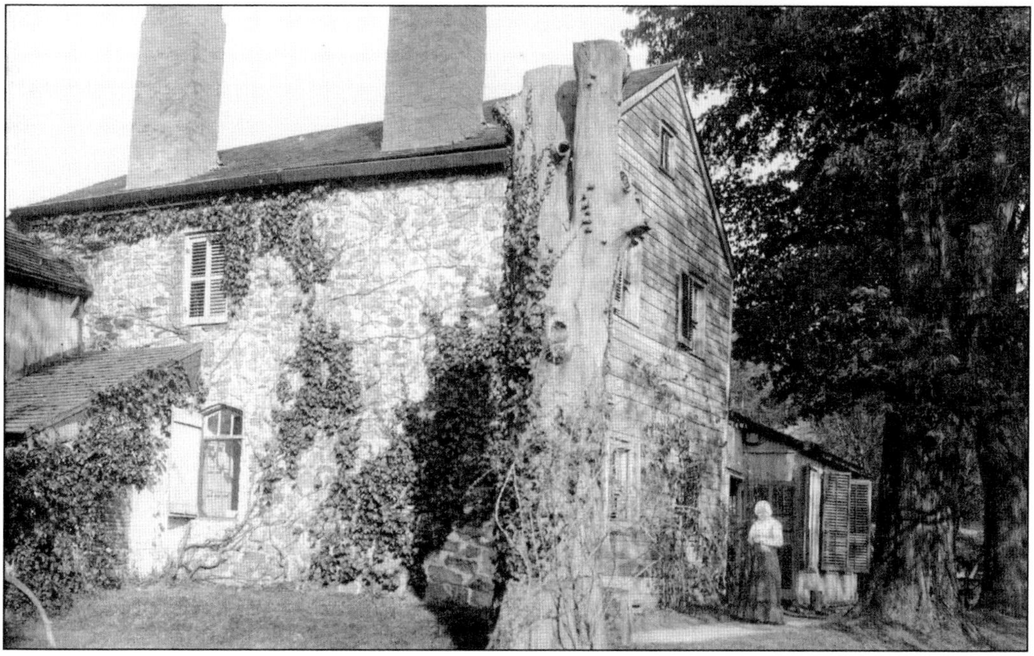

WELCOMING HOME. Dwarfed by her home, Anna waits at the front entrance. Cadets enjoyed the warmth of her hospitality. "The homelike atmosphere of the old historical Warner house," said one tribute, "has been to its visitors from the Corps a constant reminder of their own homes and of their own home folks." Aside from Bible class, small groups of cadets were regularly invited to dinner or afternoon tea.

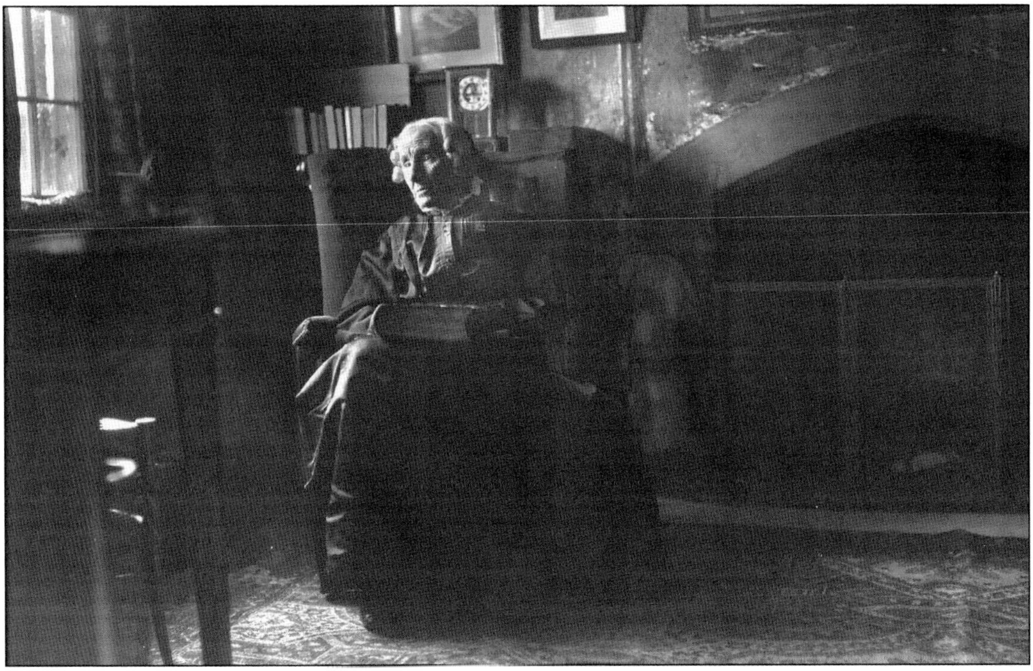

BIBLES. Sitting peacefully in the old Revolutionary sitting room, Anna Warner holds a large Bible. In a bookcase in this room, she kept a large collection of Bibles for her cadet students. Susan Warner had collected Bibles, and the sisters owned copies in every size and many foreign languages. (USMA Library.)

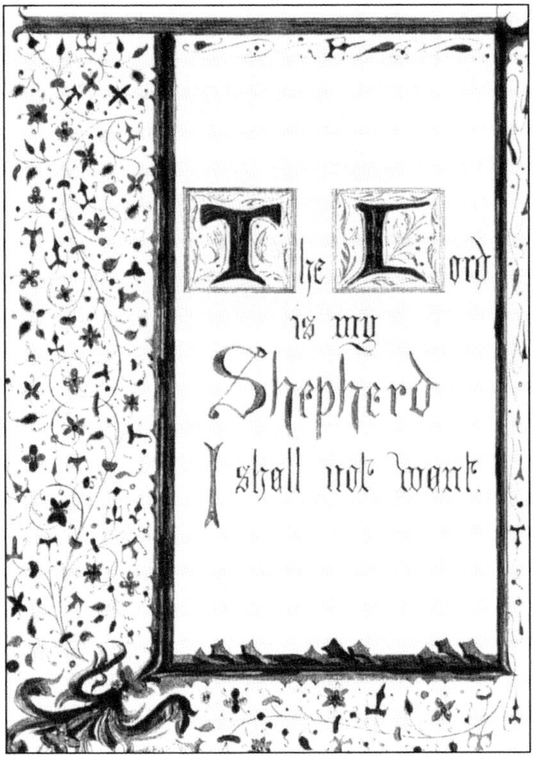

TWENTY-THIRD PSALM. One of the loveliest of Anna's artistic endeavors was a series of illustrations based on the 23rd Psalm. Meticulously drawn and colored, her artwork resembles an illuminated manuscript.

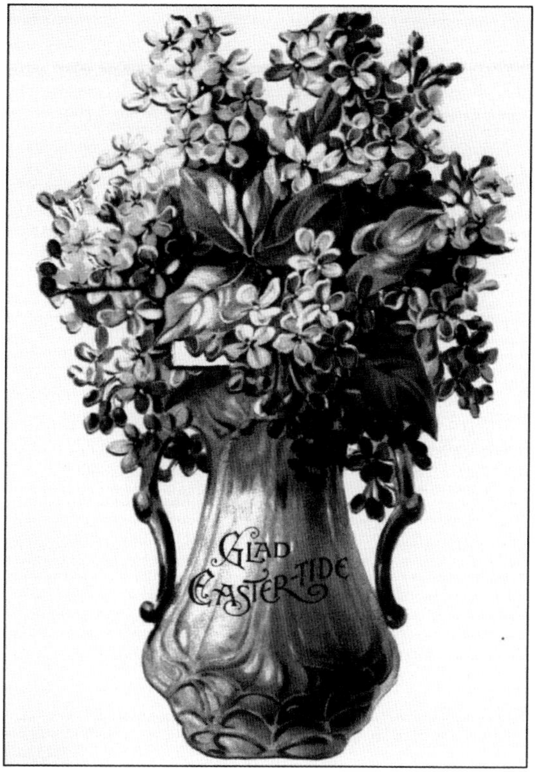

Greeting Cards. Greeting cards became popular during the 19th century. Anna saved many of hers as did her maid and companion, Bertha Buckner. The die-cut Easter card seen at right is signed "To Bertha from your friend Miss Belle." The hearty greetings for the new century were for Anna.

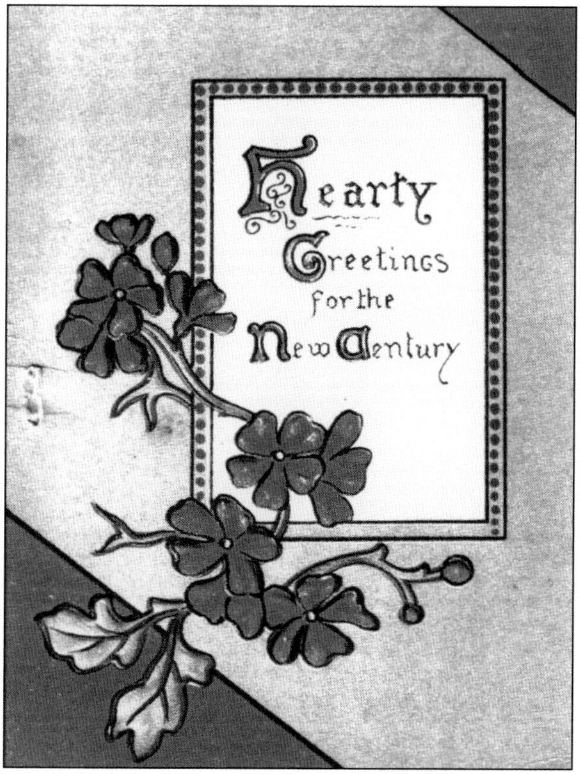

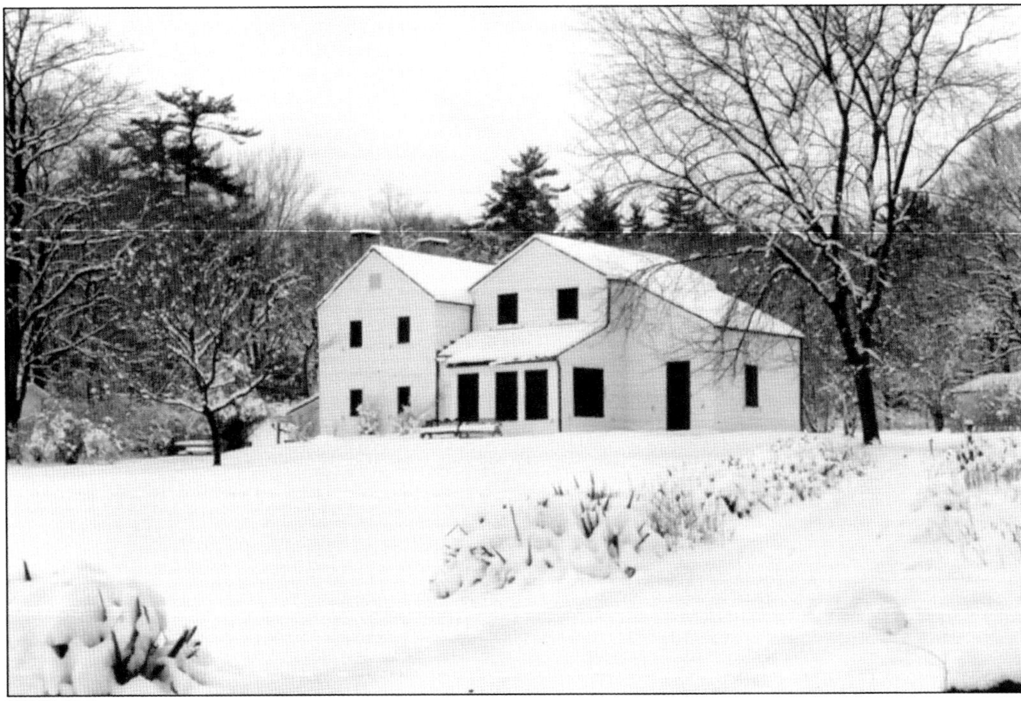

WINTER. The Warners preferred not to spend the winter on the island. They generally closed their house and remained away from December to early April. At various times they wintered in New York City, West Point, Rhinebeck, and Highland Falls.

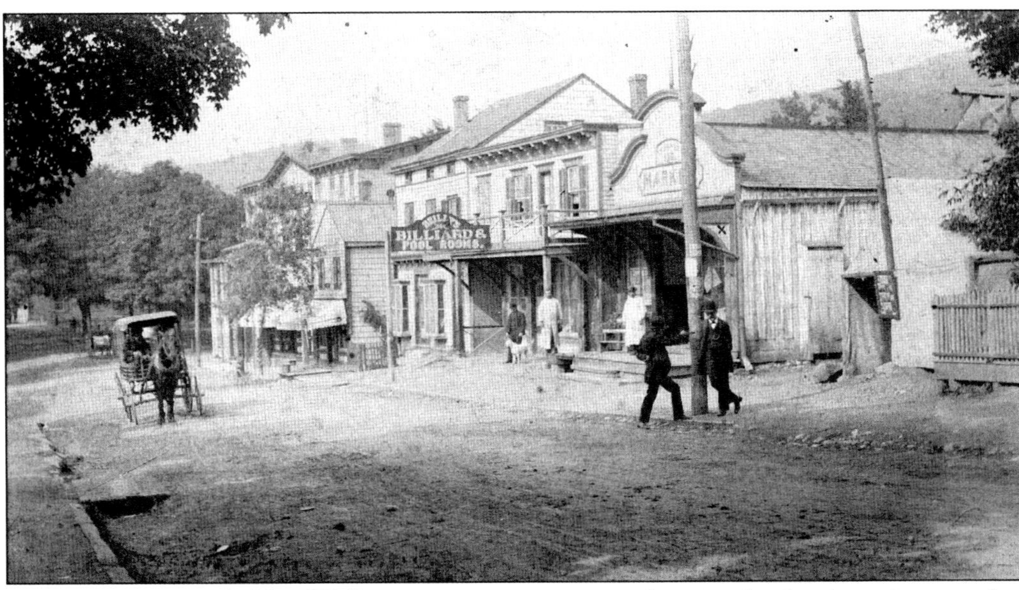

HIGHLAND FALLS. Highland Falls was a convenient winter location for the sisters because they were in traveling distance to West Point for the Sunday classes. The house occupied by the Warners was a short distance from these stores on Main Street. As Anna Warner got older, the cadets rode to the village on horseback for their lessons. (Parry collection.)

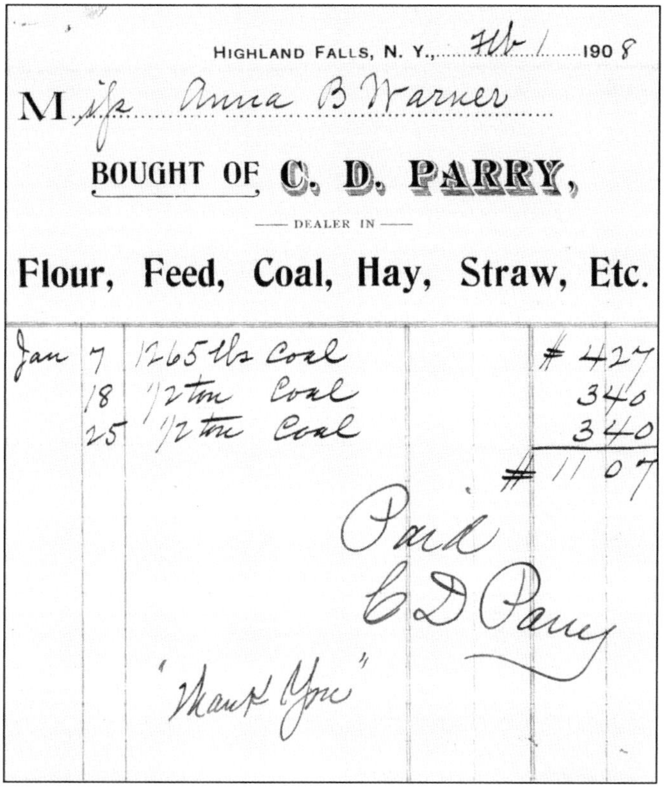

HIGHLAND FALLS, N. Y., Feb 1 1908

Miss Anna B Warner

BOUGHT OF C. D. PARRY,

DEALER IN

Flour, Feed, Coal, Hay, Straw, Etc.

Jan	7	1265 lbs coal	$4 27
	18	1/2 ton Coal	3 40
	25	1/2 ton Coal	3 40
			$11 07

Paid
C D Parry

"Thank You"

COAL BILL. During the winter of 1908, Anna resided in Highland Falls, New York, in the gatehouse of the estate of John Bigelow. The bill seen at right indicates that she purchased the coal from C. D. Parry, a prominent supplier of fuel, flour, and feed, whose family business had begun as a large flour mill at the base of Buttermilk Falls. The coal was used to heat the charming gatehouse, seen below, just off Main Street, which was the home of the Warners for several winters. Susan Warner died there in the winter of 1885. Anna died in Highland Falls during the winter of 1915.

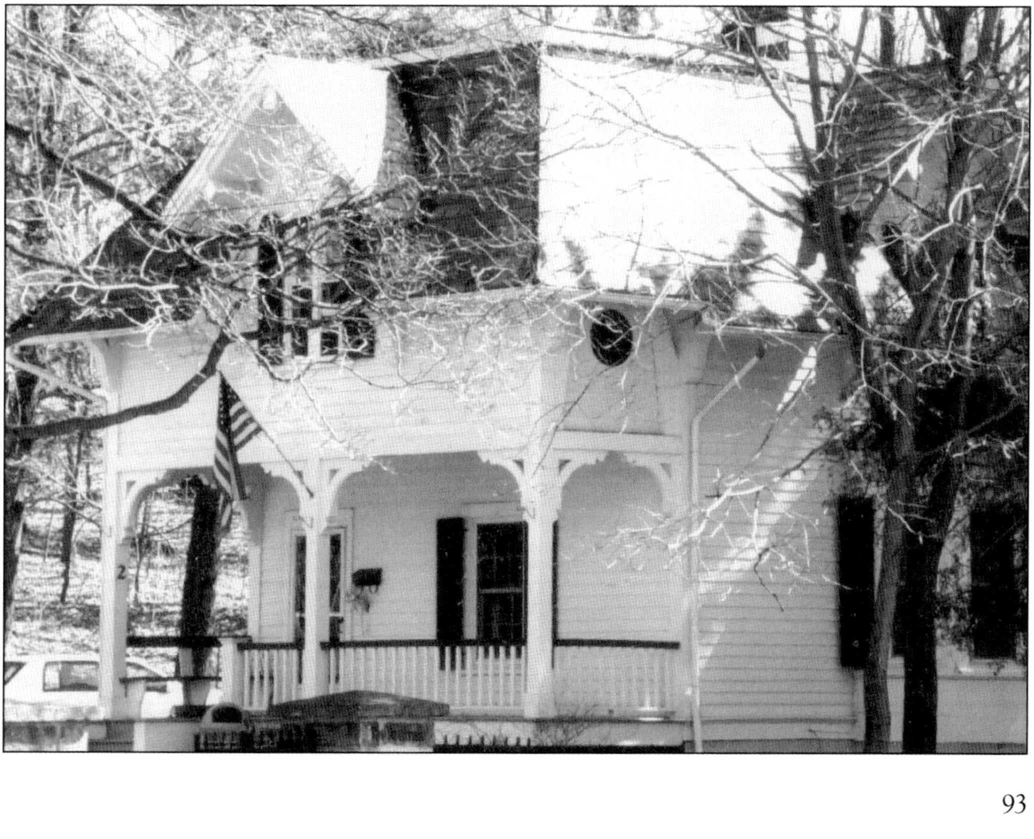

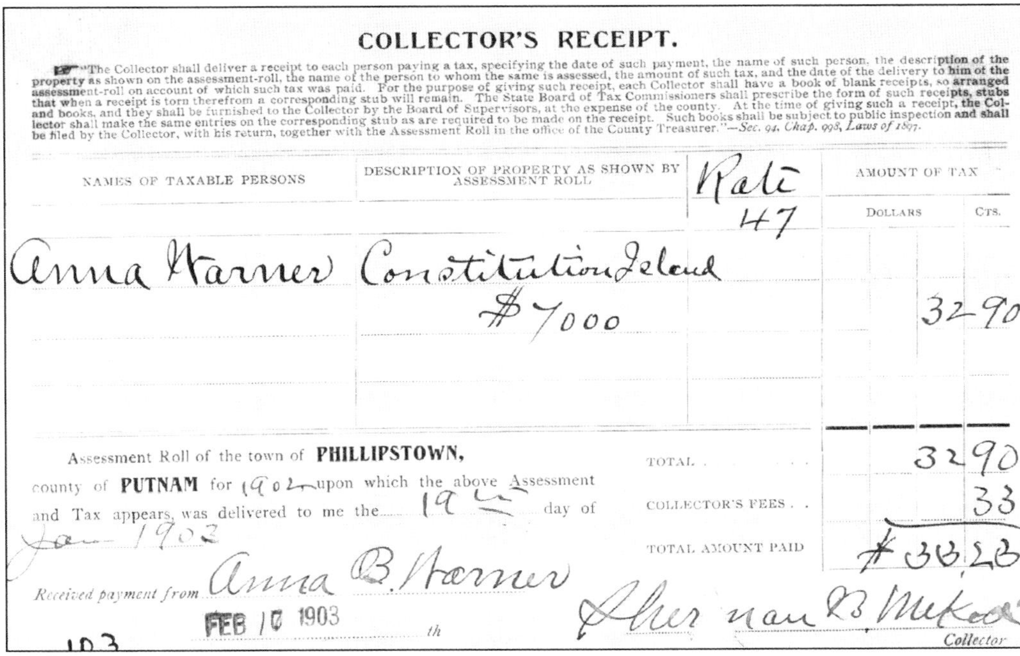

COLLECTOR'S RECEIPT.

"The Collector shall deliver a receipt to each person paying a tax, specifying the date of such payment, the name of such person, the description of the property as shown on the assessment-roll, the name of the person to whom the same is assessed, the amount of such tax, and the date of the delivery to him of the assessment-roll on account of which such tax was paid. For the purpose of giving such receipt, each Collector shall have a book of blank receipts, so arranged that when a receipt is torn therefrom a corresponding stub will remain. The State Board of Tax Commissioners shall prescribe the form of such receipts, stubs and books, and they shall be furnished to the Collector by the Board of Supervisors, at the expense of the county. At the time of giving such a receipt, the Collector shall make the same entries on the corresponding stub as are required to be made on the receipt. Such books shall be subject to public inspection and shall be filed by the Collector, with his return, together with the Assessment Roll in the office of the County Treasurer."—*Sec. 94, Chap. 998, Laws of 1897.*

NAMES OF TAXABLE PERSONS	DESCRIPTION OF PROPERTY AS SHOWN BY ASSESSMENT ROLL	Rate 47	AMOUNT OF TAX DOLLARS	CTS.
Anna Warner	Constitution Island $7000		32	90

Assessment Roll of the town of **PHILLIPSTOWN**, county of **PUTNAM** for 1902 upon which the above Assessment and Tax appears, was delivered to me the 19th day of Jan 1903

TOTAL	32 90
COLLECTOR'S FEES	33
TOTAL AMOUNT PAID	$33.23

Received payment from Anna B. Warner

FEB 10 1903 *th*

Sherman B. McKeel
Collector

103

TAX BILL. Dated February 10, 1903, this bill for the taxes on Constitution Island lists the assessment at $7,000, well below its actual value. During this time, Anna Warner was struggling financially but refused offers to sell the island to entrepreneurs. Desiring that her land become part of West Point, she hoped that the federal government would buy it, but bills proposing the purchase did not pass in Congress.

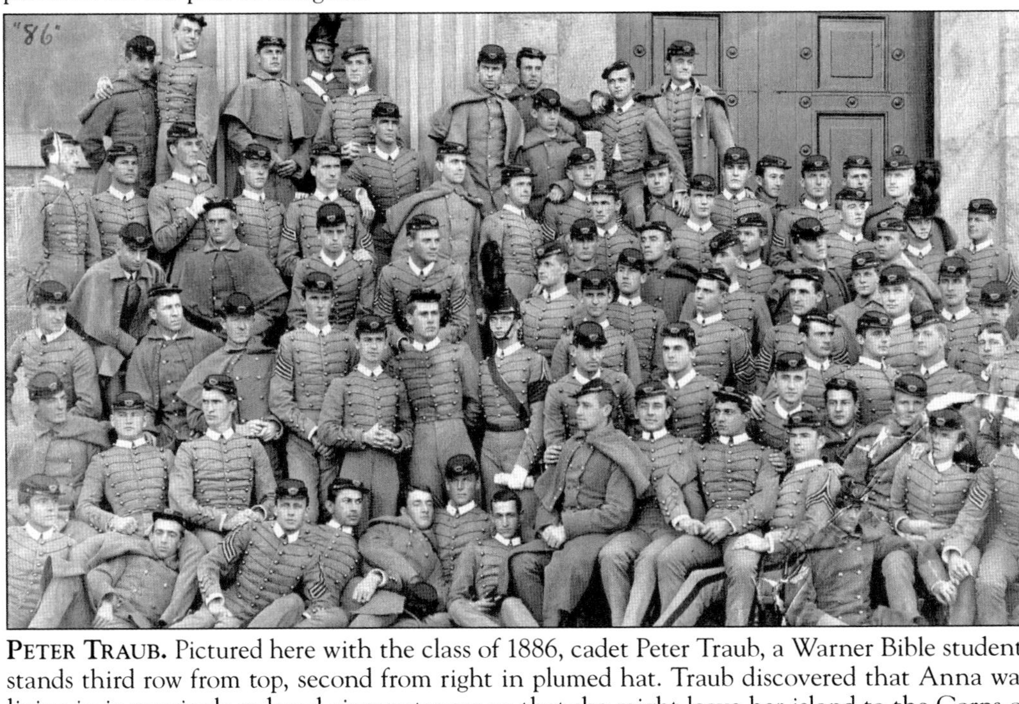

PETER TRAUB. Pictured here with the class of 1886, cadet Peter Traub, a Warner Bible student, stands third row from top, second from right in plumed hat. Traub discovered that Anna was living in increasingly reduced circumstances so that she might leave her island to the Corps of Cadets and decided to help her.

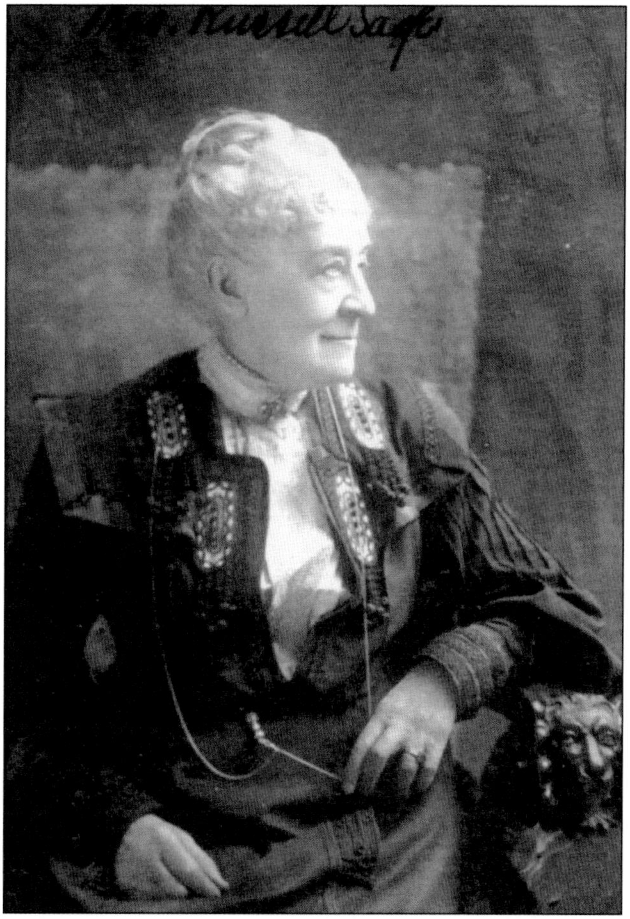

MRS. RUSSELL SAGE. Before Susan Warner's death, the sisters decided that they wanted to give their island to the government for the cadets. Anna had several lucrative offers from entrepreneurs to buy the island but repeatedly declined. Bills were introduced in Congress for the federal government to buy the island, but they never got to a vote. Anna's former student Peter Traub approached noted philanthropist Margaret Sage. Sage devised a plan to buy the island from Anna for $150,000 and give the island to the government. In a 1908 letter to Pres. Theodore Roosevelt, Sage wrote, "Sir, I take pleasure in tendering as a gift to the United States from myself and Miss Anna Bartlett Warner, Constitution Island, opposite West Point." Anna was allowed to remain on the island for the rest of her life. The gift was commemorated in postcards.

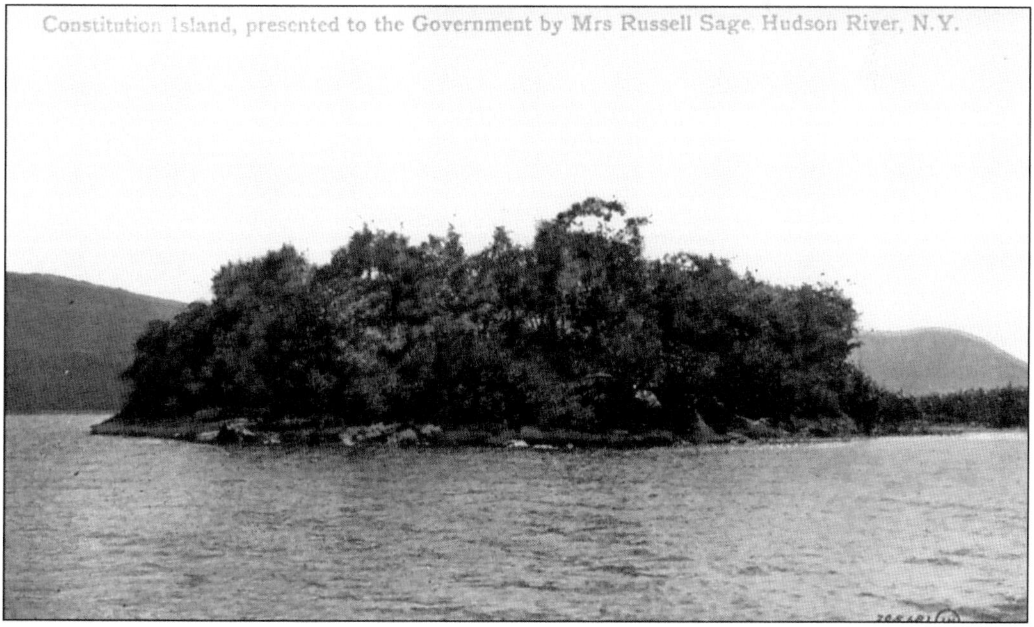

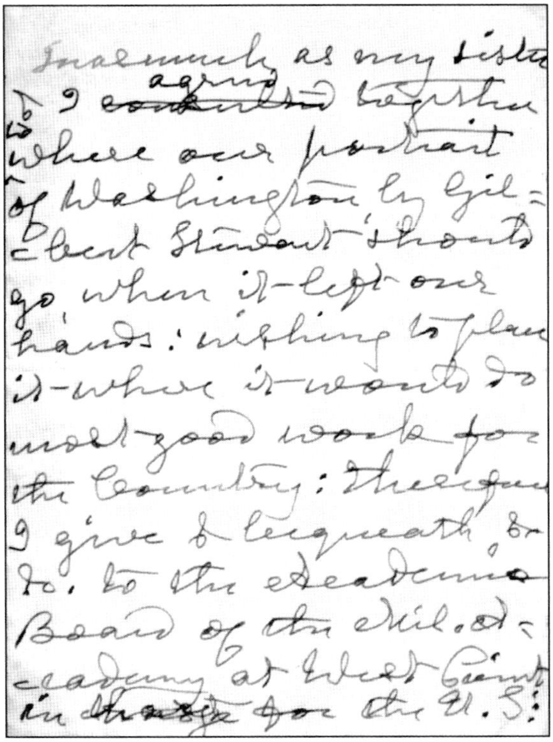

Inasmuch as my sister
& I agreed together
where our portrait
of Washington by Gil=
bert Stuart should
go, when it left our
hands: wishing to place
it where it would do
most good work for
the Country: therefore
I give & bequeath &c.
&c. to the Academic
Board of the Mil. A=
cademy at West Point
in charge for the U. S:

NOTES. While preparing her will, Anna Warner penned these notes to her lawyer. Along with the island, the Warner sisters also wished to donate the portrait of George Washington by Gilbert Stuart to the place "where it would do the most good work for the country: therefore, I give and bequeath it to the Academic Board of the Military Academy at West Point."

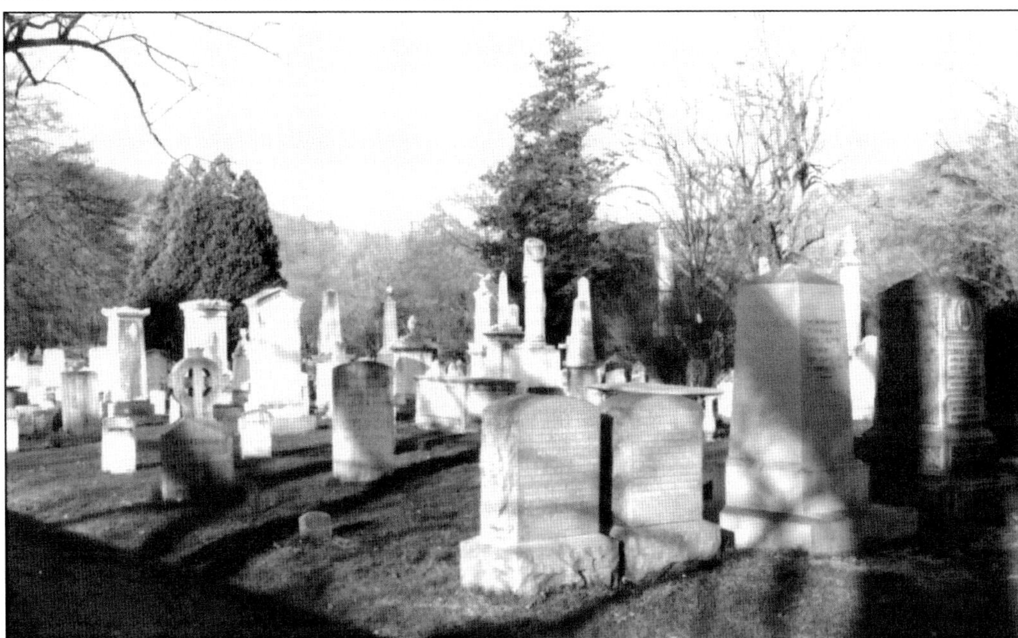

CEMETERY. Two identical gravestones mark the resting place of the Warner sisters. By special permission of the army, Susan and Anna Warner were buried at West Point. A mourner at Anna's funeral wrote, "It was wonderfully touching. The cadets whom she loved so well hadn't allowed anyone but themselves to touch the coffin. As they lowered into the ground, Taps was sounded." From their grave site, one can look out at Constitution Island.

Seven

The Constitution Island Association

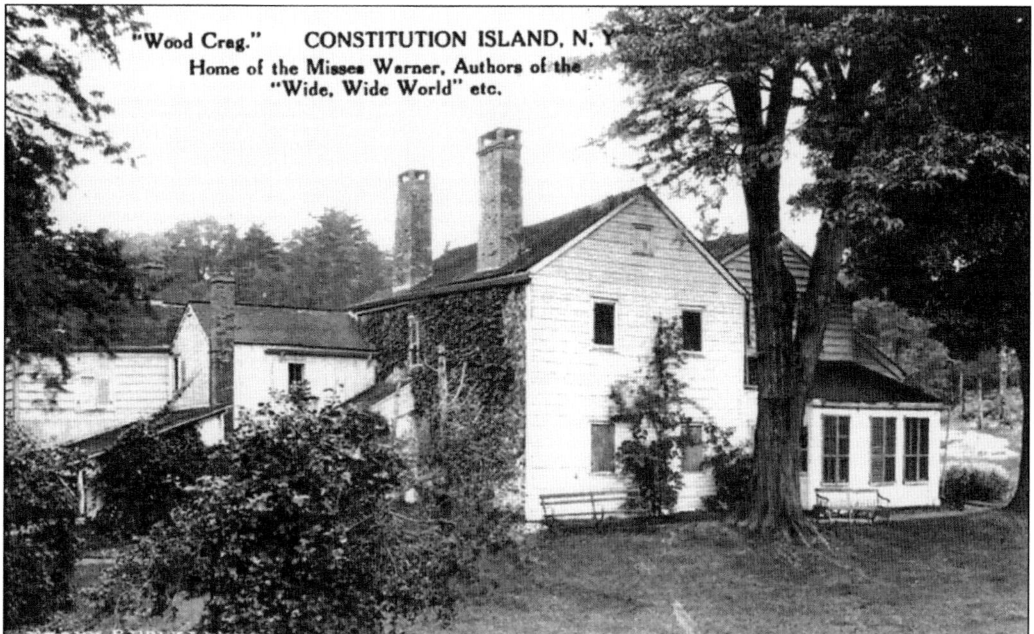

Martelaer's Rock Association, 1916. Shortly after Anna Warner's death, friends and admirers, in collaboration with the USMA, united to form the Martelaer's Rock Association to preserve the Warner House and its historic grounds. Original members included former students, commanding officers of the academy, and a litany of notable New York State families. The association held events on the island and published detailed annual reports. (Gunza collection.)

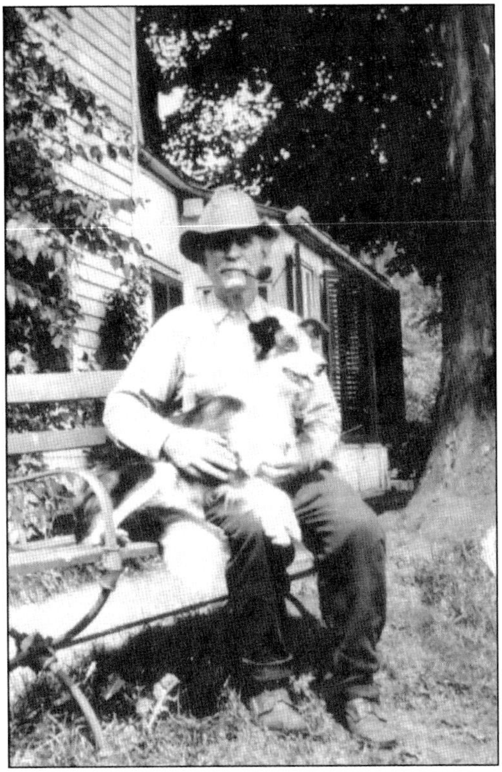

CARETAKER, C. 1918. Seated in front of the Warner House is Charles Clark, who labored on the island prior to Anna Warner's death and remained as caretaker from 1915 to 1933. After Anna's death, he and his family occupied the six oldest rooms of the house, sealing off the remainder. Clark maintained the house and grounds and helped the association with special events. After commending his work, one association report complimented him for rescuing 22 chairs from the Hudson River, which had been thrown overboard from one of the steamships, adding that they would be useful at the next annual meeting. Below Charles's wife, Vick, sits for a moment beside the well.

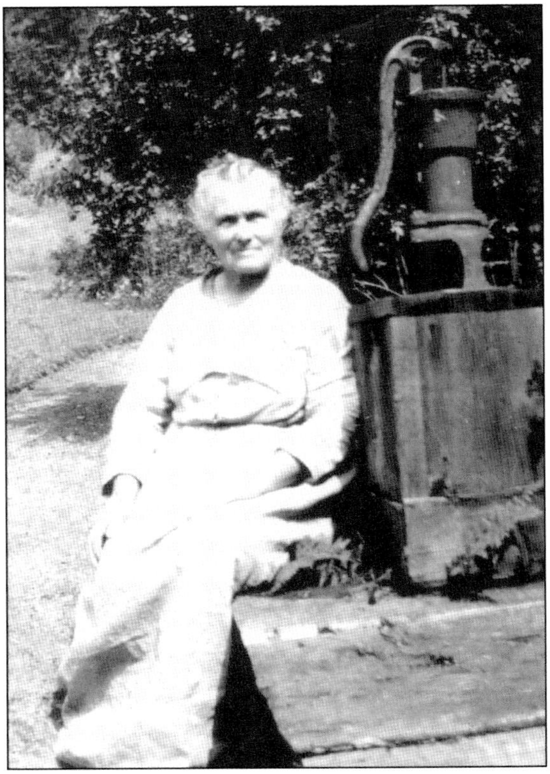

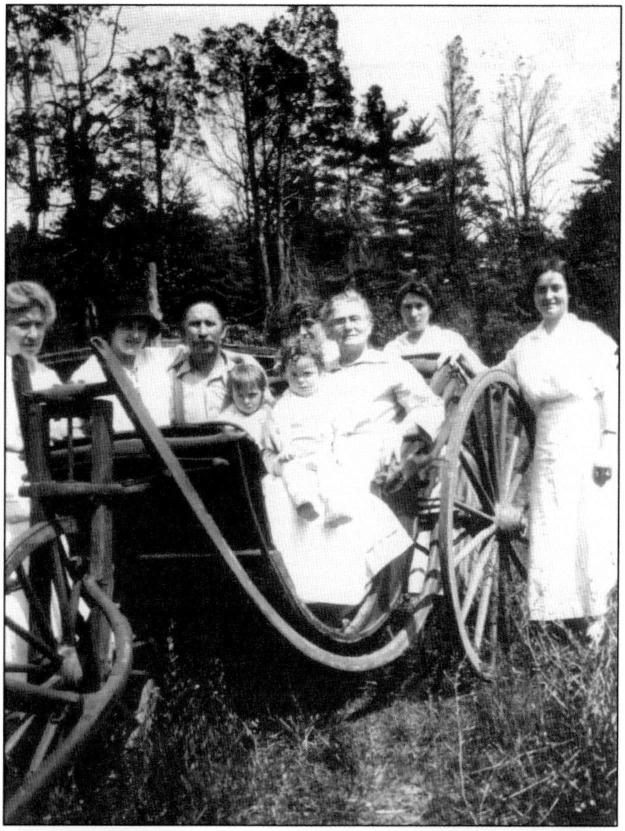

CLARK FAMILY. Flanked by family members, Charles, third from left, and his wife, Vick, third from right, pose for a group photograph in the three-wheeled chaise in 1916. The extended Clark family enjoyed outings on the island for the 17 years that Charles was caretaker. Family members spent time swimming, exploring, and picnicking.

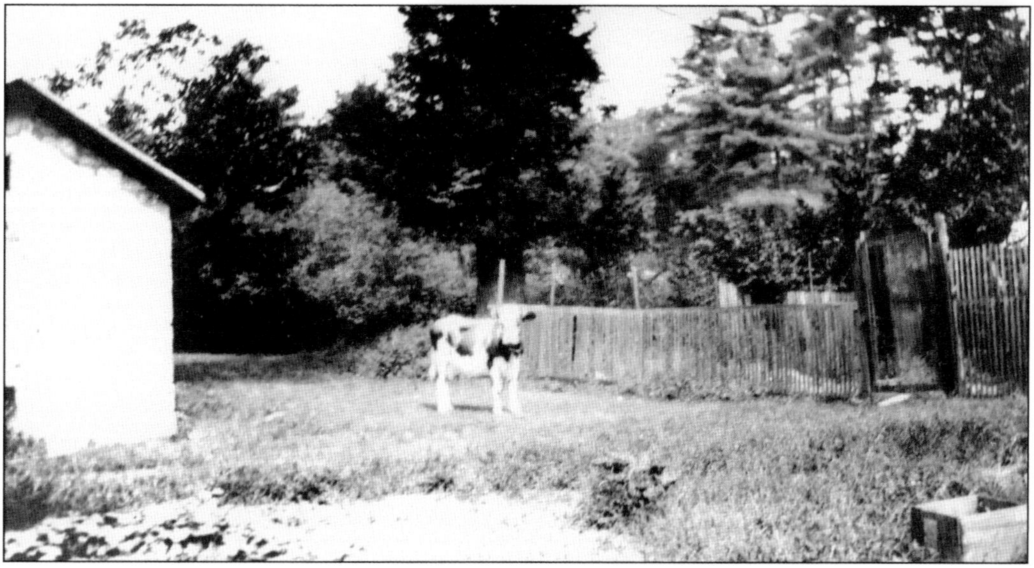

MOLLY. Charles's cow Molly seems to be posing for a photograph behind the Warner house. At left, part of the stone carriage shed is visible. Charles continued the Warner practice of maintaining a large garden and farm animals. The Constitution Island Association (CIA) annual report of 1931 states, "Clark is a faithful guardian of our interests here and we owe him a debt of thanks." The CIA gave Charles a yearly stipend.

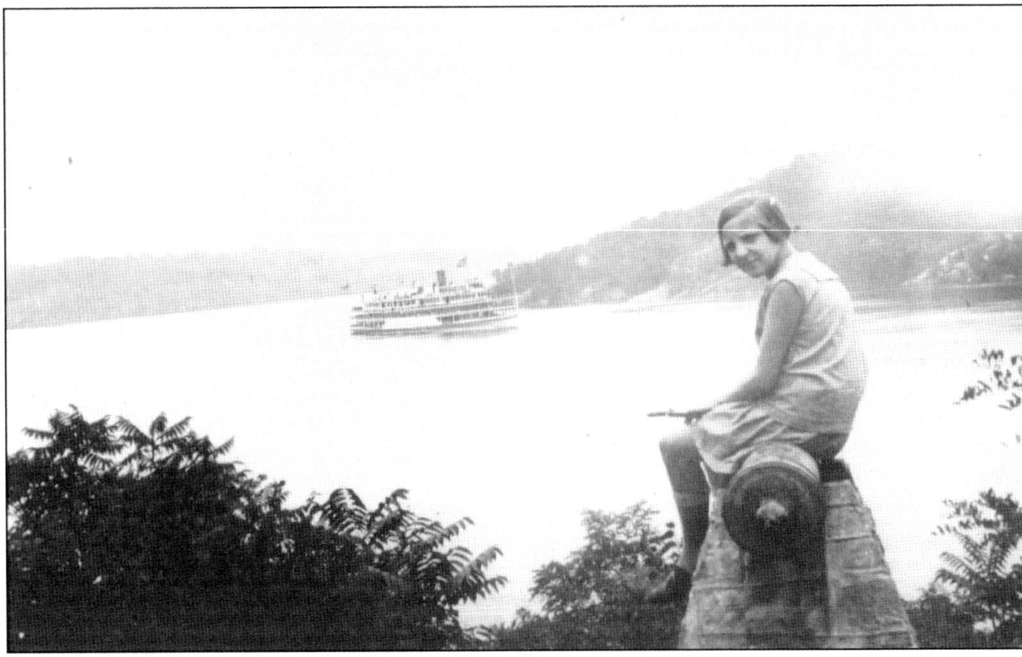

Mae Overfield. Pictured here is Mae Overfield, one of the younger generation of the Clark family. She sits atop the Revolutionary War–period cannon near the site of the original blockhouse on Constitution Island about 1932. Along the opposite shore at West Point, the Hudson River Day Line's *Robert Fulton* rounds Gee's Point en route north to Poughkeepsie and Kingston.

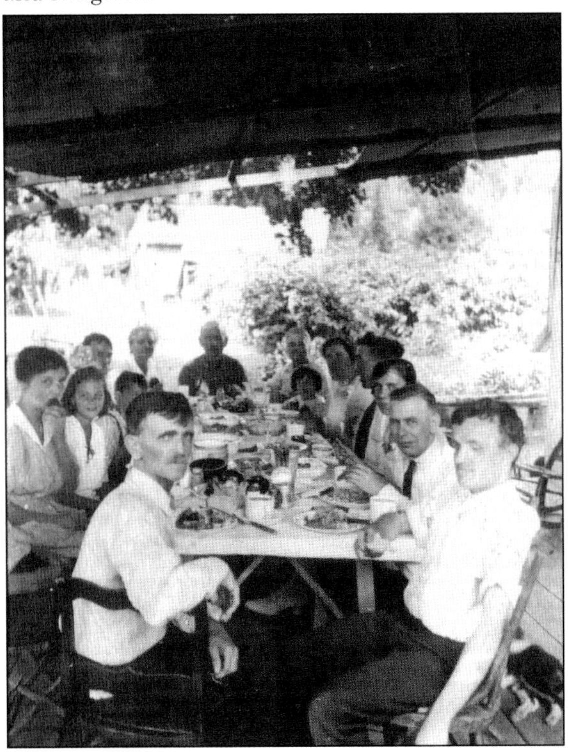

Family Picnic. Caretaker Charles Clark, seated at the head of the table, hosts a meal for his children and grandchildren on a pleasant summer day under the lean-to. The photograph is labeled simply "Family picnic, 1919."

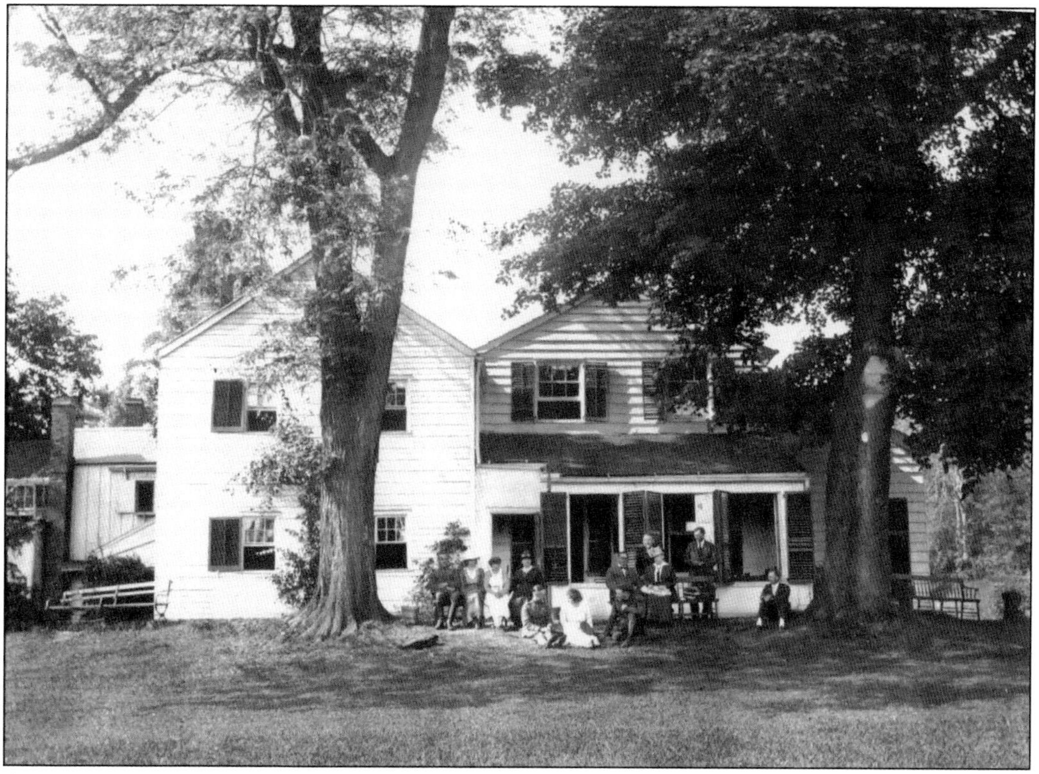

ASSOCIATION, 1919. By 1919, The Martelear's Rock Association had adopted a by-law to have two annual meetings on the island, a garden party in June and the official yearly meeting in the autumn. Members could also organize picnic parties for a visit at other times. In the photograph above, 11 visitors, probably picnickers, enjoy a shady spot in front of the Warner House. The 1919 annual report recorded, "In spite of the war, we have maintained our membership and kept alive the desire to perpetuate the memory of the Warner sisters." The treasurer's report noted that $51 had been earned from interest on Liberty Bonds. The yearly dues contribution was set at $1. The photograph below shows members at one of the 1922 meetings.

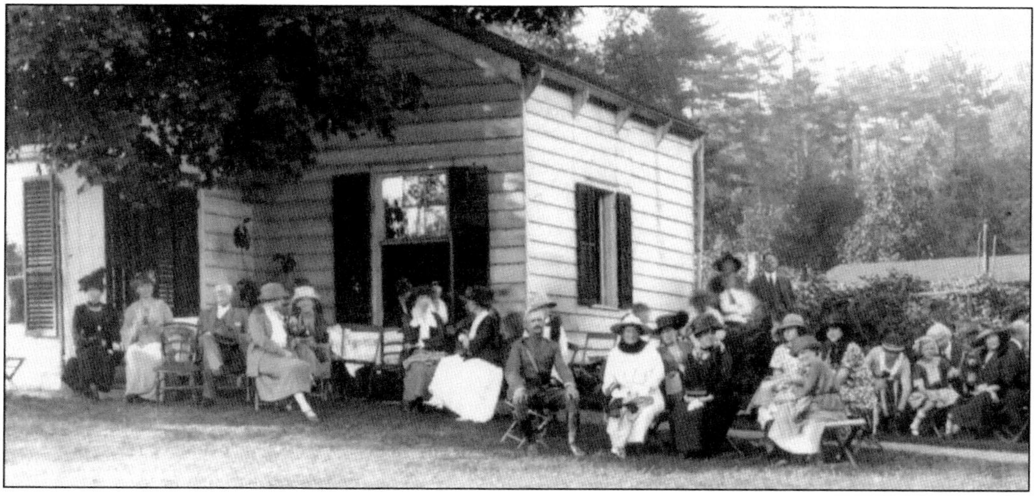

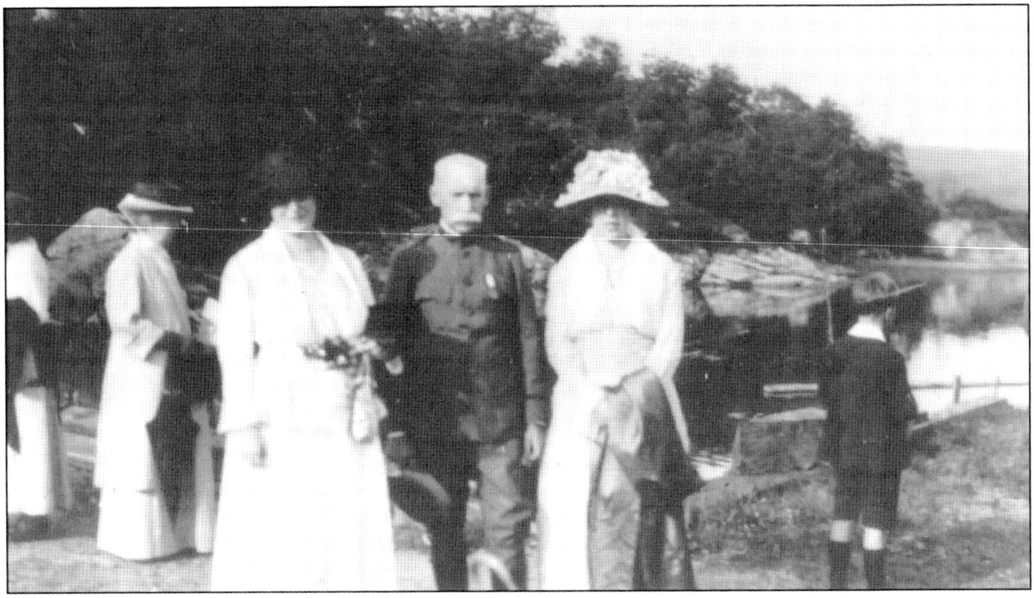

General Tillman. The 1919 garden party on the island was attended by Gen. Samuel Escue Tillman. A member of the class of 1869, he was superintendent of the USMA from 1917 to 1919. Mrs. Tillman is on the left. The lady at right is unidentified. Tillman was the guest speaker and delivered his address on the 50th anniversary of his graduation from West Point.

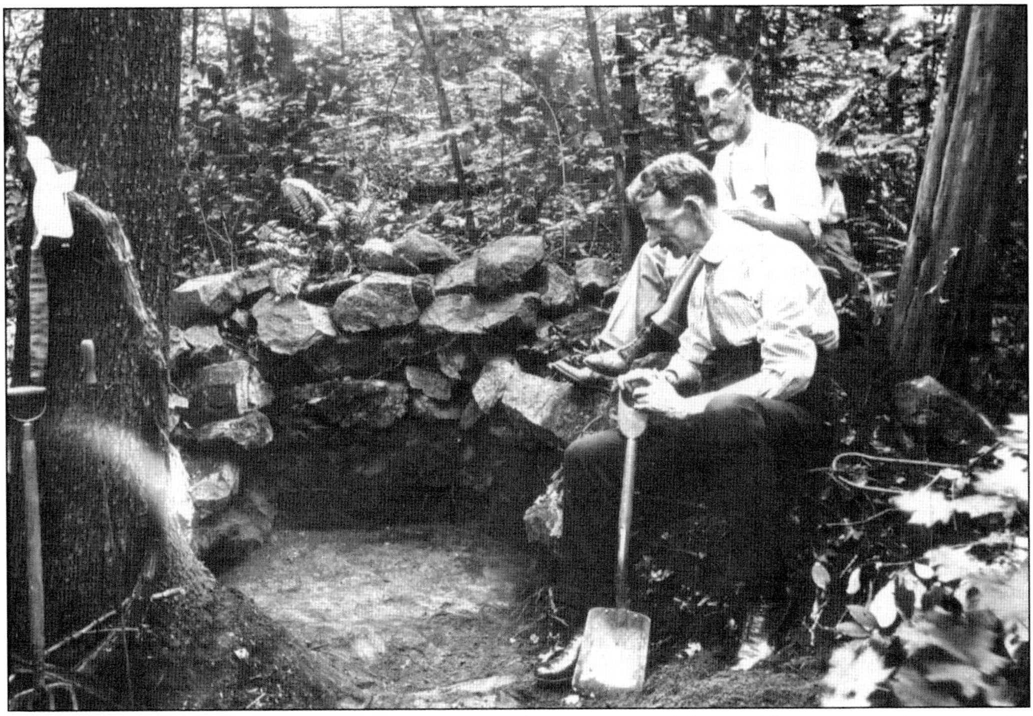

Excavation. In 1917, a group of association members examined the visible remains of stoneworks and earthworks on the island. Among their discoveries were a stone parapet, the debris of brick buildings, and a rubbish pile of bones and clamshells. They also unearthed hut sites in an excellent state of preservation.

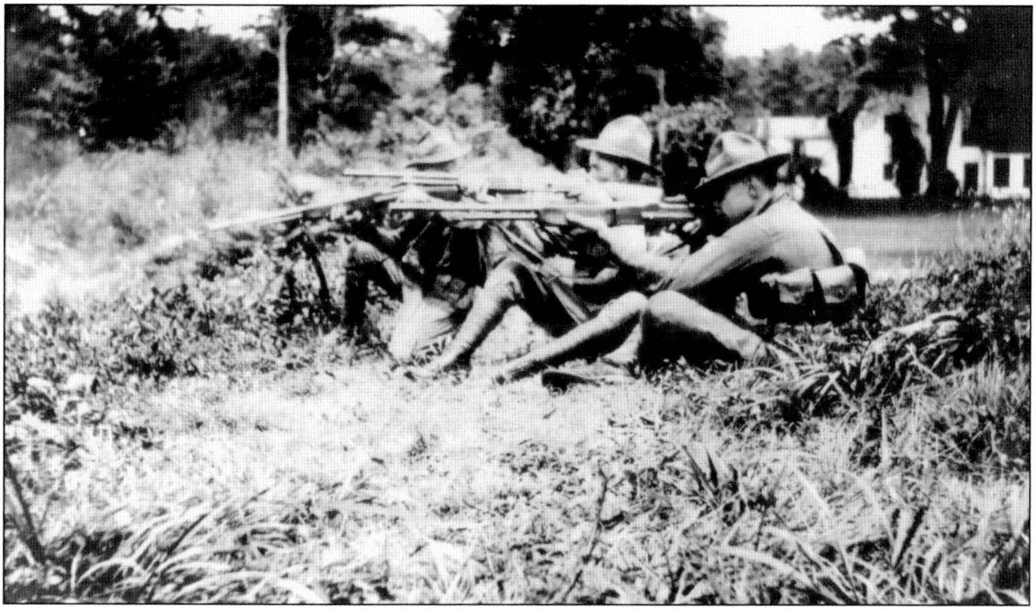

Rifle Practice. In sight of the Warner House, cadets engaged in rifle practice in 1922. The island has also served the academy as a venue for teaching military history lessons related to the Revolutionary War.

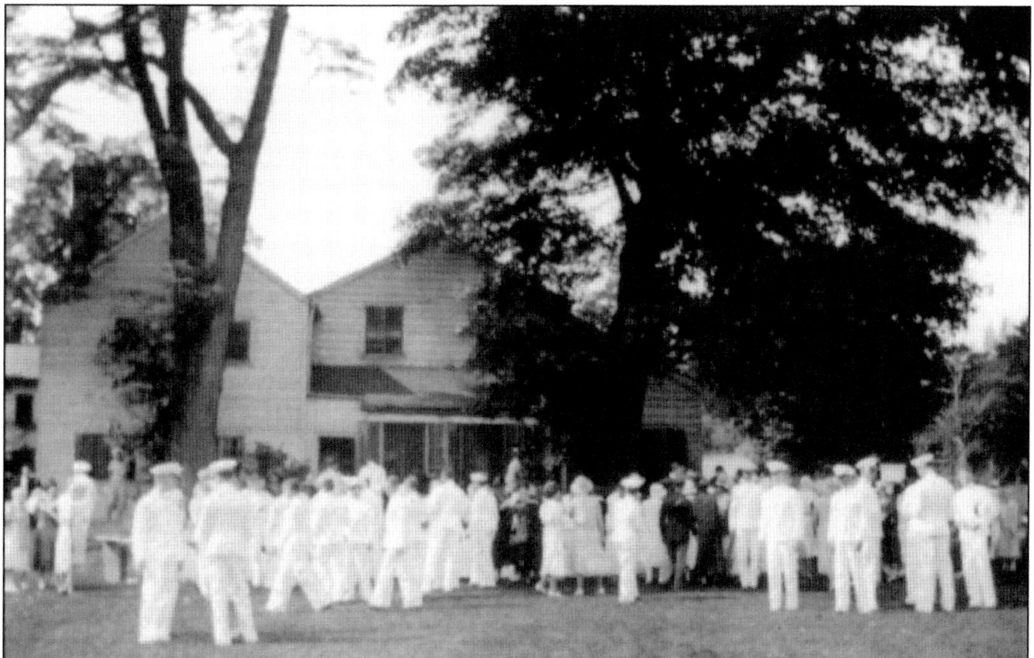

Garden Party. Cadets and guests crowd the front lawn of the Warner House in June 1924. For more than two decades, the association held an annual garden party for cadets at the end of the academic year. More recently, the island accommodates a large number of cadets and families for Plebe-Parent Weekend in October.

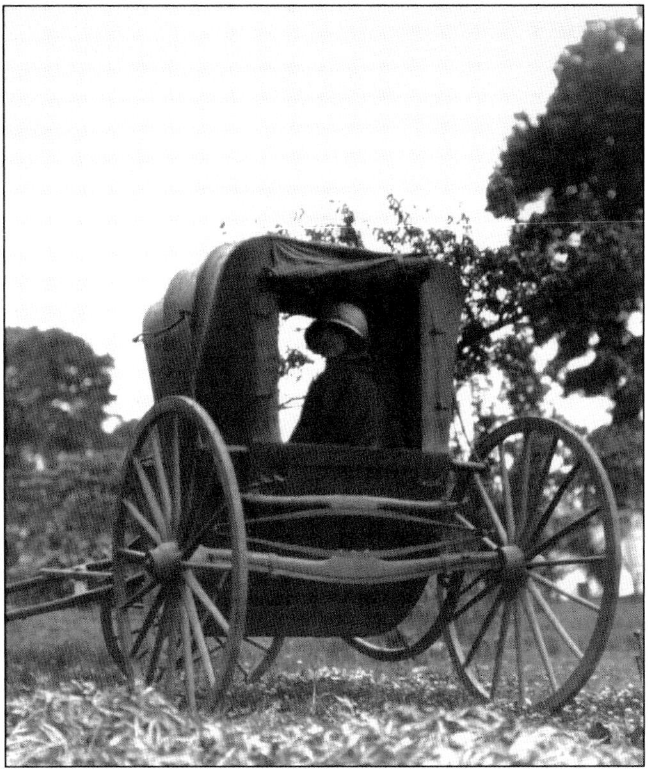

CARRIAGE. A young woman peeks out of the rear window of the Warner's unusual three-wheeled chaise. The photograph was taken by Dr. Edward Partridge on a visit to the island in the early 1900s. Partridge was a friend of Anna Warner's. After her death, he became a trustee of the Martelaer's Rock Association.

In case the weather is unfavorable, the meeting will be held at Cullum Hall, West Point.

The Annual Meeting of

The Constitution Island Association

Instituted for the commemoration of the associations, legendary, historic, literary and artistic, of

The Hudson River Valley

Will be held at MARTELAER'S ROCK, on Constitution Island

Saturday, October 9th, 1926, at 11:30 A. M.

Addresses will be delivered on

The United States Military Academy at West Point

By BRIGADIER GENERAL SAMUEL E. TILLMAN

and on

The History of West Point Prior to the Institution of the Academy

By MAJOR GEO. HAVEN PUTNAM

ANNUAL PROGRAM. In 1925, the name of the organization was changed to the Constitution Island Association. Traditionally the annual meeting was held on the island in autumn. Launches were provided by the military academy and occasionally by members. Mrs. J. Pierpont Morgan and Mrs. William Church Osborn loaned their boats when necessary. The program, like this one in 1926, always included a scholarly address on an aspect of Hudson Valley history.

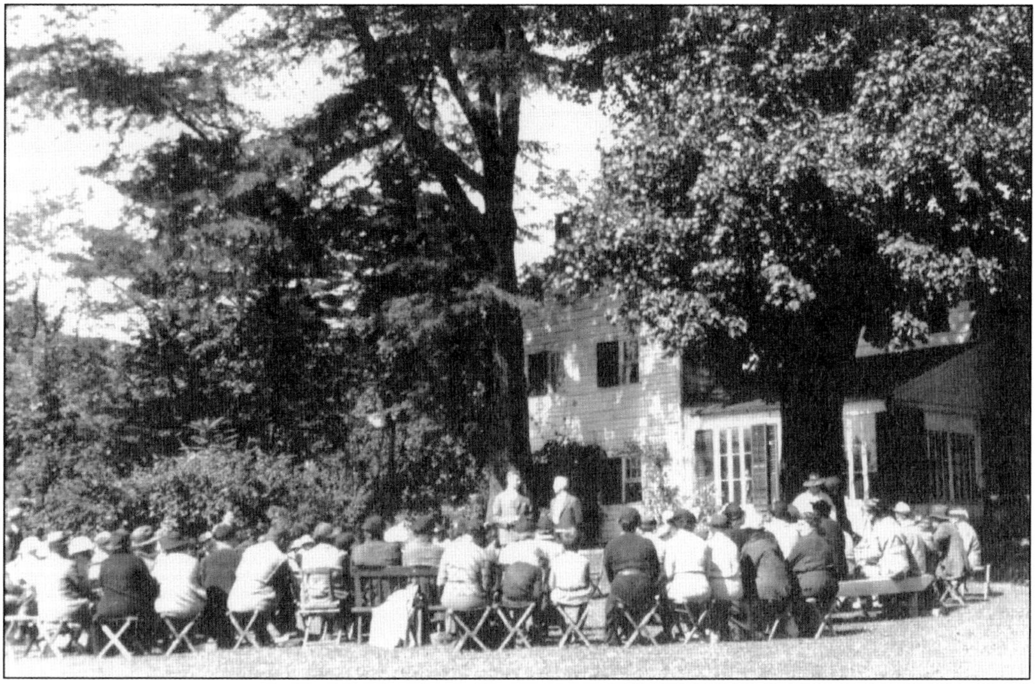

ANNUAL MEETING, 1934. Members who attended the annual meeting of the CIA in 1934 had much to enjoy. The Warner House had been painted in a fresh coat of white, and the Philipstown Garden Club had worked on the borders and garden walk. An address was given by Lt. Col. Robert Richardson on the history of West Point.

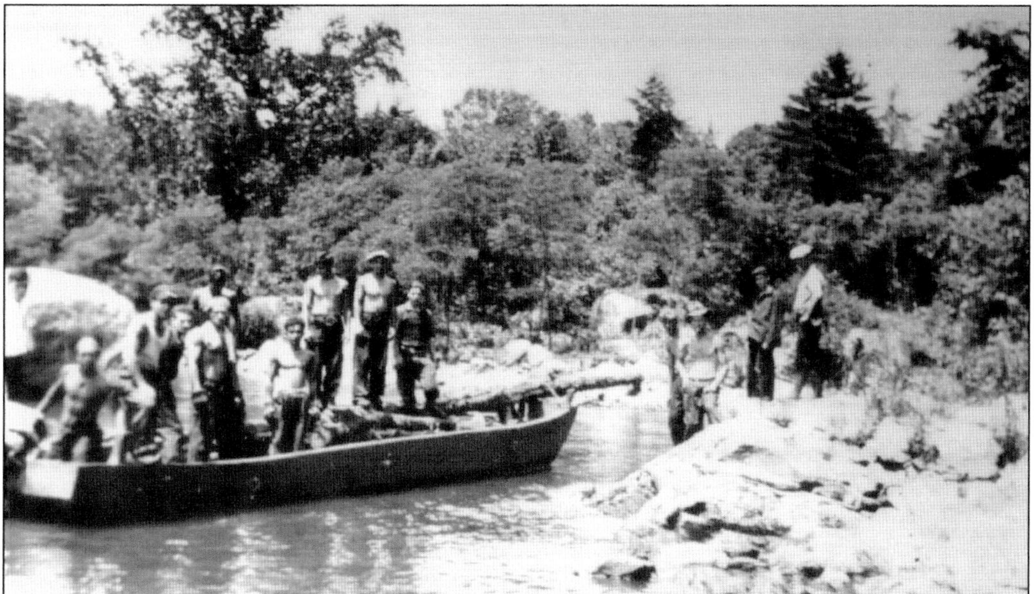

CIVILIAN CONSERVATION CORPS. Standing in their pontoon boat, a crew of the CCC arrives at the island in 1935. During the summers of 1935 and 1936, the CCC worked to preserve the Revolutionary War–era ruins. They cleared and widened trails, removed brush, and drained stagnant water to reduce mosquitoes. The boys were transported daily from a camp in Cornwall.

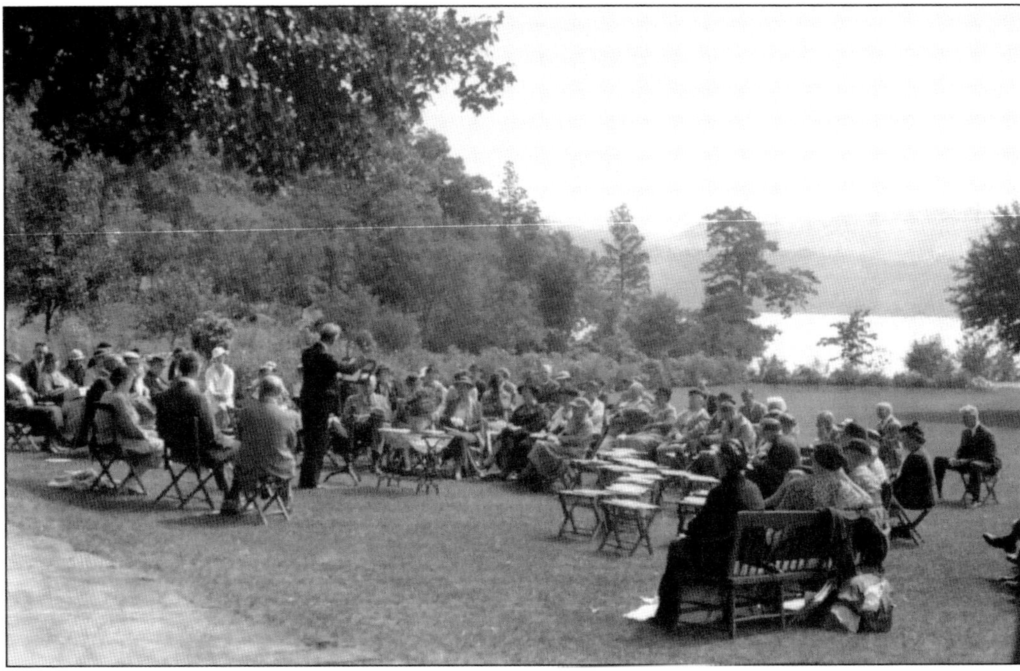

ANNUAL MEETING, 1935. In September 1935, 75 members attended the CIA annual meeting. The work of the CCC was discussed. They had found Native American and Revolutionary War–era artifacts that would be preserved. Attention was drawn to the fact that the island was an outstanding bird refuge.

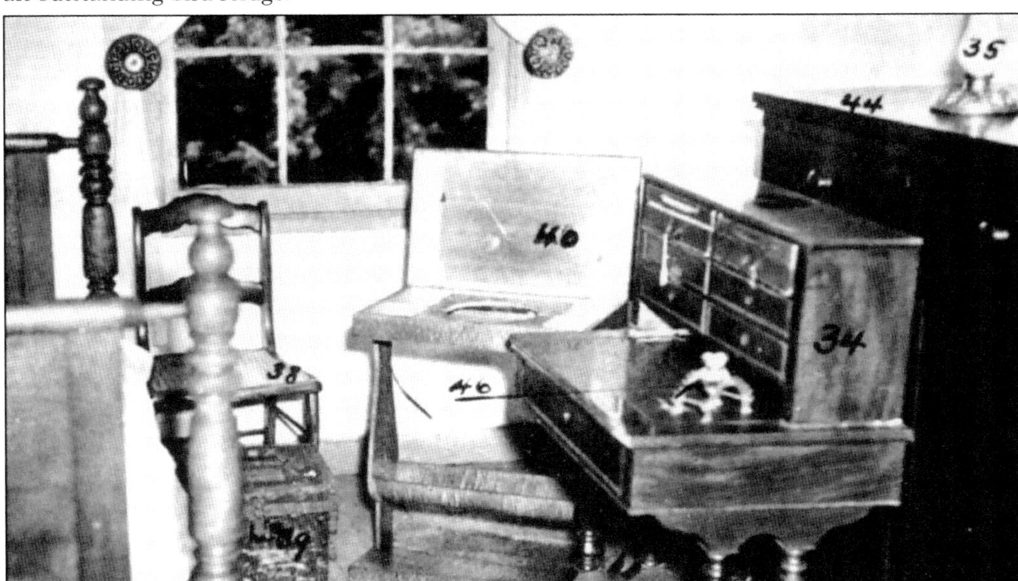

INVENTORY. In 1939, an inventory of the Warner House furnishings was performed. Items were photographed in groups, then numbered and catalogued. In the annual report that year, CIA chairman Brig. Gen. John Delafield thanked General Benedict and Colonel Scowden, the quartermaster, for their "splendid cooperation" with the association in such a worthwhile accomplishment. The 1939 inventory continues to serve as a valuable resource.

ANNUAL REPORT. The CIA has published a report annually or biannually from 1916 to the present. A fascinating historic record, the annual reports contain name of members, minutes of meetings, summaries of work accomplished, repairs, treasurer's reports, photographs and scholarly articles.

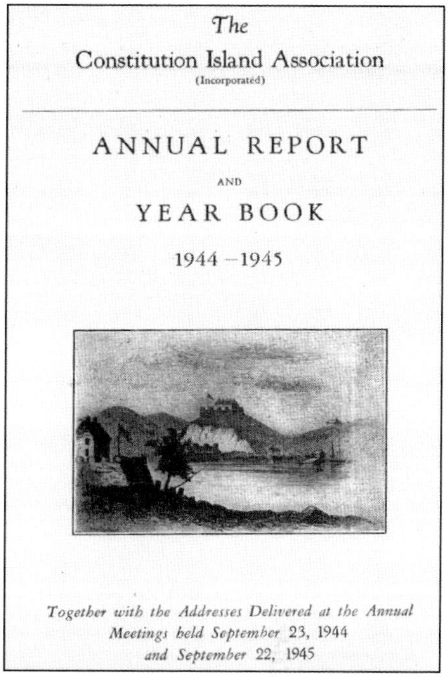

The
Constitution Island Association
(Incorporated)

ANNUAL REPORT
AND
YEAR BOOK
1944 – 1945

Together with the Addresses Delivered at the Annual Meetings held September 23, 1944 and September 22, 1945

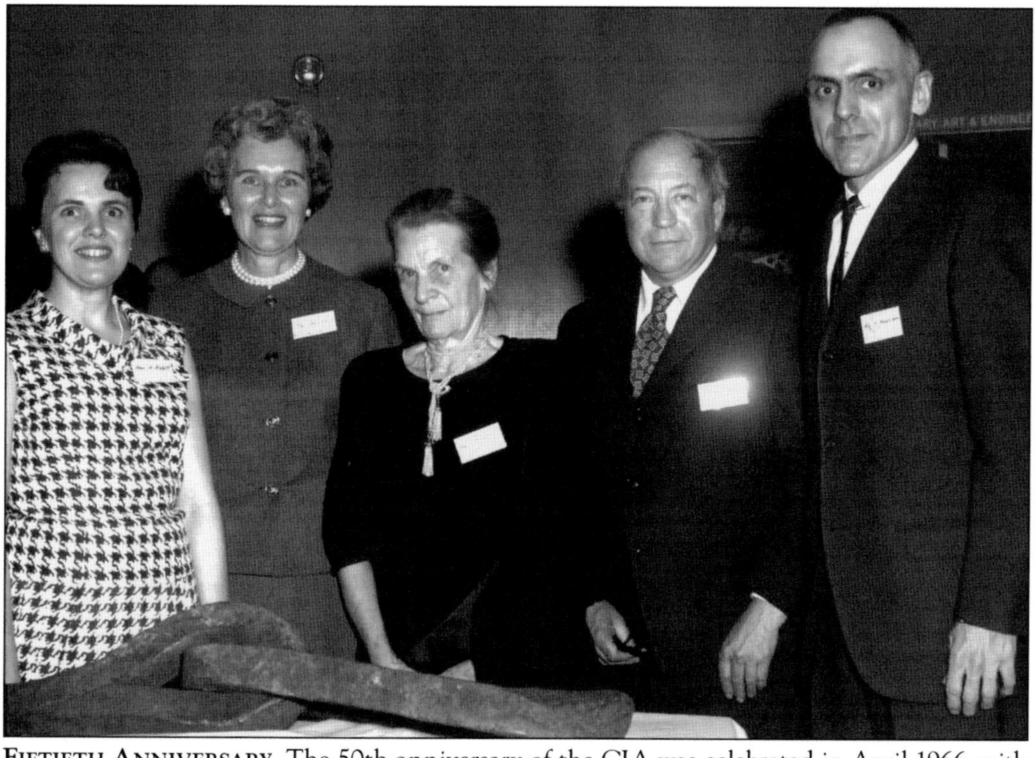

FIFTIETH ANNIVERSARY. The 50th anniversary of the CIA was celebrated in April 1966, with a major event attended by 325 guests. Among those present are, from left to right, Mrs. Ardis Abbott, executive director Genevieve Lewis, Mrs. S. C. Eristoff, B. W. Frazier, and Maj. Andrew Mansinne, who gave a lecture on the West Point chain. A link of the chain was on display courtesy of Ben Frazier of Boscobel Restoration.

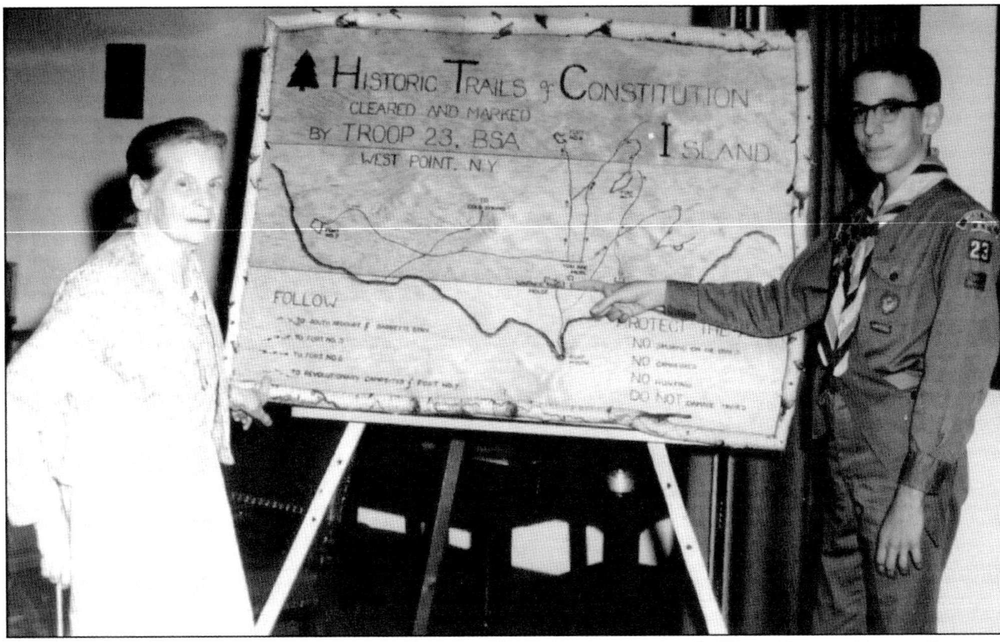

TRAIL MAP. Mrs. Simon C. Eristoff, poses beside a map with Boy Scout Steve Capps. In 1966, Troop 23 at West Point cleared and marked trails on Constitution Island. At the end of the summer, the scouts presented the CIA with a large map of the trails burned on wood for display.

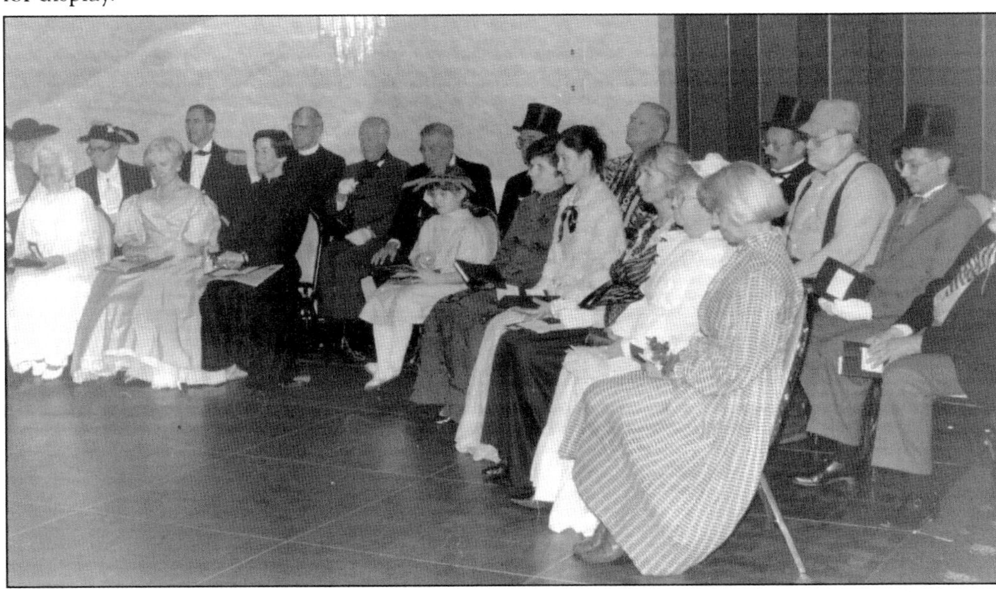

HISTORICAL PROGRAM. For the 1995 annual meeting, members of the CIA board of trustees and volunteers presented a program on notable 19th-century figures that influenced the Warner sisters. Seen here from left to right are (first row) Blair Davies, Helen Blewett, Eleanor Peters, Juliet Coffey, Faith Herbert, Jane Weiss, Judith Sibley, Betty Rasmussen, and Virjean Camp; (second row) Constantine Sidamon-Eristoff, Philip Hoblin, Michael Peters, Richard Camp, Blair Davies, Merl Hutto, Richard Gruenther, Elliott Cutler, David Gordon, Kevin Coffey, Anthony Marchesani, and Chester Logan.

TOURS. For many years, through the combined efforts of CIA volunteers in cooperation with USMA Harborcraft Division, Constitution Island has been open for tours on a limited basis. Tours for school-age children, known as the Little American Program, are given in May and June. Public tours run from mid-June to early October on certain weekday afternoons and occasional weekends. Reservations are recommended.

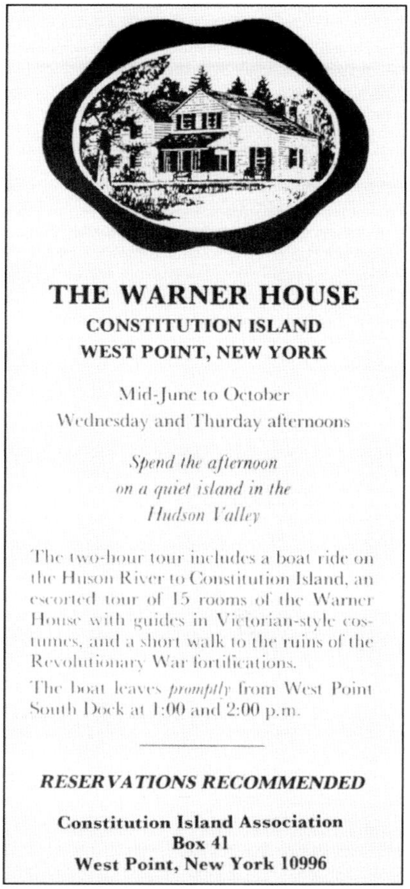

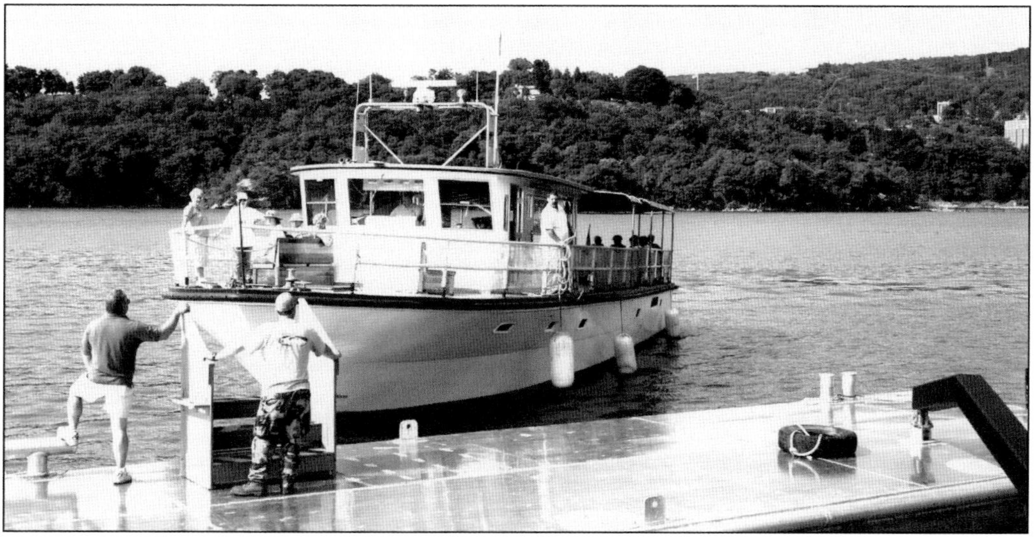

Q-BOAT. Transporting volunteers to work in the early morning, the USMA's Q-Boat prepares to dock at the island. Harbormaster Richard Camarda is at the helm. Charles Herd handles the lines, while island caretaker Roddy MacLeod, left, and Micah Johnson assist on the dock. (Vacek collection.)

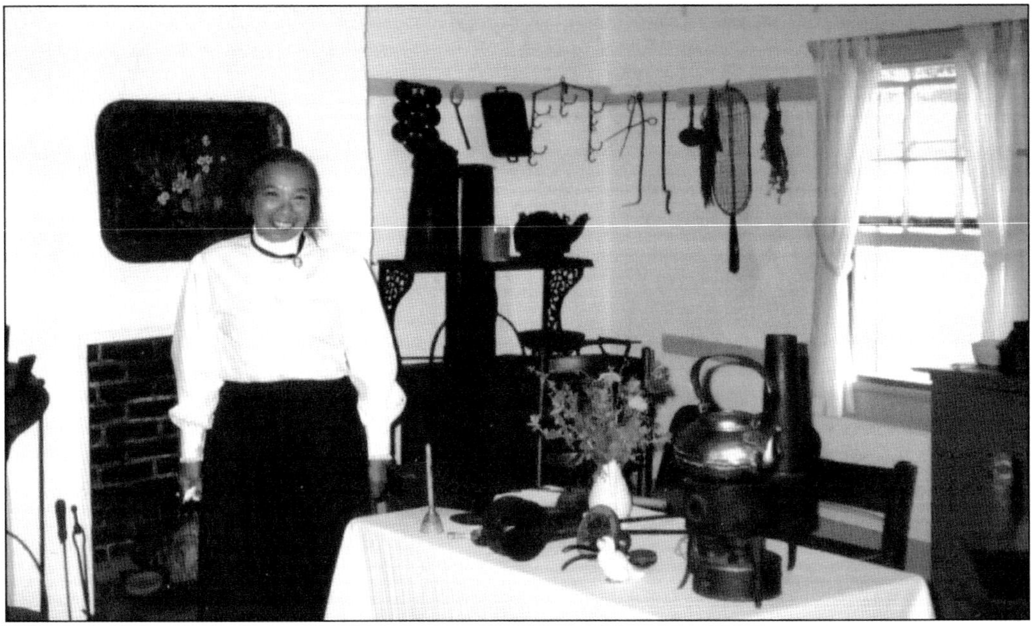

KITCHEN TOUR. Docent Francine Ashby stands beside a table in the Warner House kitchen. Among the implements on display are a wood stove, corn popper, bellows, sausage grinder, butter mold, Anna Warner's gardening tools, and a special device for watering violets. All docents are volunteers who are trained to interpret the house and the fortifications.

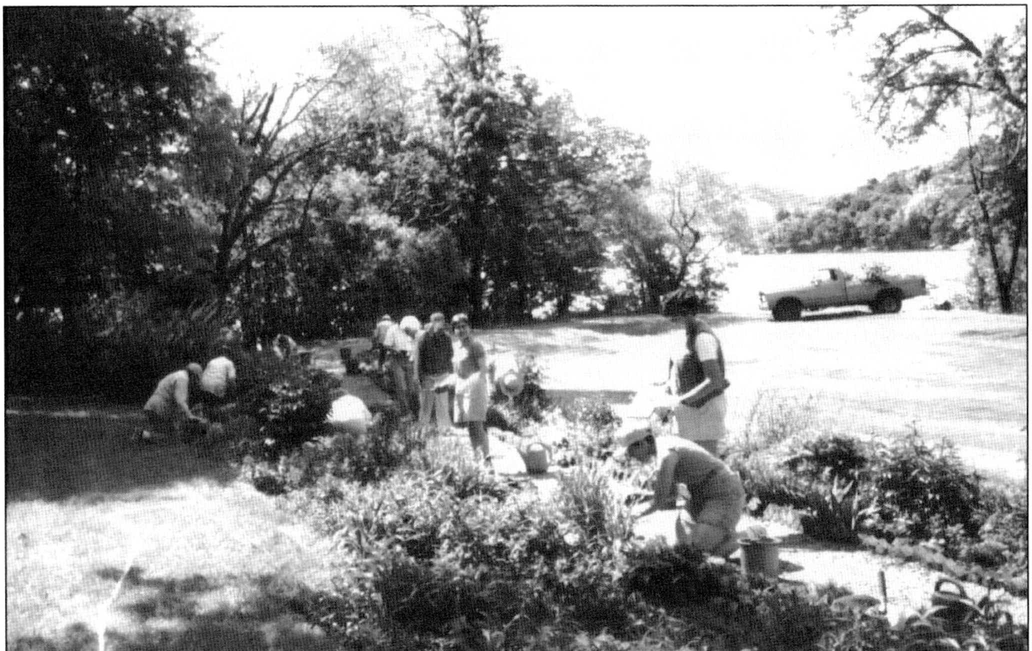

GARDENING BY THEMSELVES. Throughout spring and summer, volunteer gardeners maintain the flower garden, rose bushes, shrubs, a grape arbor, and an herb garden. They also make fresh flower arrangements each week for the rooms of the Warner House. Above they are hard at work in the Anna B. Warner Memorial Garden along the path in front of the house.

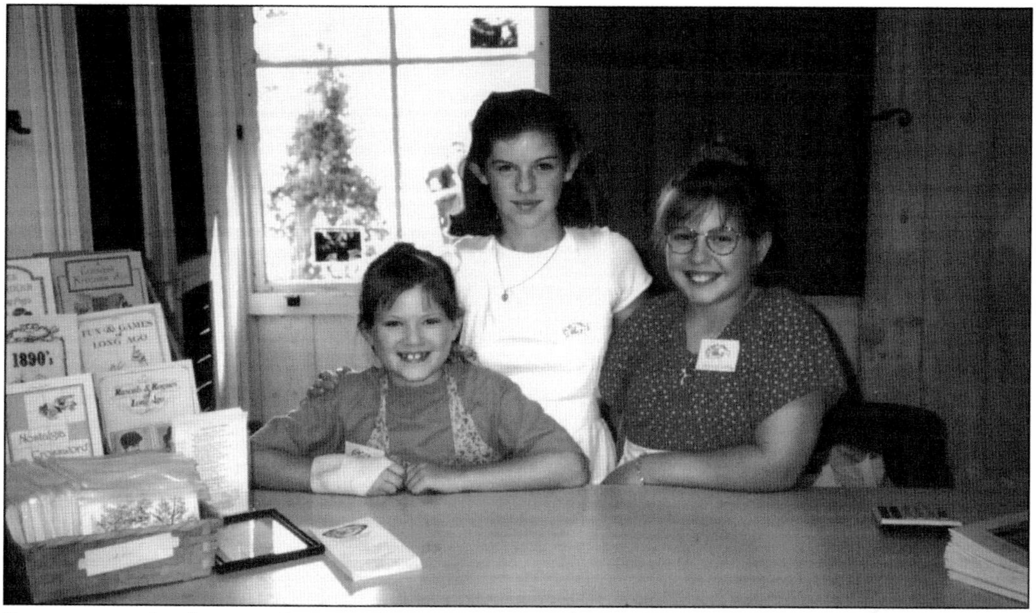

BOOKSHOP. At the conclusion of a tour, visitors have the opportunity to browse through the bookshop. Copies of *The Wide, Wide World*, *Gardening by Myself*, *Private Yankee Doodle*, *Constitution Island*, and other books about the Warner family and the island are for sale, along with postcards, gifts, and souvenirs. Pictured here from left to right are Juliet Coffey, Meredith Rose, and Veronica Coffey, helping in the bookshop on a summer day.

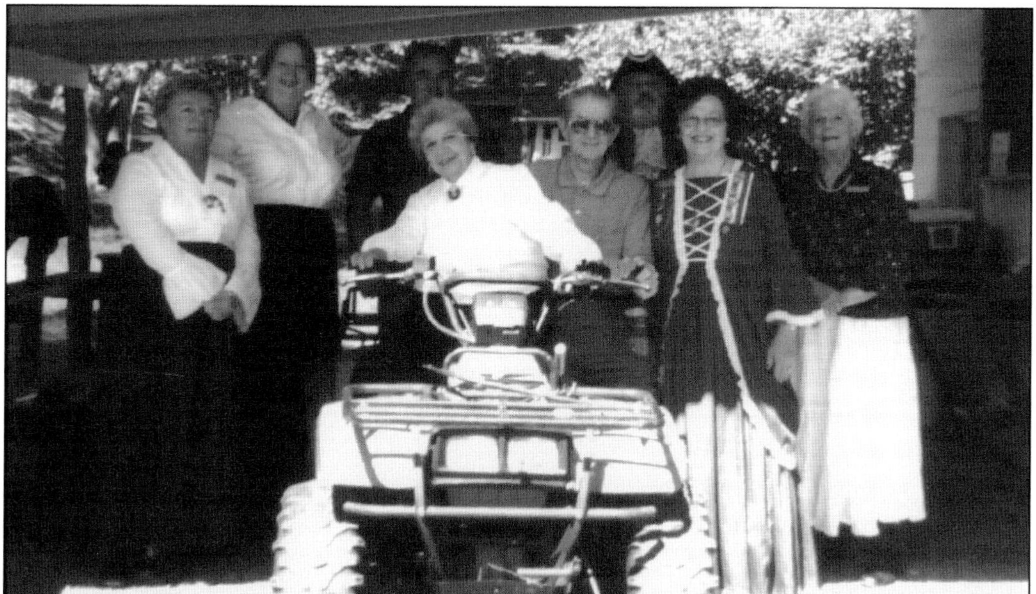

OLD AND NEW. Costumed volunteers gather with caretaker Roddy MacLeod, standing third from left, for a whimsical photograph representing old and new. While the docents interpret the traditions of the past, MacLeod uses his modern ATV to help protect and manage the resources of the island in the present. Seated on the vehicle are Anna Policastri, left, and Frank Murphy. Standing are, from left to right, Barbara Miller, Alexina de Koster, MacLeod, Ted Wisner, Phyllis Murphy, and Susan Crowfoot. (Murphy collection.)

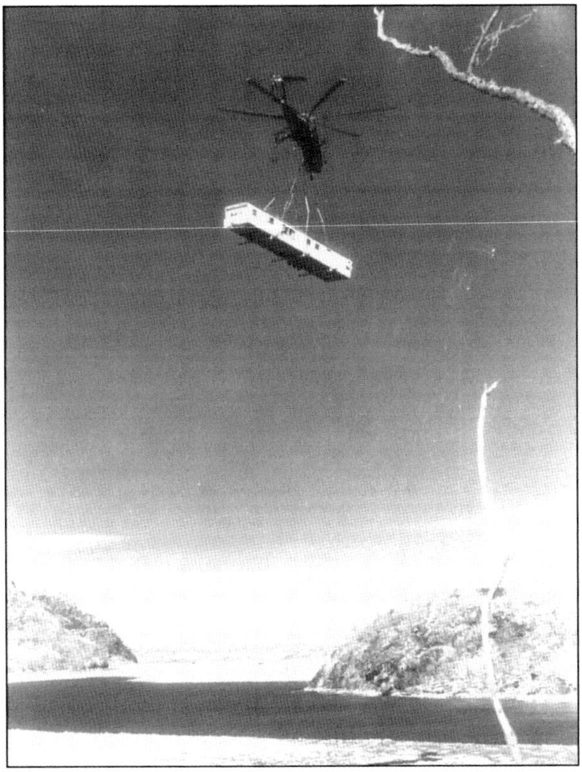

AIRLIFT. In February 1987, high above the ice floes of the Hudson, a U.S. Army helicopter transported a house trailer from the North Dock of West Point to Constitution Island. The narrow causeway and winding dirt road from Cold Spring to the island was inadequate for moving the trailer by land. It served as the home of caretaker Roddy MacLeod, below, for three years until 1990 when a permanent cabin was built.

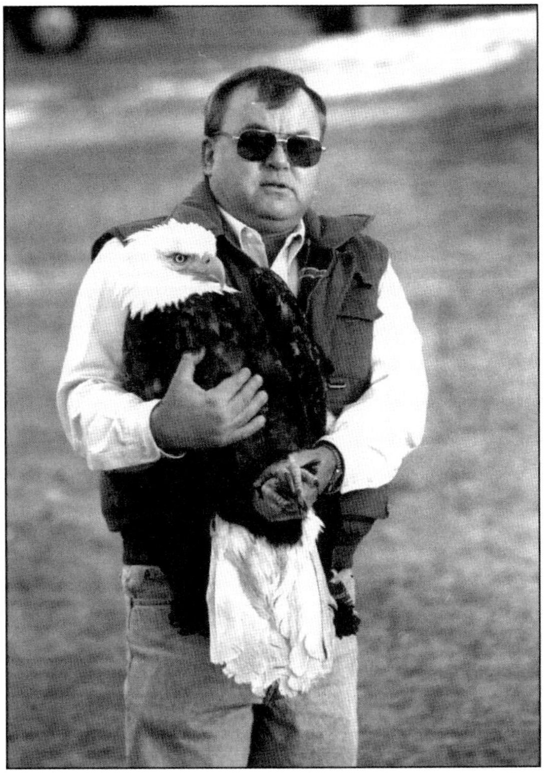

ISLAND CARETAKER. MacLeod, resident manager of Constitution Island, holds a bald eagle moments before its release. MacLeod had assisted with an eagle banding project on the island in 1999. The project was a joint effort between the USMA and the Department of Environmental Conservation. (MacLeod collection.)

Eight

LIVING LEGACY

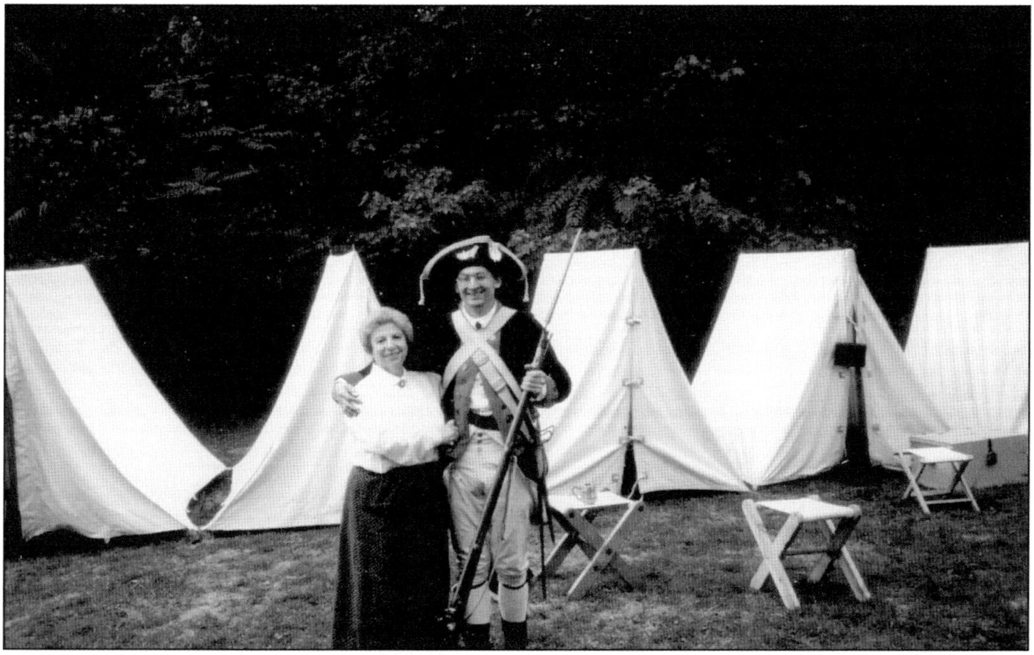

LEGACY. Standing side by side, these two costumed interpreters symbolize a history of remarkable people and events at Constitution Island. Docent Anna Policastri, left, and a smartly uniformed Continental soldier enact stories of patriotism, courage, loyalty, family, dedication, and resourcefulness in times gone by. Volunteers like these support tours and events that keep the legacy of Constitution Island alive.

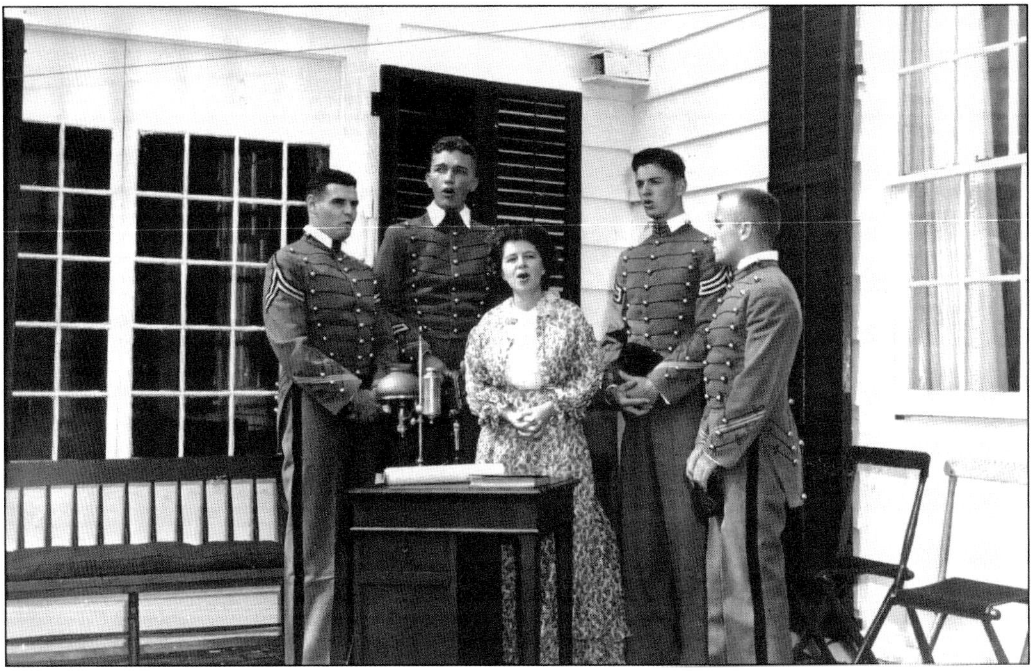

BIBLE CLASS REENACTMENT. A September 1951 program at the island consisted of a reenactment of a cadet Sunday school class. Mrs. C. E. Covell played the part of Anna Warner surrounded by her students. They were portrayed by cadets Kenney, Christman, Fialo, and Gray. The ensemble concluded with the singing of *Jesus Loves Me*.

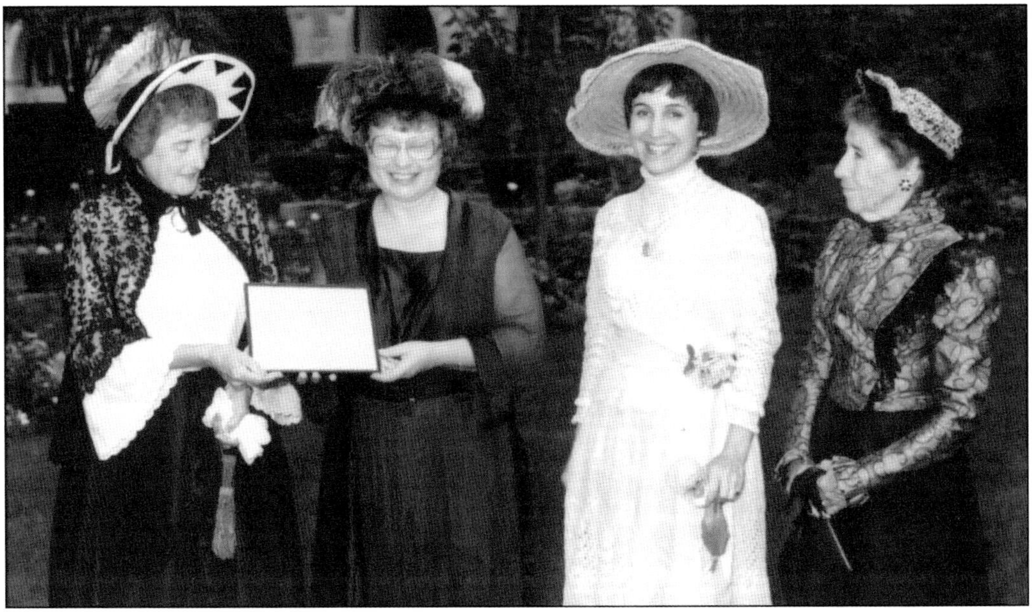

MEMORIAL. A highlight for CIA members in 1985 was a memorial service held in September to commemorate Susan, Anna, and Fanny Warner. Volunteers in Victorian costume included Carolyn Osborn, Carol Bryan, Mary Katherine McIntosh, and Emma O'Gorman. Members assembled in the Old Cadet Chapel for a service and then to the garden of the USMA superintendent for a reception featuring the Warner sisters' own recipes.

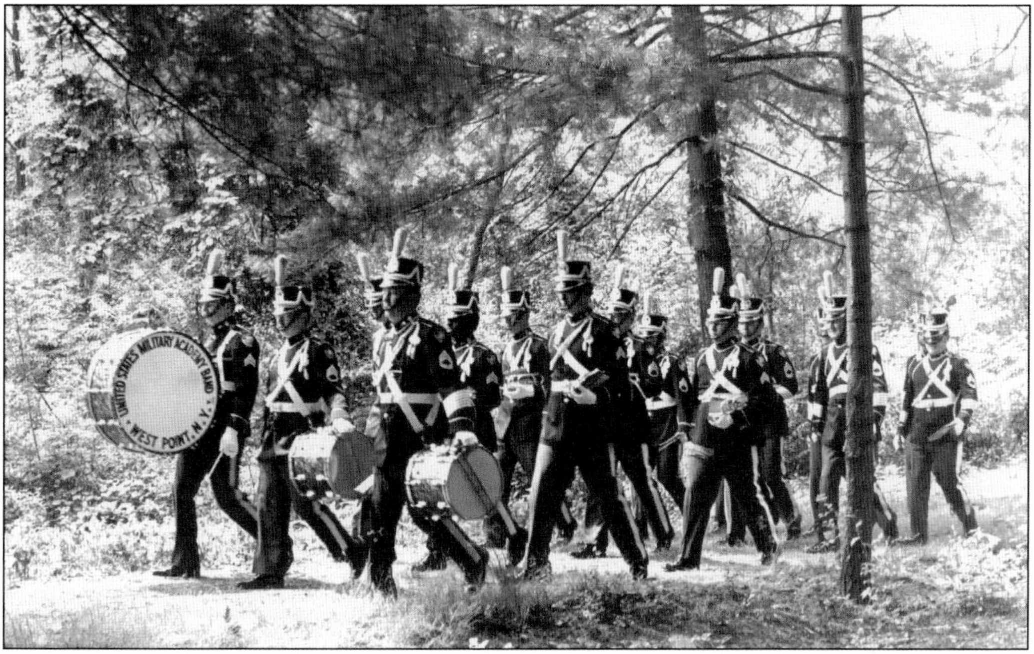

USMA BAND. From the early days of the association, the USMA Band actively supported events on Constitution Island. The Hellcats, above, are an ensemble of drummers and buglers whose history of providing field music at the academy dates back over 220 years. They are pictured marching through a patch of woods to a performance location on the front lawn.

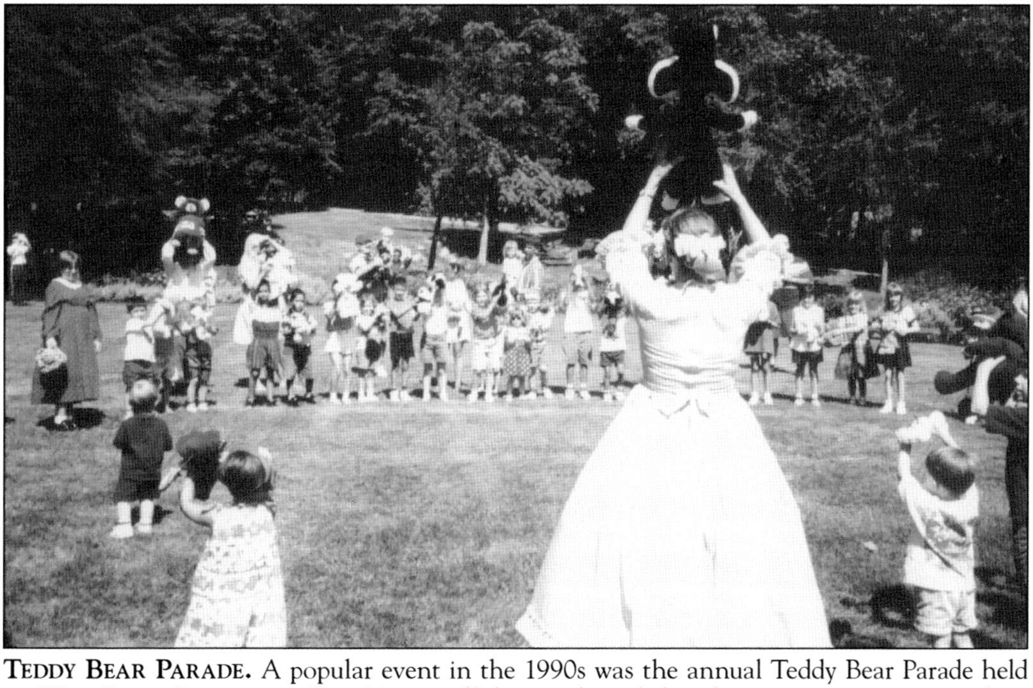

TEDDY BEAR PARADE. A popular event in the 1990s was the annual Teddy Bear Parade held on West Point Community Day. Here stuffed animals and their human companions get their marching orders from executive director Ronnie Coffey. The USMA Hellcats saved a rousing tune for the grand parade.

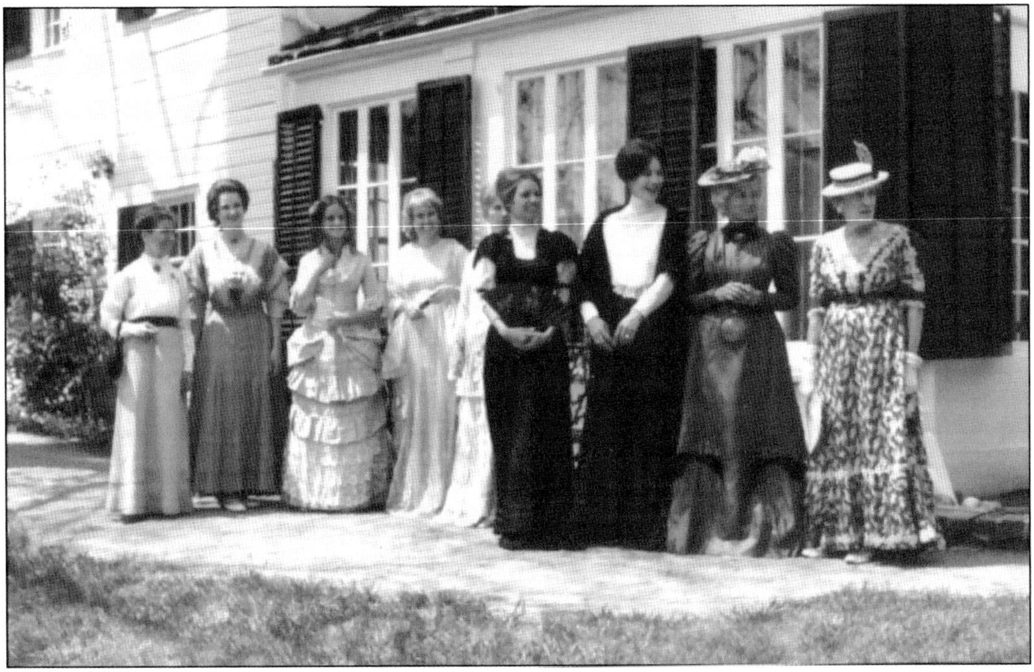

VICTORIAN DAY. Docent Emma O'Gorman, left, was joined by a group of elegantly attired CIA volunteers on Victorian Day in 1975. This first annual Victorian Day began with a coffee at the West Point Train Station, followed by a picnic on the island with docent hostesses wearing items from the costume collection, an assortment of lovely antique dresses donated to the association over the years.

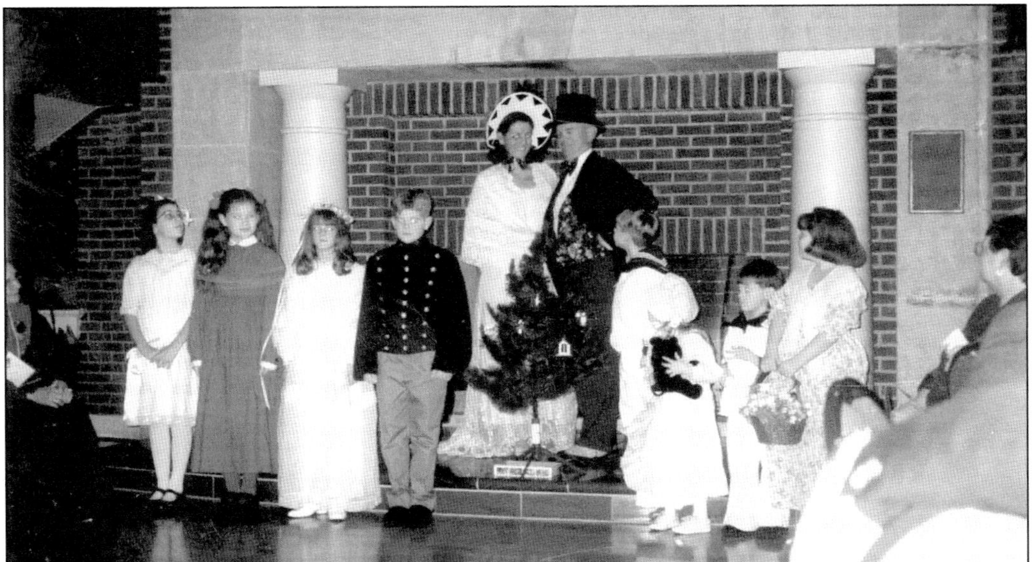

FASHION SHOW. Utilizing reproduction and authentic costume to illuminate history, the CIA had a tradition of fashion shows put on by the volunteers. This one took place in the Association of Graduates building at West Point in 1996. Seated far left is Mary Betty Sergent. Portraying members of a 19th-century family are, from left to right, Amy Donaldson, Juliet Coffey, unidentified, Timothy Rose, Jill Rose, Edward Rose, Patrick Rose, Sarah Taylor, Frank Taylor, and Megan Kane.

FASHION DEMONSTRATION. Laura Stewart takes a deep breath as her mother, Doumina Stewart, tightens the laces of her corset. As part of the 1996 fashion show, Laura demonstrated the discomfort endured by 19th-century women in order to be properly dressed. After a slight adjustment of her hoops, Laura was ready to slip on her gown.

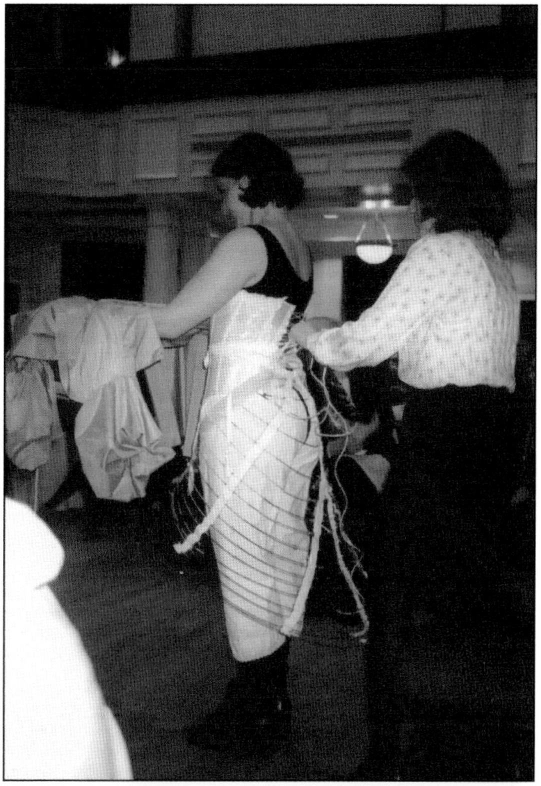

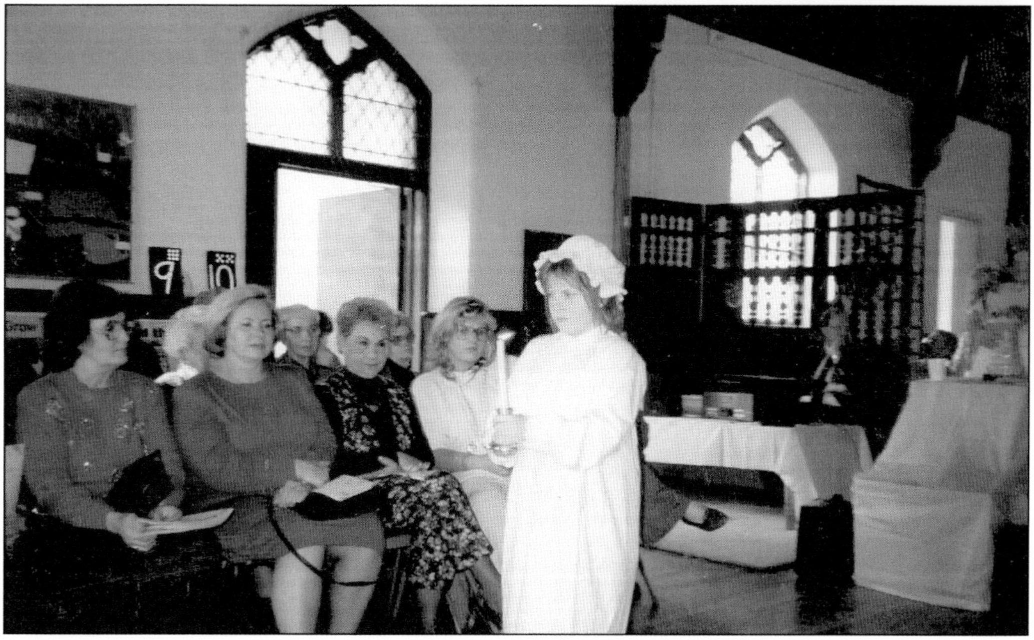

EDUCATIONAL FASHION SHOW. The three educational fashion shows held during the 1990s raised funds to support the work of the CIA. This 1993 program was presented at St. Philip's Church in Garrison, New York. Veronica Coffey modeled a Victorian nightgown and sleeping cap.

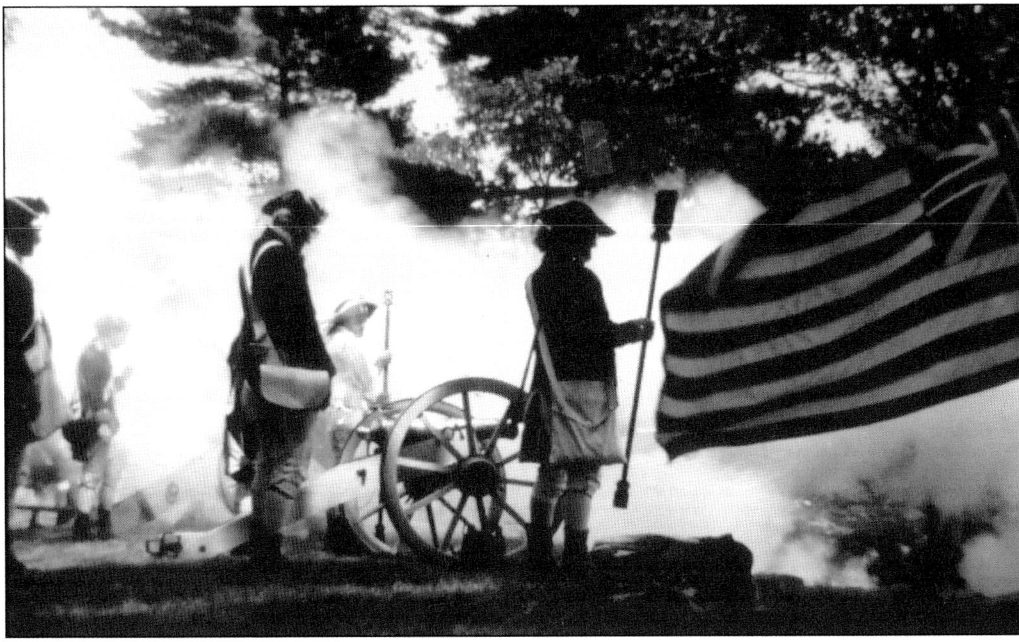

REENACTMENTS. Reenactments are always exciting events on Constitution Island. The reenactors take pleasure in spending time at such a beautiful, historic location and the public gets a chance to travel back in time. Here a unit of Revolutionary War artillerymen demonstrates the loading and firing of cannons. Visitors enjoy talking with the reenactors and visiting their tents to learn about camp life.

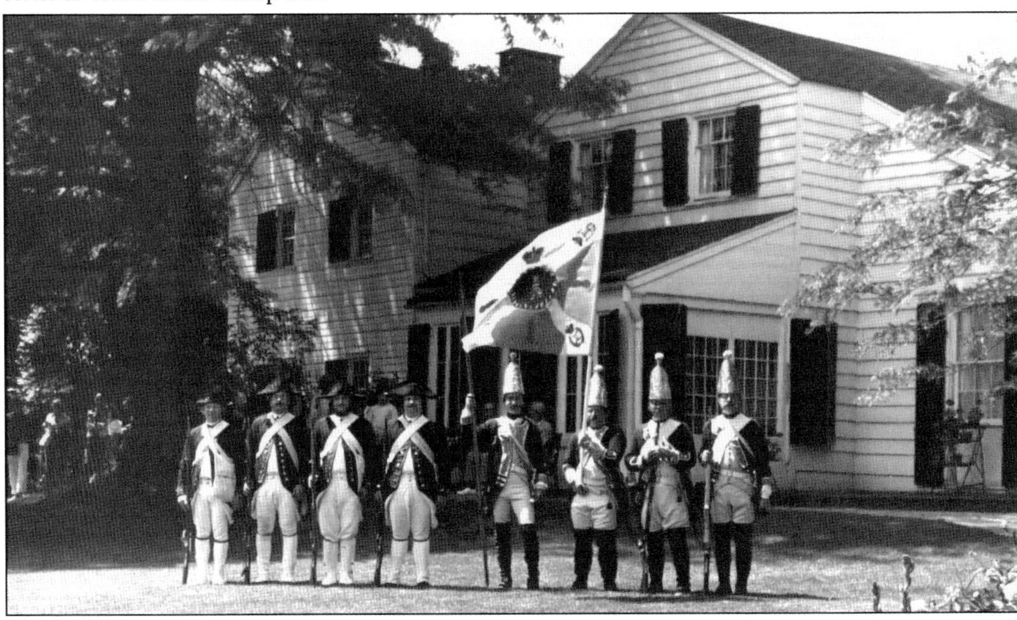

THE BRITISH ARE COMING. A unit of reenactors portraying British soldiers prepares for inspection in front of the Warner House. In 1777, the British occupied Constitution Island for one month after defeating the colonists at the Battle of Fort Montgomery. Reenactors have included Revolutionary War–era British and Continental soldiers and Native Americans. Civil War groups have also participated.

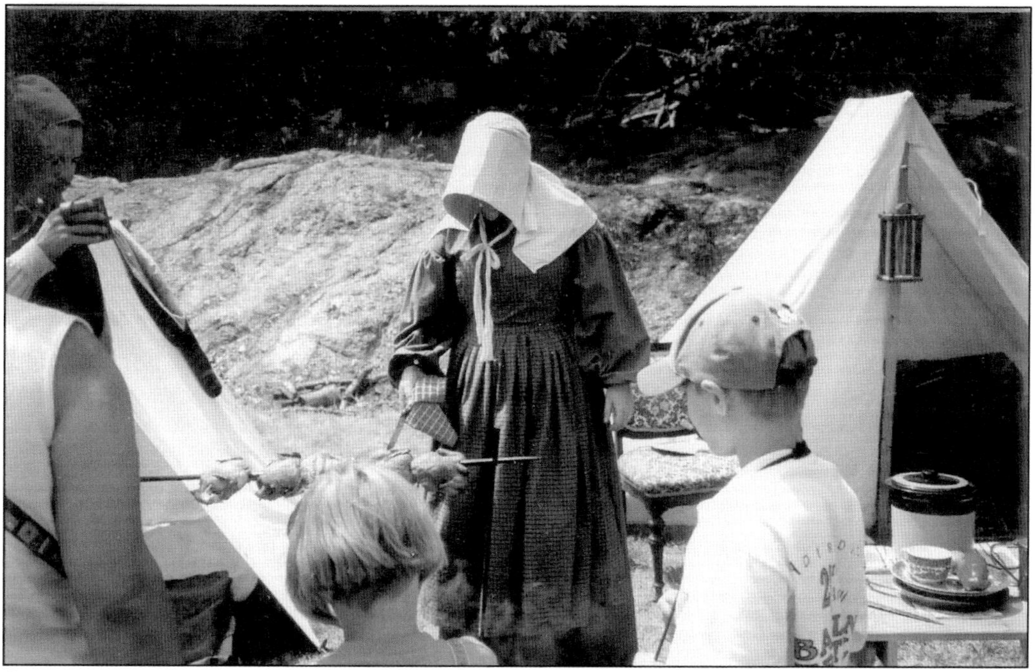

Camp Life. Basting five chickens is guaranteed to capture the attention of young visitors, as this reenactor knows. At an outdoor kitchen near a line of tents, she cooks over an open fire. Revolutionary soldiers were often accompanied by family members and other civilians so reenactments include these fascinating portrayals of camp life.

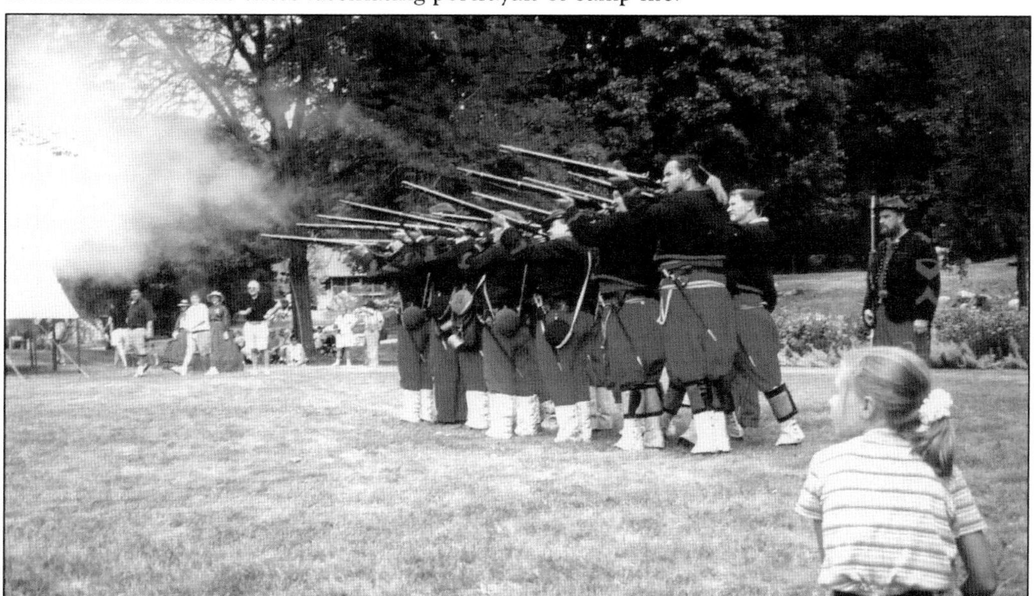

Civil War Soldiers. Ready, aim, fire. Civil War reenactors of a Zouave regiment fascinate a young visitor with a demonstration of musket firing. Reenactments often feature displays, marching, musical performances, and exhibitions of 18th- and 19th-century trades. The strong connection between Constitution Island and military history are highlighted on these days.

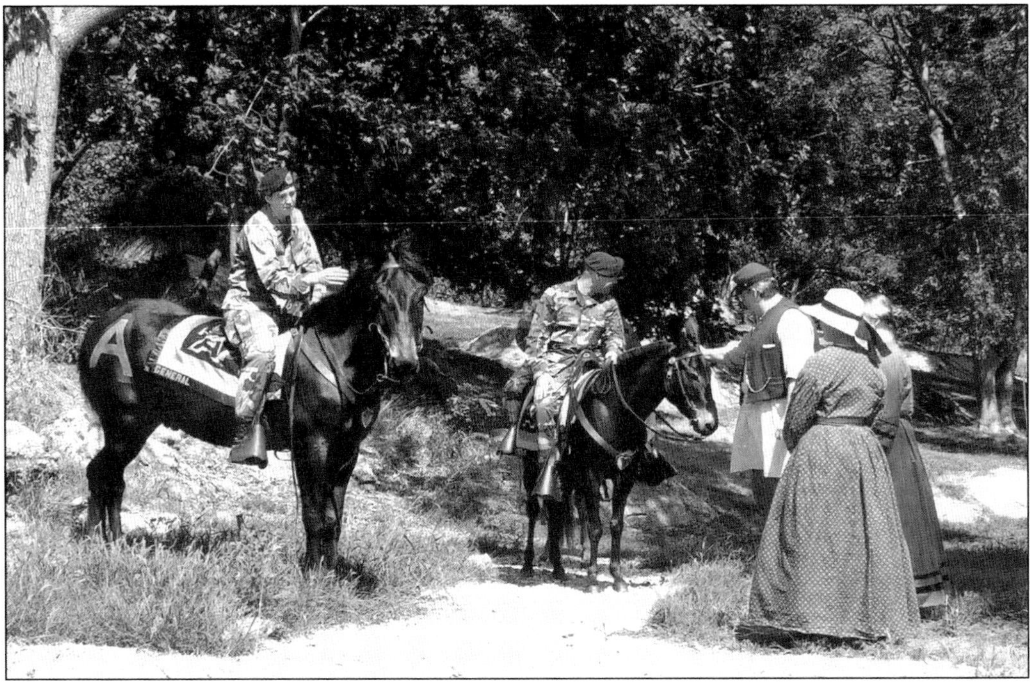

ARMY MULES. Army mules and their cadet riders make occasional appearances at the island to add interest to public events. Here the army mascots enjoy the attention of Civil War reenactors.

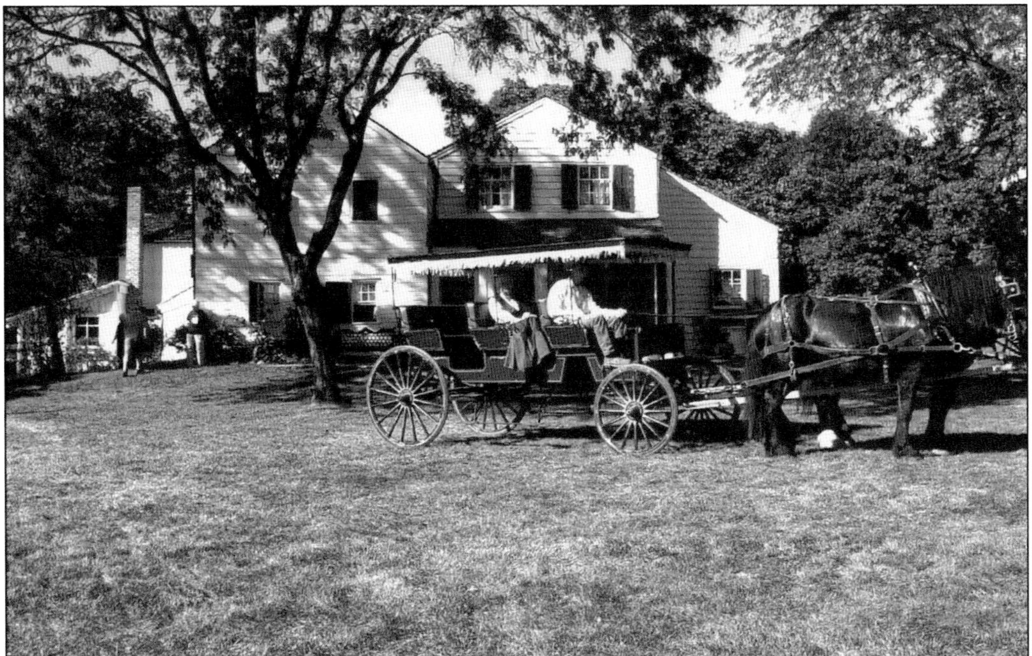

SURREY. Docent Susan Crowfoot takes a leisurely ride in a charming surrey at Outdoor Day, a September event. The CIA continues to take pride in its multifaceted relationship with the USMA and its tradition of creative events to accomplish its mission to commemorate associations legendary, historic, literary, and artistic of the Hudson River Valley.

Nine

TIMELESS

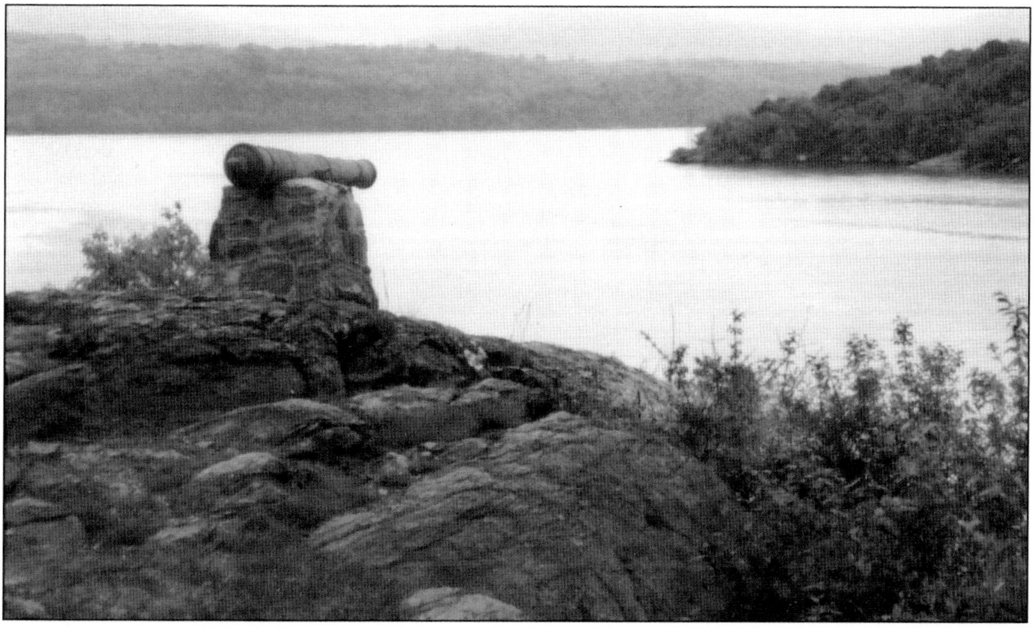

REVOLUTIONARY CANNON. This cannon marks the site of a blockhouse built by Bernard Romans, the first military engineer on Constitution Island. Captured from the British at Saratoga, it stands as a memorial to those who fought for American independence. It sits peacefully overlooking the Hudson River more than two centuries later.

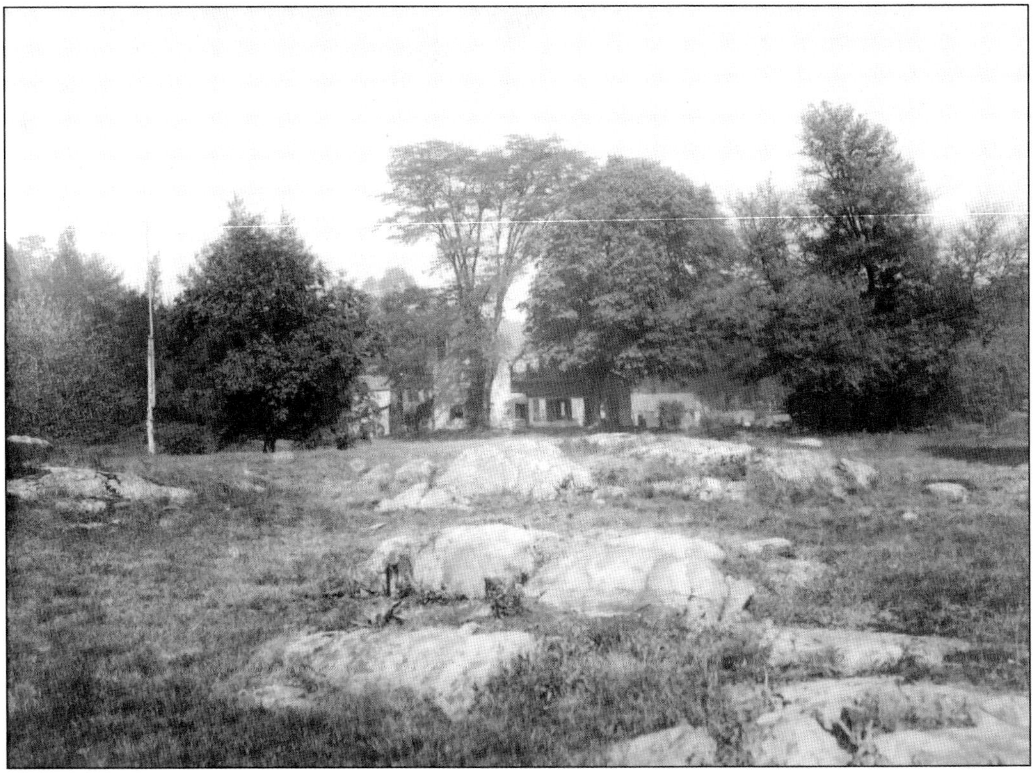

ROCK OF AGES. The simple loveliness and serenity of Martelaer's Rock have not changed over time. Bible student Crampton Jones wrote, "To rest his eyes on such natural beauty and have his nerves calmed by the peace which ruled that home would make any man thankful."

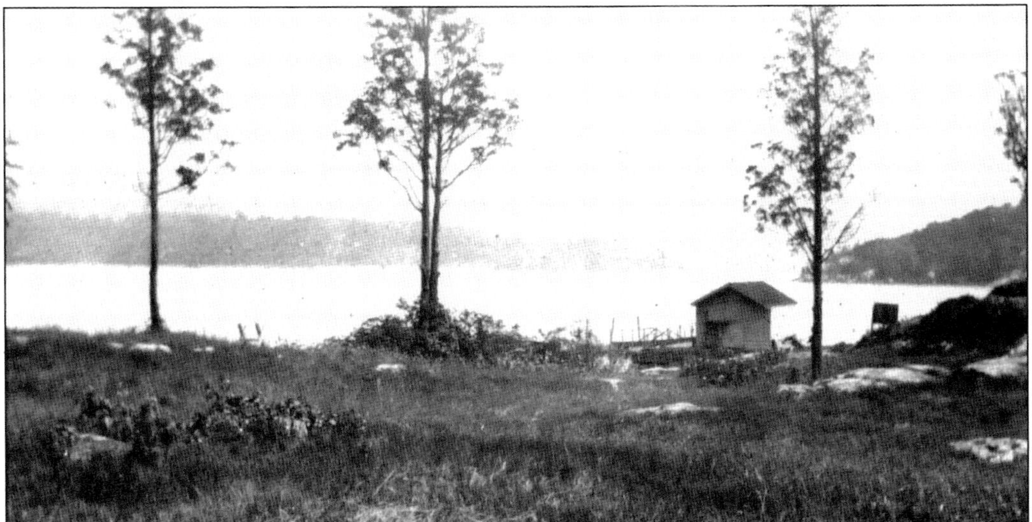

REFLECTION. Despite all the difficulties she faced on the island, Susan Warner came to appreciate its charm. After traveling to New York City for a visit she wrote, "I thought as I sailed quietly down the river that morning, that our place was a very fair one and that I should be not desirous to change it for another."

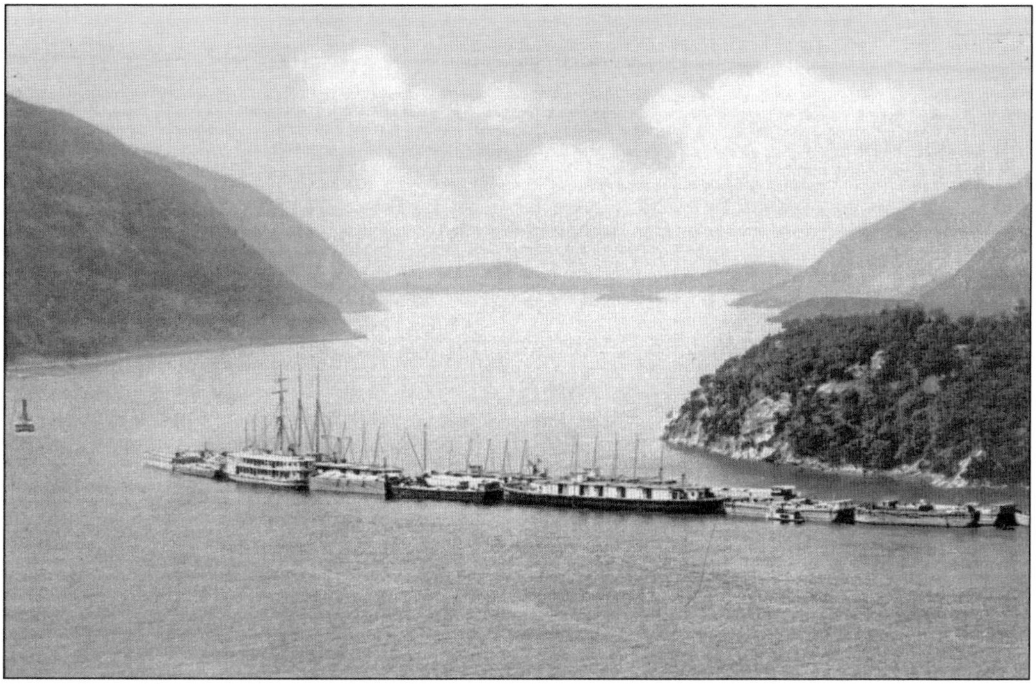

TUG BOAT. Although not as common today as in the early 20th century, the sight of a tug boat pulling barges past Constitution Island remains impressive, evoking a past when the river was the main thoroughfare through the Hudson Highlands. (Donnery collection.)

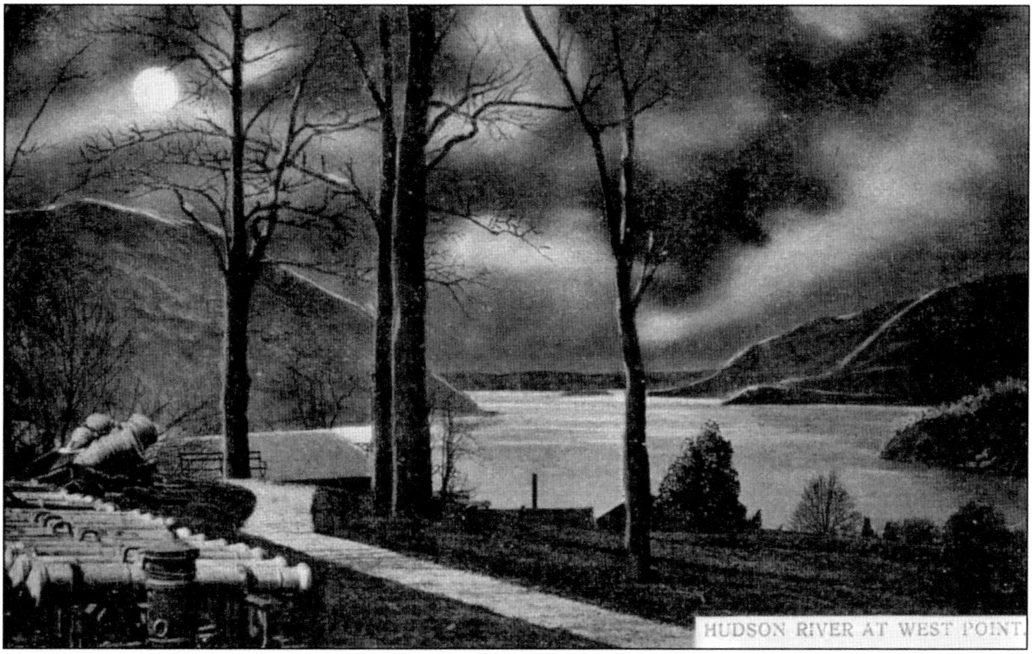

MOONLIT NIGHT. Before Constitution Island became their home, the Warners had often seen it by moonlight from Trophy Point. The view is as awe-inspiring today as it was then. Electric lights have not dimmed the majesty of the Hudson Highlands. (Donnery collection.)

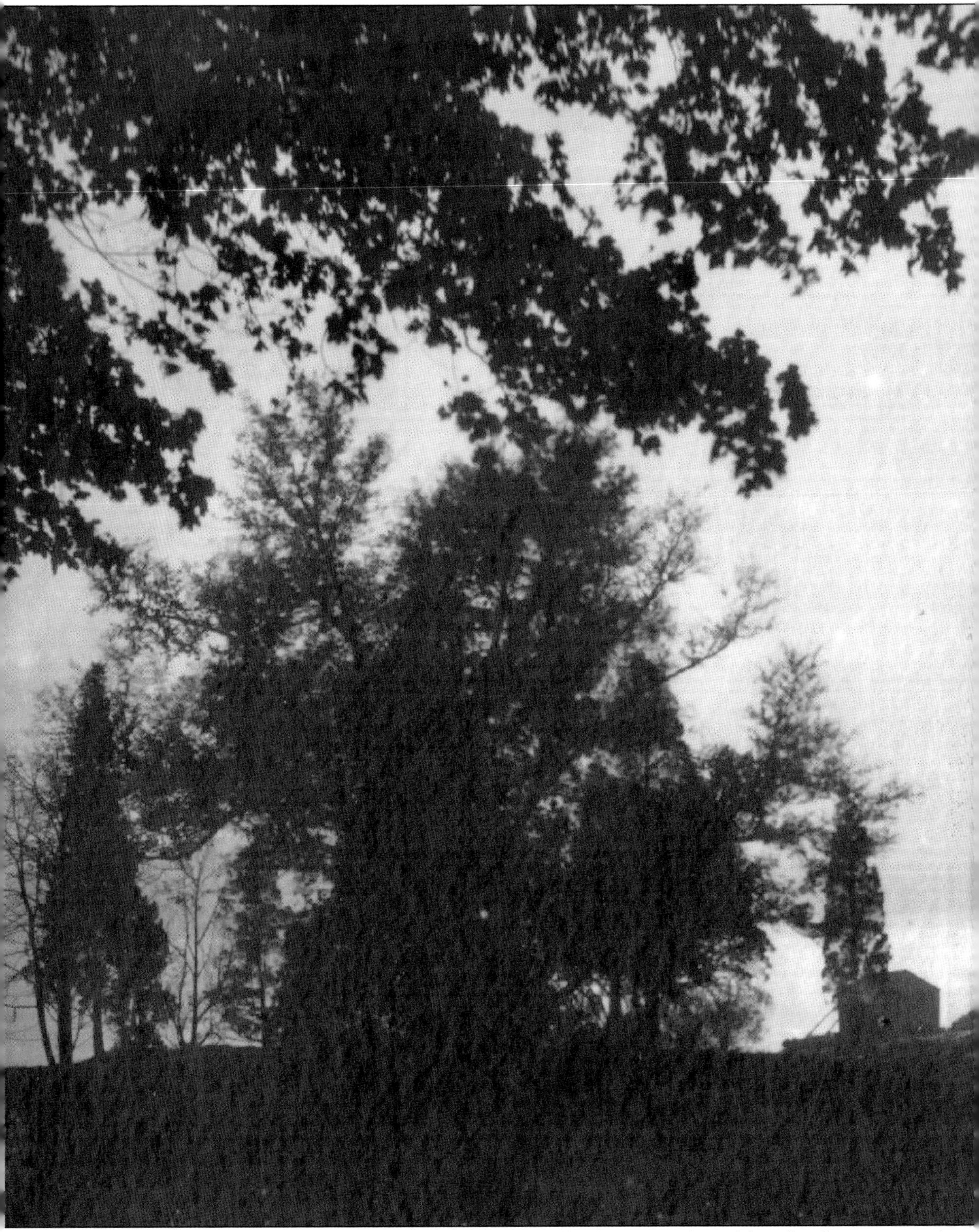

EVENING ON CONSTITUTION ISLAND. As darkness falls, the tranquility of the island is juxtaposed against the moonlit river. Anna Warner once remarked to a friend that the main reason the

island maintained its great natural beauty was because her family "never had sufficient means to spoil it."

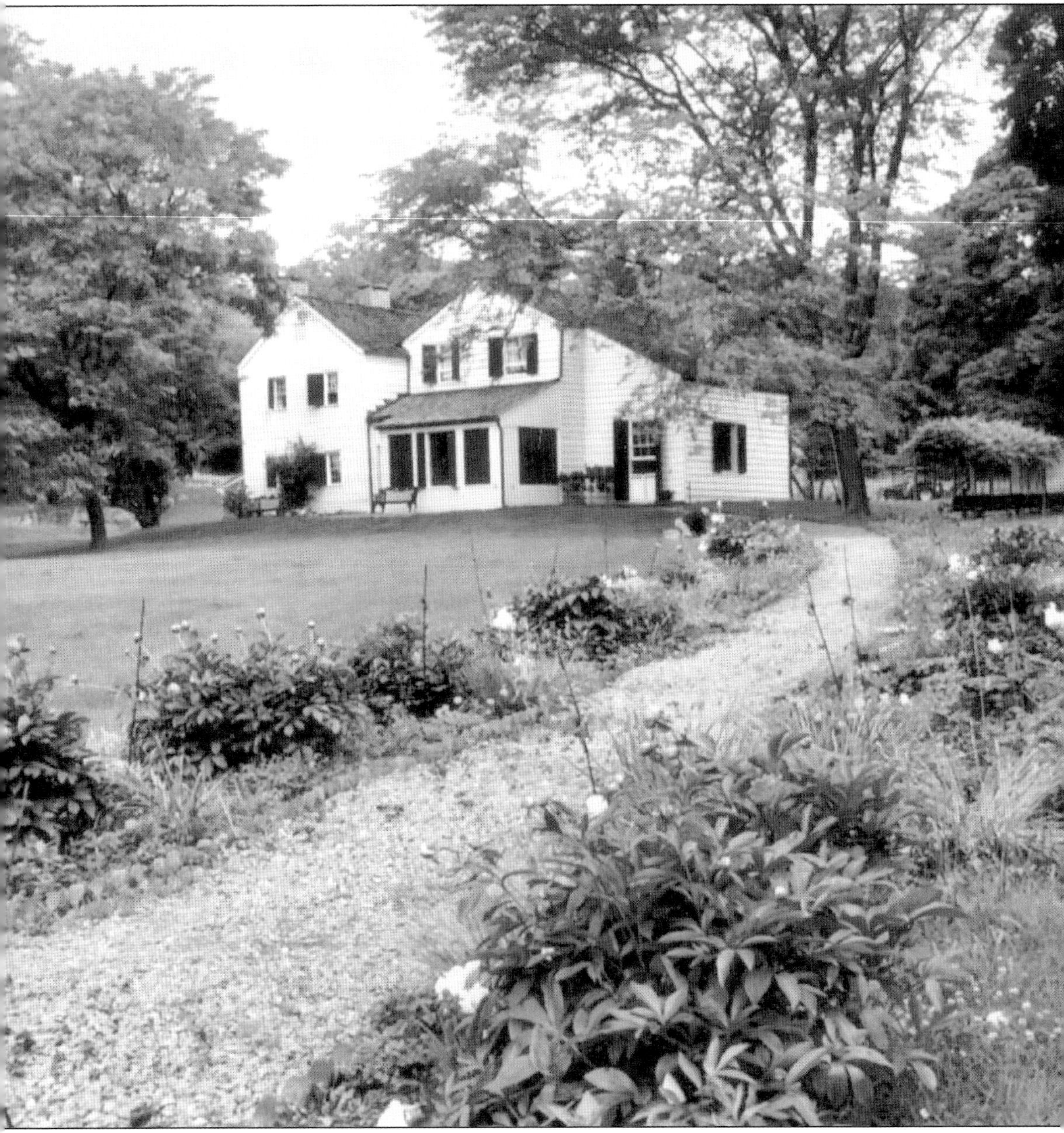

TIMELESS CHARM. The timeless charm of the Warner House and its magnificent setting—the Hudson Highlands—have been preserved to be enjoyed today. As visitors depart, they might find themselves musing, as Anna Warner did in 1910: "What place could ever have been so dear to us as our old Revolutionary house?"

BIBLIOGRAPHY

Baker, Mabel. *Light in the Morning.* West Point: Constitution Island Association Press, 1978.

———. *The Warner Family and the Warner Books.* West Point: Constitution Island Association Press, 1971.

Church, Albert E. *Personal Reminiscences of the Military Academy from 1824–1831.* West Point: United States Military Academy Press, 1879.

Diamant, Lincoln. *Chaining the Hudson: The Fight for the River in the American Revolution.* New York: Fordham University Press, 2004.

Foster, Edward Halsey. *Susan and Anna Warner.* Boston: Twayne Publishers, 1978.

Historic Structures Inventory United States Military Academy (HABS), West Point, New York. Washington, D. C.: U.S. Department of Interior, 1984.

Howell, William Thompson. *The Hudson Highlands.* New York: Walking News, 1982.

Lossing, Benson. *Pictorial Field Book of the Revolution.* New York: Harper and Brothers, 1852.

Lyle, Charles T. *Analysis of the Period Furnishings at the Warner House.* West Point: Constitution Island Association, 2006.

Martin, Joseph Plumb. *Private Yankee Doodle.* New York: Signet, 1999.

Sheffield, Merle. *The Fort That Never Was.* West Point: Constitution Island Association, 1969.

Stokes, Olivia Phelps. *Recollections of Miss Susan and Miss Anna Warner.* West Point: Constitution Island Association, 1948.

Warner, Anna. *Gardening by Myself.* West Point: Constitution Island Association, 1972.

———. *Susan Warner.* New York: George Putnam and Sons, 1910.

Weiss, Jane. "Many Things Take My Time: The Journals of Susan Warner." PhD diss., University of the City of New York, 1995.